Rick ®

SNAPSHOT

Naples & the Amalfi Coast

with Pompeii

D'Errico Giuseppe

CONTENTS

Introduction 1

Naples 3

- Orientation to Naples 5
- Tours in Naples 14
- Archaeological Museum Tour . . 15
- Naples Walk 25
- Sights in Naples 36
- Sleeping in Naples 54
- Eating in Naples 55
- Naples Connections 64

Pompeii & Nearby 67

- Pompeii 67
- Herculaneum 86
- Vesuvius 91

Sorrento & Capri 94

- Sorrento 94
- Capri 117

Amalfi Coast & Paestum 132

- Amalfi Coast 133
- Amalfi Coast Tour 137
- Positano 143
- Amalfi Town 153
- Ravello 161
- Paestum 165

Practicalities 179

- Money 179
- Staying Connected 180
- Sleeping 181
- Eating 182
- Transportation 183
- Helpful Hints 184
- Resources from Rick Steves . . 186
- Additional Resources 187
- How Was Your Trip? 187
- Italian Survival Phrases 189

Index 191

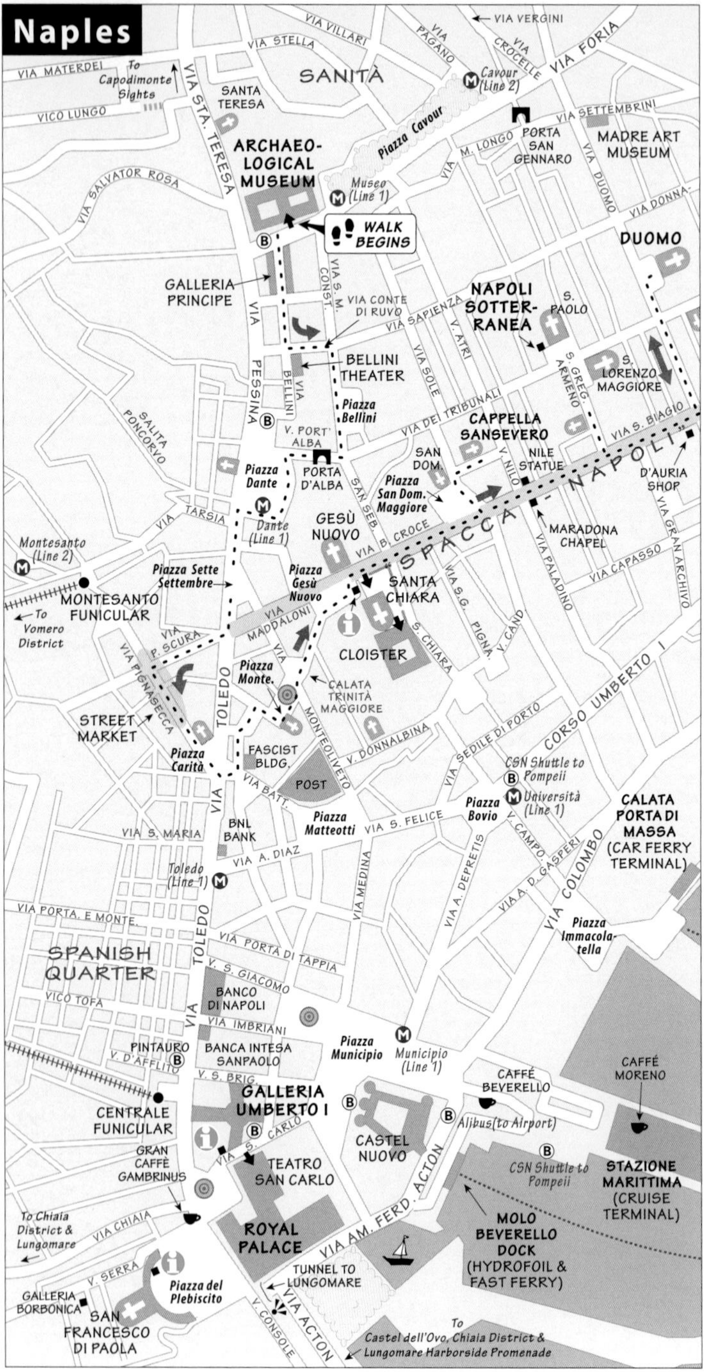
Naples
VIA VERGINI
VIA VILLARI
VIA STELLA
VIA PAGANO
VIA CROCELLE
VIA FORIA
SANITÀ
VIA MATERDEI
To Capodimonte Sights
Cavour (Line 2)
VIA STA. TERESA
SANTA TERESA
VICO LUNGO
Piazza Cavour
VIA SETTEMBRINI
PORTA SAN GENNARO
MADRE ART MUSEUM
ARCHAEO-LOGICAL MUSEUM
VIA M. LONGO
VIA SALVATOR ROSA
Museo (Line 1)
VIA DUOMO
VIA DONNA-
WALK BEGINS
DUOMO
GALLERIA PRINCIPE
VIA S. M. CONST.
VIA CONTE DI RUVO
VIA SAPIENZA
NAPOLI SOTTER-RANEA
S. PAOLO
VIA PESSINA
BELLINI THEATER
VIA BELLINI
V. ATRI
VIA SOLE
S. GREG. ARMENO
S. LORENZO MAGGIORE
SALITA PONCORVO
Piazza Bellini
VIA DEI TRIBUNALI
CAPPELLA SANSEVERO
VIA S. BIAGIO
V. PORT' ALBA
PORTA D'ALBA
SAN DOM.
V. NILO
NILE STATUE
D'AURIA SHOP
Piazza Dante
Piazza San Dom. Maggiore
SAN SEB.
SPACCA - NAPOLI
VIA TARSIA
Dante (Line 1)
GESÙ NUOVO
VIA B. CROCE
MARADONA CHAPEL
Montesanto (Line 2)
Piazza Sette Settembre
Piazza Gesù Nuovo
SANTA CHIARA
VIA S.G. PIGNA.
VIA PALADINO
VIA CAPASSO
VIA GRAN ARCHIVIO
MONTESANTO FUNICULAR
VIA MADDALONI
V. CAND.
To Vomero District
VIA P. SCURA
CLOISTER
S. CHIARA
CORSO UMBERTO I
VIA PIGNASECCA
Piazza Monte.
CALATA TRINITÀ MAGGIORE
VIA TOLEDO
STREET MARKET
VIA MONTEOLIVETO
VIA SEDILE DI PORTO
V. DONNALBINA
Piazza Carità
FASCIST BLDG.
CSN Shuttle to Pompeii
POST
VIA BATT.
Università (Line 1)
Piazza Bovio
CALATA PORTA DI MASSA (CAR FERRY TERMINAL)
BNL BANK
Piazza Matteotti
VIA S. FELICE
VIA S. MARIA
VIA A. DIAZ
VIA CAMPO
VIA A. D. GASPERI
VIA COLOMBO
Toledo (Line 1)
VIA MEDINA
VIA A. DEPRETIS
VIA PORTA. E MONTE.
Piazza Immacolatella
VIA PORTA DI TAPPIA
SPANISH QUARTER
V. S. GIACOMO
BANCO DI NAPOLI
VICO TOFA
VIA IMBRIANI
PINTAURO
BANCA INTESA SANPAOLO
Piazza Municipio
Municipio (Line 1)
V. D'AFFLITO
V. S. BRIG.
CAFFÈ BEVERELLO
CAFFÈ MORENO
CENTRALE FUNICULAR
GALLERIA UMBERTO I
CASTEL NUOVO
Alibus (to Airport)
VIA S. CARLO
TEATRO SAN CARLO
GRAN CAFFÈ GAMBRINUS
CSN Shuttle to Pompeii
STAZIONE MARITTIMA (CRUISE TERMINAL)
VIA AM. FERD. ACTON
To Chiaia District & Lungomare
VIA CHIAIA
ROYAL PALACE
MOLO BEVERELLO DOCK (HYDROFOIL & FAST FERRY)
V. SERRA
TUNNEL TO LUNGOMARE
Piazza del Plebiscito
GALLERIA BORBONICA
SAN FRANCESCO DI PAOLA
V. CONSOLE
VIA ACTON
To Castel dell'Ovo, Chiaia District & Lungomare Harborside Promenade

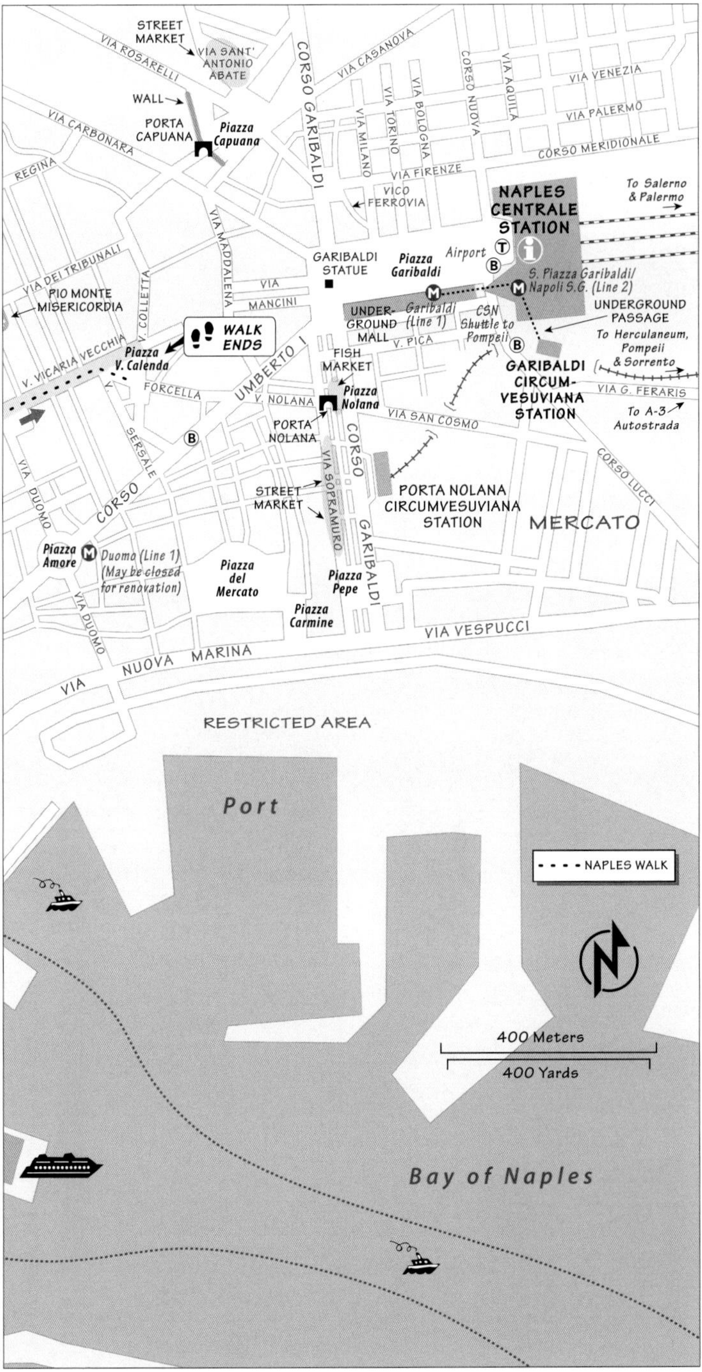
STREET MARKET
VIA SANT' ANTONIO ABATE
VIA ROSARELLI
WALL
PORTA CAPUANA
Piazza Capuana
VIA CARBONARA
REGINA
CORSO GARIBALDI
VIA CASANOVA
VIA MILANO
VIA TORINO
VIA BOLOGNA
CORSO NUOVA
VIA AQUILA
VIA VENEZIA
VIA PALERMO
CORSO MERIDIONALE
VIA FIRENZE
VICO FERROVIA
NAPLES CENTRALE STATION
To Salerno & Palermo
VIA MADDALENA
VIA DEI TRIBUNALI
PIO MONTE MISERICORDIA
V. COLLETTA
GARIBALDI STATUE
Piazza Garibaldi
Airport
S. Piazza Garibaldi/ Napoli S.G. (Line 2)
VIA MANCINI
UNDER-GROUND MALL
Garibaldi (Line 1)
CSN Shuttle to Pompeii
UNDERGROUND PASSAGE
To Herculaneum, Pompeii & Sorrento
WALK ENDS
Piazza V. Calenda
V. VICARIA VECCHIA
UMBERTO I
FISH MARKET
V. PICA
GARIBALDI CIRCUM-VESUVIANA STATION
VIA G. FERARIS
FORCELLA
V. NOLANA
Piazza Nolana
PORTA NOLANA
VIA SAN COSMO
To A-3 Autostrada
SERSALE
CORSO LUCCI
VIA DUOMO
CORSO
STREET MARKET
VIA SOPRAMURO
PORTA NOLANA CIRCUMVESUVIANA STATION
MERCATO
Piazza Amore
Duomo (Line 1) (May be closed for renovation)
Piazza del Mercato
Piazza Pepe
Piazza Carmine
VIA VESPUCCI
VIA NUOVA MARINA
RESTRICTED AREA
Port
NAPLES WALK
400 Meters
400 Yards
Bay of Naples

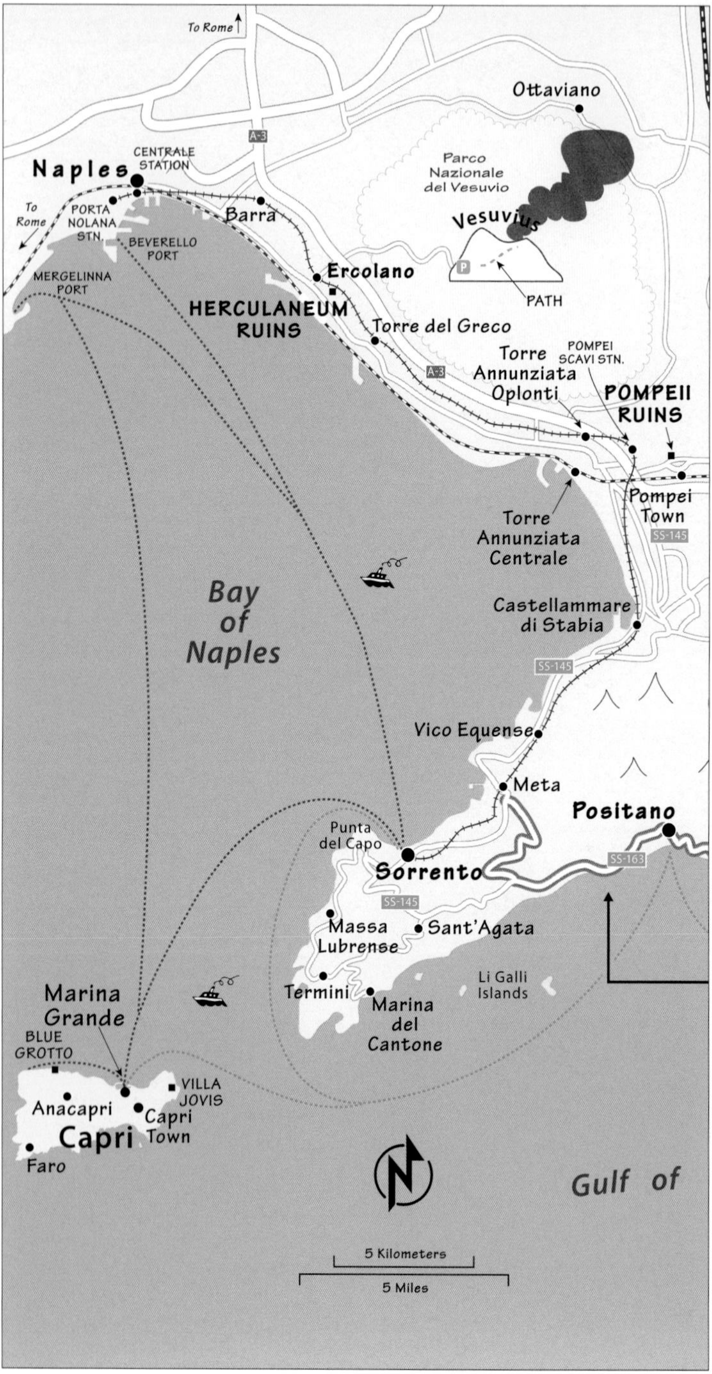

To Rome
Ottaviano
A-3
Parco Nazionale del Vesuvio
Naples
CENTRALE STATION
To Rome
PORTA NOLANA STN.
BEVERELLO PORT
Barra
Vesuvius
P
PATH
MERGELINNA PORT
Ercolano
HERCULANEUM RUINS
Torre del Greco
Torre Annunziata Oplonti
POMPEI SCAVI STN.
POMPEII RUINS
A-3
Pompei Town
SS-145
Torre Annunziata Centrale
Bay of Naples
Castellammare di Stabia
SS-145
Vico Equense
Meta
Positano
Punta del Capo
Sorrento
SS-163
SS-145
Massa Lubrense
Sant'Agata
Termini
Marina del Cantone
Li Galli Islands
Marina Grande
BLUE GROTTO
VILLA JOVIS
Anacapri
Capri Town
Capri
Faro
Gulf of
5 Kilometers
5 Miles

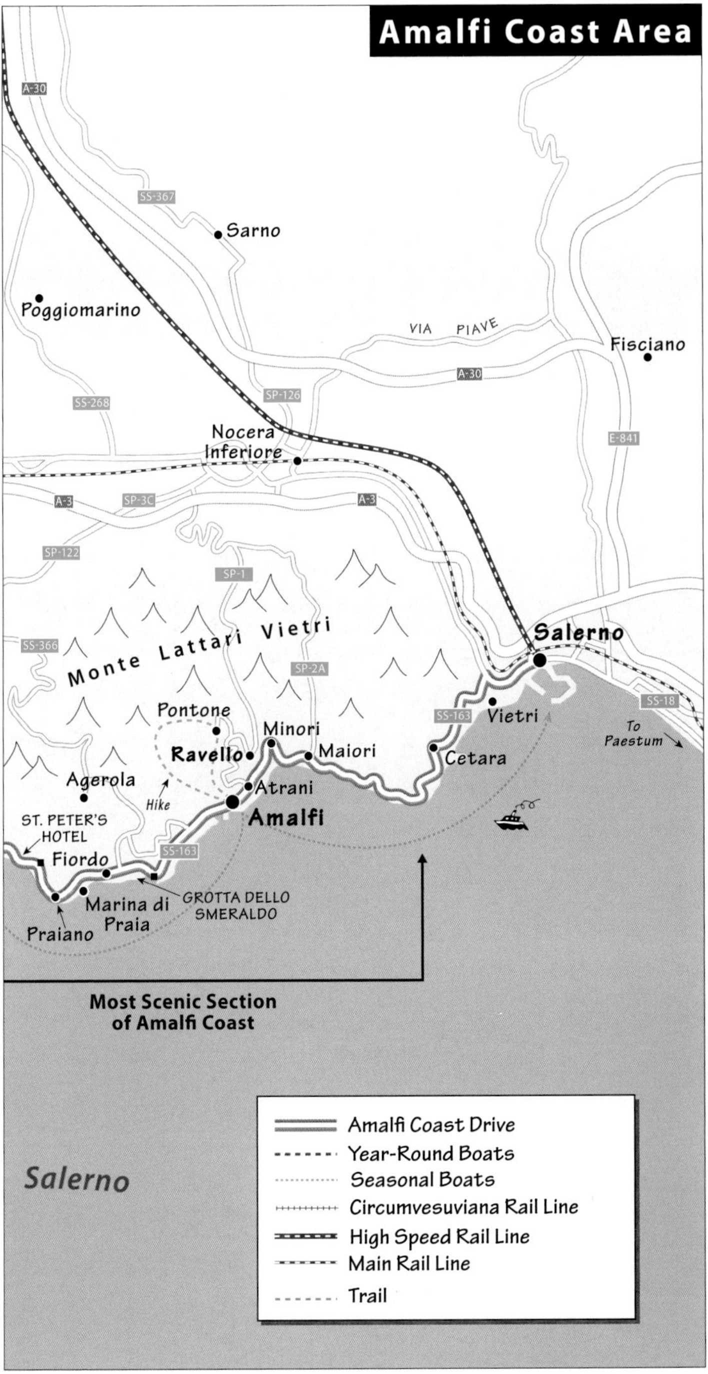
Amalfi Coast Area
A-30
SS-367
Sarno
Poggiomarino
VIA PIAVE
Fisciano
A-30
SS-268
SP-126
E-841
Nocera Inferiore
A-3
SP-3C
A-3
SP-122
SP-1
Monte Lattari Vietri
SS-366
SP-2A
Salerno
Pontone
Minori
SS-163
Vietri
SS-18
To Paestum
Ravello
Maiori
Cetara
Agerola
Atrani
Hike
Amalfi
ST. PETER'S HOTEL
Fiordo
SS-163
GROTTA DELLO SMERALDO
Marina di Praia
Praiano
Most Scenic Section of Amalfi Coast
Salerno
Amalfi Coast Drive
Year-Round Boats
Seasonal Boats
Circumvesuviana Rail Line
High Speed Rail Line
Main Rail Line
Trail

INTRODUCTION

This Snapshot guide, excerpted from my guidebook *Rick Steves Italy,* introduces you to Naples, Pompeii, and the Amalfi Coast. The gritty, historic port city of Naples is arguably Italy's wildest urban jungle, with a uniquely vibrant street life. Enjoy a pizza in its birthplace, and explore the city's excellent Archaeological Museum. Then head into the countryside to unearth ancient history at Pompeii and Herculaneum, well-preserved Roman towns in the shadow of the steaming Mt. Vesuvius.

An hour to the south, Sorrento kicks off the gloriously scenic Amalfi Coast, where buses filled with white-knuckle tourists take turns squeezing along an impossibly narrow sea-view road. Relax in stylish Sorrento or hilly Positano, and side-trip to the glitzy Amalfi Town and Ravello, the ancient Greek temples at Paestum, or the jet-set isle of Capri, with its otherworldly Blue Grotto.

To help you have the best trip possible, I've included the following topics in this book:

• **Planning Your Time,** with advice on how to make the most of your limited time

• **Orientation,** including tourist information (abbreviated as TI), tips on public transportation, local tour options, and helpful hints

• **Sights,** with ratings and strategies for meaningful and efficient visits

• **Sleeping** and **Eating,** with good-value recommendations in every price range

• **Connections,** with tips on trains, buses, and driving

Practicalities, near the end of this book, has information on money, staying connected, hotel reservations, transportation, and other helpful hints, plus Italian survival phrases.

To travel smartly, read this little book in its entirety before you go. It's my hope that this guide will make your trip more meaningful and rewarding. Traveling like a temporary local, you'll get the absolute most out of every mile, minute, and dollar.

Buon viaggio!

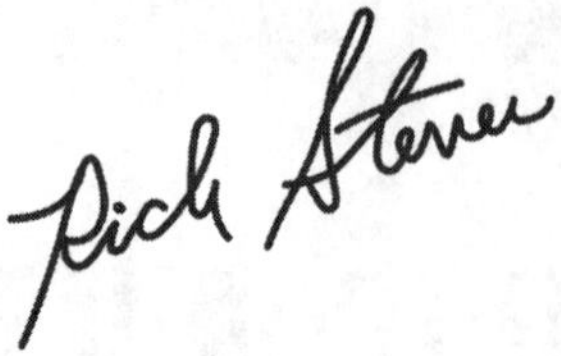

NAPLES

Napoli

If you like Italy as far south as Rome, go farther south—it gets better. If Italy is getting on your nerves, stop at Rome. Italy intensifies as you plunge deeper. Naples is Italy in the extreme—its best (birthplace of pizza) and its worst (home of the Camorra, Naples' "family" of organized crime).

Before Italy unified in the late 1800s, Naples was the country's richest city. But Naples' fortunes nosedived when the capital of modern Italy was established in Rome. Things got so bad that many of its residents emigrated. The Italy America knows—pizza, spaghetti, and "O Sole Mio"/"Santa Lucia"—came from 19th-century Naples, as brought to the US by all those immigrants.

Today, Naples impresses visitors with one of Europe's top archaeological museums (showcasing the artistic treasures of Pompeii), fascinating churches that convey the city's unique personality and powerful devotion, an underground warren of Greek and Roman ruins, fine works of art (including pieces by Caravaggio, who lived here for a time), and evocative Nativity scenes (called *presepi*). Of course, Neapolitans make great pizza and tasty pastries (try the crispy, ricotta-stuffed *sfogliatella*). But more than anything, Naples has a brash and vibrant street life—"Italy in your face" in ways both good and bad. Walking through its colorful old town is one of my favorite experiences anywhere in Europe. For a grand overlook, head to the hilltop viewpoint (San Martino) for sweeping views of the city and its bay.

Naples is southern Italy's leading city, the third-largest city in Italy, and Europe's most densely populated city, with more than one million people and few open spaces or parks. While in many ways it feels like an urban jungle, Naples surprises the observant

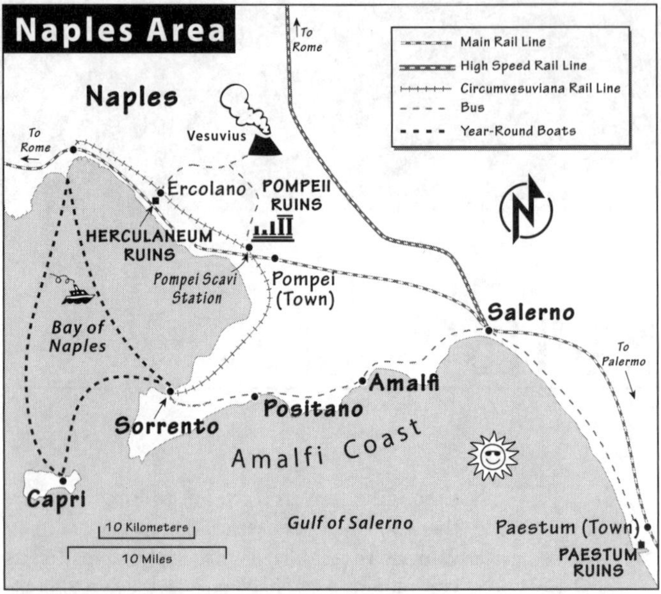

traveler with its impressive knack for living, eating, and raising children with good humor and decency. Overcome your fear of being run down or ripped off long enough to talk with people. Enjoy a few smiles and jokes with the man running the neighborhood tripe shop, or the woman taking her daycare class on a walk through the traffic.

The pulse of Italy throbs in Naples. Like Cairo or Mumbai, it's shocking and captivating at the same time, the closest thing to "reality travel" that you'll find in Western Europe. But this tangled mess still somehow manages to breathe, laugh, and sing—with a joyful Italian accent. Thanks to its reputation as a dangerous place, Naples doesn't get nearly as many tourists as it deserves. While the city has its problems, it has improved a lot in recent years. And even though it remains a bit edgy, I feel comfortable here. Naples richly rewards those who venture in.

Naples is also the springboard to an array of nearby sightseeing treats (covered in the next three chapters and easy to reach by train, bus, or boat): Just beyond Naples are the remarkable ruins of Herculaneum and Pompeii, and the brooding volcano that did them both in, Mount Vesuvius. A few more miles down the road is the pleasant resort town of Sorrento and the offshore escape isle of Capri. Next comes the dramatic scenery of the Amalfi Coast. Plunging even farther south, you'll reach the Greek temples of Paestum.

PLANNING YOUR TIME

Naples is an ideal day trip either from Rome or from the comfortable home base of Sorrento, each just over an hour away. Or you can stow your bag at the station and see Naples in a few hours while you change trains here on the way between Rome and Sorrento. For some, a little Naples goes a long way. If you're not comfortable in chaotic and congested cities, think twice before spending the night here. But those who are intrigued by the city's sights and street life enjoy overnighting in Naples.

On a quick visit, start with the Archaeological Museum (closed Tue), follow my self-guided Naples Walk, and celebrate your survival with pizza. With more time, dip into more churches, go underground to see Greek and Roman ruins, trek to Capodimonte to see art treasures, or ascend San Martino for the view. Spend an early evening strolling Naples' romantic Lungomare harborside promenade.

For a blitz tour from Rome, you could have breakfast on an early Rome-Naples express train (usually daily 7:35-8:45), zip to Pompeii by bus or train, return to Naples and hit the Archaeological Museum, and be back in Rome before you turn into a zucchini. That's exhausting, but more memorable than a fourth day in Rome.

Yes, Naples is huge. But if you stick to my suggestions and grab a cab when you're lost or tired, it's fun. Treat yourself well in Naples; the city is cheap by Italian standards. Splurging on a sane and comfortable hotel is a worthwhile investment.

On summer afternoons, Naples' street life slows and many churches, museums, and shops close as the temperature soars. The city comes back to life in the early evening.

Orientation to Naples

Naples is set deep inside the large, curving Bay of Naples, with Mount Vesuvius looming just five miles away. Although Naples is a sprawling city, its fairly compact core contains the most interesting sights. The tourist's Naples is a triangle, with its points at the Centrale train station in the east, the Archaeological Museum to the west, and Piazza del Plebiscito (with the Royal Palace) and the port to the south. Steep hills rise above this historic core, including San Martino, capped with a mighty fortress.

Planning Your Time in the Region

Give the entire area—including Sorrento and Naples—a minimum of three days. If you use Sorrento as your sunny springboard, you can spend a day in Naples, a day exploring the Amalfi Coast, and a day split between Pompeii and the town of Sorrento. While Paestum (Greek temples), Mount Vesuvius, Herculaneum (an ancient Roman site like Pompeii), and the island of Capri are fine destinations, they are worthwhile only if you have more time.

The **Campania ArteCard** regional pass may save you a few euros, but it also saves the time and hassle of buying tickets. Consider it if you're here for two or three days, use public transportation, and visit multiple major sights (such as Pompeii, Herculaneum, Paestum, Naples' Archaeological Museum, and several other museums in Naples). The **three-day Campania** version (€32) is good if you'll be visiting both Naples and Sorrento; it includes free entry to two sights, a 50 percent discount off others, and transportation within Naples, on the Circumvesuviana train (but not the Campania Express), the Metropolitana, and on Amalfi Coast buses. The **seven-day Campania** version (€34) covers five sights and discounts on others, but no transportation. If you're focusing on Naples, the **three-day Napoli** version (€21) covers transportation within Naples and three city sights, plus discounts on others, but doesn't cover outlying ancient sites. The card is sold at participating sights and at some Naples TIs; you can also buy an electronic version online (cards activate on first use, expire 3 or 7 days later at midnight, www.campaniartecard.it).

TOURIST INFORMATION

Central Naples has various small TIs, none of them particularly helpful—just grab a map and browse the brochures. The main branch, open all year, is in the city center on Spaccanapoli, across from the **Church of Gesù Nuovo** (Mon-Sat 9:00-18:00, likely closed Sun, +39 081 551 2701). Seasonally, you may also find TI branches at the **Centrale train station,** at the **cruise port,** and at the **airport**—look around when you arrive. For information online, the best overall website is www.inaples.it.

ARRIVAL IN NAPLES

No matter how you arrive, expect some chaos. Instead of getting frustrated, consider it part of the charm of Naples—as most locals do. If you're connecting to another destination from Naples, see the "Getting Around the Region" sidebar on page 62.

By Train

Naples has several train stations, but all trains coming into town stop at either Napoli Centrale station or Garibaldi station—which are essentially the same place, with Centrale on top of Garibaldi. Stretching in front of this station complex is the vast Piazza Garibaldi, with an underground shopping mall and Metro entrance.

Centrale station, on the ground floor, is the slick, modern main station, with intercity connections across Italy. Baggage check (*deposito bagagli,* run by Kipoint) is near track 2; pay WCs are down the stairs across from track 13. A nice Food Hall Napoli is located near tracks 2-8; other shops and eateries are mainly concentrated on the underground level. In high season, a TI may be set up somewhere in the station; the inStazione desk is a private agency but can be helpful in a pinch. Out the front door to the left, you'll find a big bookstore (La Feltrinelli) and a good supermarket (Sapori & Dintorni).

Garibaldi station, on the lower level, is used exclusively by the narrow-gauge Circumvesuviana commuter train and the Campania Express (options you can use to connect to Sorrento or Pompeii; to get here from Centrale, follow signs to *Circumvesuviana* and *Linee Vesuviane*). Note that this is not the terminus for the Circumvesuviana; that's one stop farther downtown, at the station called Porta Nolana.

To add to the confusion, **"Stazione Piazza Garibaldi,"** or "Napoli S.G." for short, is a stop on Trenitalia's Metropolitana (part of Naples' Metro line 2—see next); these tracks are downstairs near the middle of Centrale station (follow signs for *M Linea 2*). In addition to stops in Naples, some of these trains go all the way out to Pompei (the modern town) and Salerno.

Getting Downtown: Arriving at either station, the best bet for reaching most sights and hotels is either the Metro or a taxi. **Metro** lines 1 and 2 are both downstairs—in separate areas—and signposted throughout the Centrale and Garibaldi stations. Line 1 (direction: Piscinola) is handy for city-center stops, including the cruise port (Municipio), the main shopping drag (Toledo and Dante), and the Archaeological Museum (Museo). Line 2 is slightly quicker for reaching the Archaeological Museum (direction: Campi Flegrei/Pozzuoli/Formina, go one stop to Piazza Cavour, then walk 5 minutes). For tips on navigating the Metro, see "Getting Around Naples," later.

Long rows of white **taxis** line up out front. Ask the driver to charge you the fixed rate *(tariffa predeterminata),* which varies from €9 for the old center to €15 for the most distant hotel I list.

By Plane or Cruise Ship

For information on Naples' airport, cruise ship terminal, and ferry docks, see the end of this chapter.

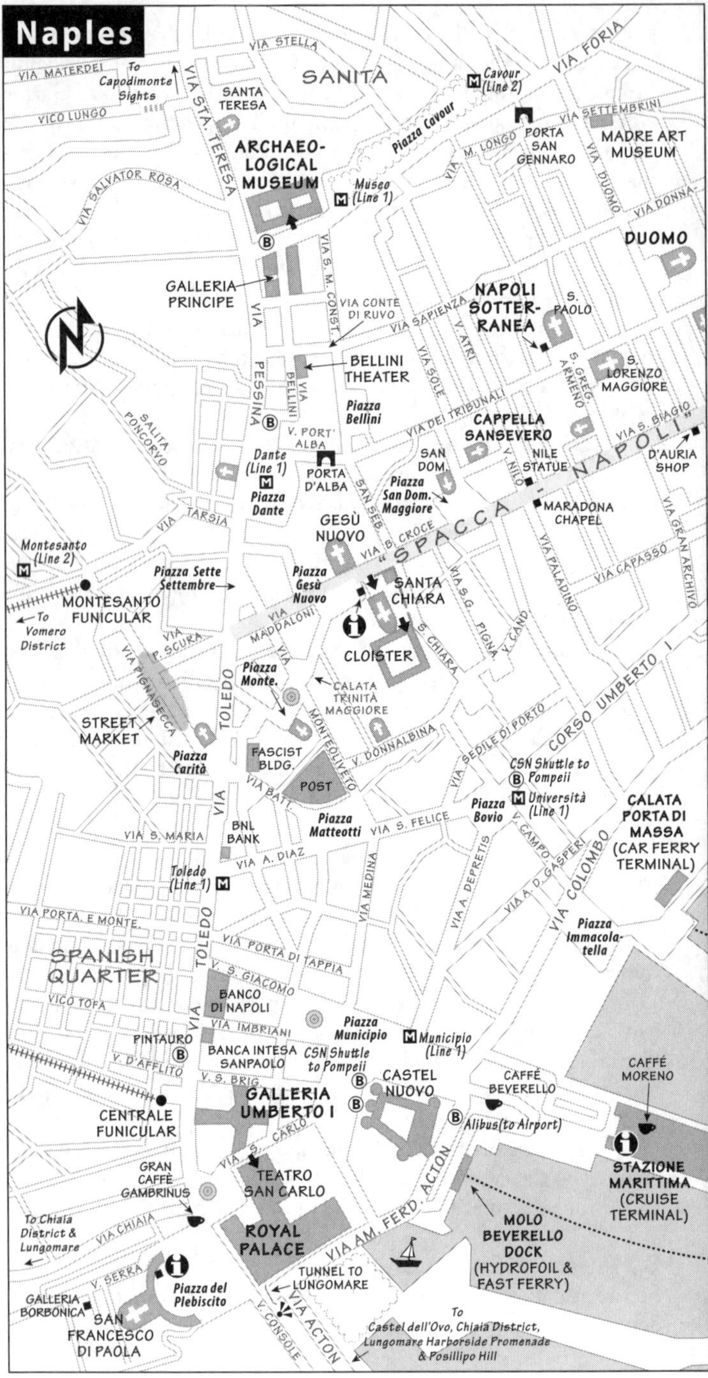
Naples
VIA STELLA
SANITÀ
VIA MATERDEI
To Capodimonte Sights
VIA STA. TERESA
SANTA TERESA
Cavour (Line 2)
VIA FORIA
Piazza Cavour
VICO LUNGO
VIA SETTEMBRINI
PORTA SAN GENNARO
MADRE ART MUSEUM
ARCHAEO-LOGICAL MUSEUM
VIA M. LONGO
VIA SALVATOR ROSA
Museo (Line 1)
VIA DUOMO
VIA DONNA-
DUOMO
VIA S. M. CONST.
GALLERIA PRINCIPE
NAPOLI SOTTER-RANEA
S. PAOLO
VIA CONTE DI RUVO
VIA SAPIENZA
VIA
V. ATRI
BELLINI THEATER
VIA SOLE
S. LORENZO MAGGIORE
PESSINA
VIA BELLINI
S. GREG. ARMENO
Piazza Bellini
VIA DEI TRIBUNALI
SALITA PONCORVO
V. PORT' ALBA
CAPPELLA SANSEVERO
VIA S. BIAGIO
D'AURIA SHOP
Dante (Line 1)
PORTA D'ALBA
SAN DOM.
V. NILO
NILE STATUE
"SPACCA - NAPOLI"
Piazza Dante
SAN SEB.
Piazza San Dom. Maggiore
MARADONA CHAPEL
VIA TARSIA
GESÙ NUOVO
VIA B. CROCE
VIA GRAN ARCHIVIO
Montesanto (Line 2)
Piazza Sette Settembre
Piazza Gesù Nuovo
SANTA CHIARA
VIA S.G.
VIA CAPASSO
VIA PALADINO
MONTESANTO FUNICULAR
To Vomero District
VIA MADDALONI
PIGNA
V. CAND
VIA P. SCURA
CLOISTER
S. CHIARA
CORSO UMBERTO I
VIA PIGNASECCA
TOLEDO
Piazza Monte.
CALATA TRINITÀ MAGGIORE
STREET MARKET
MONTEOLIVETO
VIA SEDILE DI PORTO
Piazza Carità
FASCIST BLDG.
V. DONNALBINA
CSN Shuttle to Pompeii
POST
Università (Line 1)
VIA BATT.
Piazza Bovio
CALATA PORTA DI MASSA (CAR FERRY TERMINAL)
VIA S. MARIA
BNL BANK
Piazza Matteotti
VIA S. FELICE
V. CAMPO
VIA A. DIAZ
VIA COLOMBO
Toledo (Line 1)
VIA MEDINA
VIA A. DEPRETIS
VIA A. D. GASPERI
VIA PORTA. E MONTE.
Piazza Immacolatella
SPANISH QUARTER
VIA PORTA DI TAPPIA
V. S. GIACOMO
BANCO DI NAPOLI
VICO TOFA
VIA IMBRIANI
Piazza Municipio
Municipio (Line 1)
PINTAURO
BANCA INTESA SANPAOLO
CSN Shuttle to Pompeii
V. D'AFFLITO
V. S. BRIG.
CASTEL NUOVO
CAFFÈ BEVERELLO
CAFFÈ MORENO
GALLERIA UMBERTO I
CENTRALE FUNICULAR
Alibus (to Airport)
VIA S. CARLO
TEATRO SAN CARLO
STAZIONE MARITTIMA (CRUISE TERMINAL)
GRAN CAFFÈ GAMBRINUS
VIA AM. FERD. ACTON
To Chiaia District & Lungomare
VIA CHIAIA
ROYAL PALACE
MOLO BEVERELLO DOCK (HYDROFOIL & FAST FERRY)
V. SERRA
TUNNEL TO LUNGOMARE
Piazza del Plebiscito
GALLERIA BORBONICA
SAN FRANCESCO DI PAOLA
V. CONSOLE
VIA ACTON
To Castel dell'Ovo, Chiaia District, Lungomare Harborside Promenade & Posillipo Hill

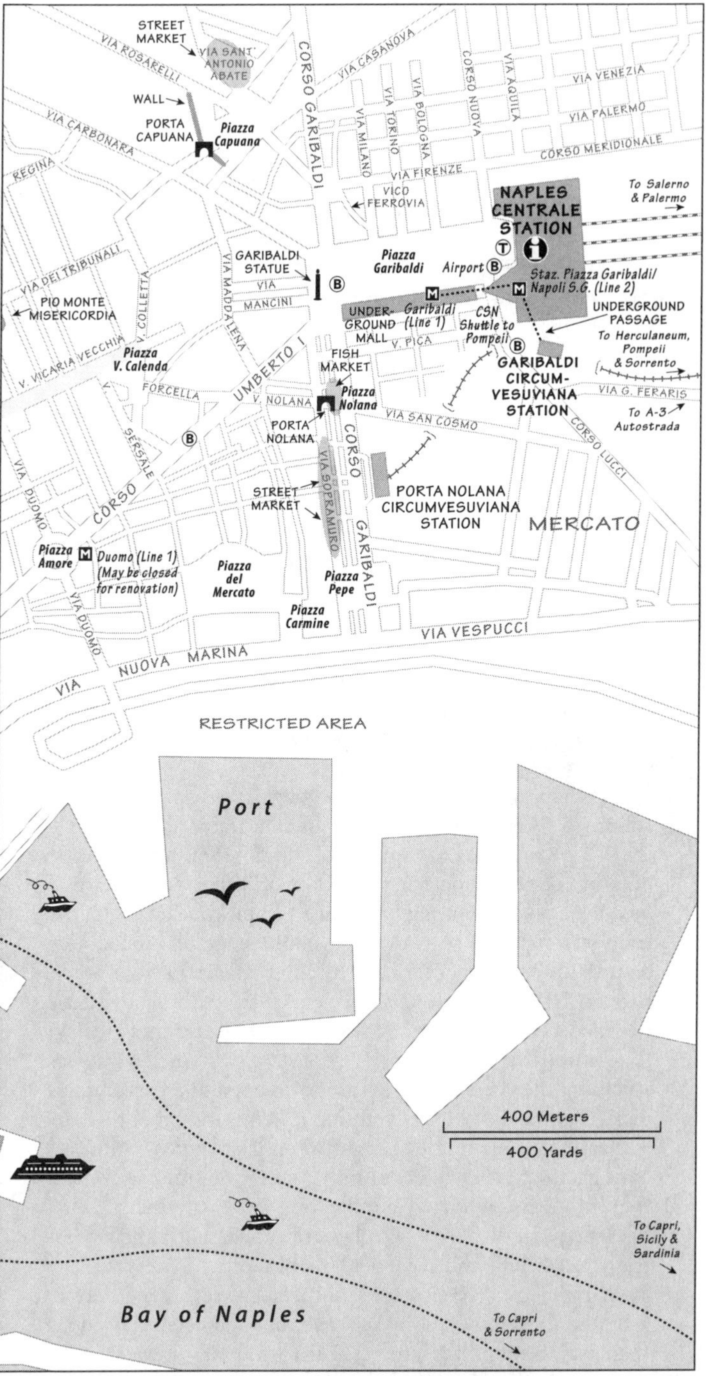
STREET MARKET
VIA SANT' ANTONIO ABATE
VIA ROSARELLI
WALL
PORTA CAPUANA
Piazza Capuana
VIA CARBONARA
REGINA
CORSO GARIBALDI
VIA CASANOVA
VIA MILANO
VIA TORINO
VIA BOLOGNA
CORSO NUOVA
VIA AQUILA
VIA VENEZIA
VIA PALERMO
CORSO MERIDIONALE
VIA FIRENZE
VICO FERROVIA
NAPLES CENTRALE STATION
To Salerno & Palermo
VIA DEI TRIBUNALI
GARIBALDI STATUE
VIA MANCINI
Piazza Garibaldi
Airport
Staz. Piazza Garibaldi/ Napoli S.G. (Line 2)
PIO MONTE MISERICORDIA
V. COLLETTA
VIA MADDALENA
UNDERGROUND MALL
Garibaldi (Line 1)
CSN Shuttle to Pompeii
UNDERGROUND PASSAGE
To Herculaneum, Pompeii & Sorrento
V. VICARIA VECCHIA
Piazza V. Calenda
V. PICA
FISH MARKET
GARIBALDI CIRCUM-VESUVIANA STATION
FORCELLA
UMBERTO I
V. NOLANA
Piazza Nolana
VIA G. FERRARIS
VIA SAN COSMO
To A-3 Autostrada
PORTA NOLANA
CORSO LUCCI
SERSALE
VIA DUOMO
CORSO
CORSO GARIBALDI
VIA SOPRAMURO
STREET MARKET
PORTA NOLANA CIRCUMVESUVIANA STATION
MERCATO
Piazza Amore
Duomo (Line 1) (May be closed for renovation)
Piazza del Mercato
Piazza Pepe
Piazza Carmine
VIA DUOMO
VIA VESPUCCI
VIA NUOVA MARINA
RESTRICTED AREA
Port
400 Meters
400 Yards
To Capri, Sicily & Sardinia
Bay of Naples
To Capri & Sorrento

HELPFUL HINTS

Theft Alert: While most travelers visit Naples safely, err on the side of caution. Be aware that thieves and con artists hang out close to where travelers tumble into Naples: the train station and the port. Although the train station itself has been nicely spruced up, its glow doesn't extend far. Remember that poor and chaotic does not necessarily mean dangerous. Don't let your first impression of the station area get in your way of enjoying Naples—the city changes drastically as you move farther away. Touristy Spaccanapoli, Capodimonte, and the posh Via Toledo shopping boulevard are more upscale—though even in its nicest areas, Naples can strike many visitors as a bit scruffy.

Stick to busy streets and beware the odd gang of hoodlums. A third of the city is unemployed, and past local governments have set an example of corruption that the Mafia would be proud of. As in most big cities, consider any jostle or commotion a possible thief-team smokescreen. Keep a low profile, carry only the bare minimum, and leave heavy bags at your hotel or at the left-luggage office in Centrale station.

Walk with confidence, as if you know where you're going and what you're doing. Use the sidewalk (even if the locals don't) and carry your belongings on the side away from the street—thieves on scooters have been known to snatch bags as they swoop by. Keep valuables buttoned up (or secure them at your hotel).

Perhaps your biggest risk of theft is while catching or riding the Circumvesuviana commuter train. While I ride the Circumvesuviana comfortably and safely, each year I hear of travelers who get ripped off on this ride. You won't be mugged—but you may be conned or pickpocketed. At the train station, carry your own bags—there are no official porters. If you're connecting from a long-distance express, you'll be going from a relatively secure compartment into an often-crowded and dingy train. Be ready for this very common trick: A team of thieves blocks the door at a stop, pretending it's stuck. While everyone rushes to try to open it, an accomplice picks their pockets. Wear your money belt, and avoid the Circumvesuviana train late at night when it's plagued by intimidating ruffians. For peace of mind, sit in the front car, where there is a driver who may be able to monitor activity.

Traffic Safety: In Naples, red lights are timed short, and pedestrians need to be wary, particularly of motor scooters that zip among the cars. Even on "pedestrian" streets, stay alert to avoid being sideswiped by scooters (or even cars) that nudge their way through the crowds. Smart tourists jaywalk in the shadow of bold locals, who generally ignore crosswalks. Wait for a break in traffic, cross with confidence, and make eye contact with approaching drivers and motor scooters. The traffic will slow to let you pass.

Free Entry Days: State museums in Italy, including the Archaeological Museum and Capodimonte Museum, are free to enter once or twice a month, usually on a Sunday. Check in advance and if possible, avoid going on a free day, which can attract huge crowds.

Bookstore: La Feltrinelli, conveniently located at Centrale station, carries a small selection of English-language books (daily 8:00-20:00, near track 24, also accessible from outside the station).

Laundry: Lav@Sciuga, a block from the Università Metro stop, is convenient but has just a few washing machines (Mon-Fri 9:00-17:00, Sat until 13:00, closed Sun, Via Sedile di Porto 54, mobile +39 327 754 6639).

GETTING AROUND NAPLES

Sightsee Naples with help from its subway (Metro), funiculars, and taxis. (There are also public buses, but these generally aren't useful for travelers.) For general transit information, maps, and fares, visit www.unicocampania.it. For schedules, your only option is the Italian-only site www.anm.it. Google Maps works as well as anything for journey planning.

Tickets and Passes: Most of Naples' public transportation system—Metro, funiculars, and buses—use the same ticket, which must be stamped as you enter (in yellow or blue machines). Tickets are sold at tobacco stores, some newsstands, clunky machines at Metro stations (these accept coins, small bills, or credit cards, but can be tricky to operate), and occasionally at station windows. Basically, anywhere you see a queue near the station, people are buying tickets.

A €1.10 single ticket *(corsa singola)* covers any ride on bus, funicular, or Metro line 1, with no transfers; for Metro line 2 you need the €1.30 version. (This ticket is a long, printed receipt with a QR code that needs to be punched at the machine—fold your ticket in half and insert.) A *giornaliero* day pass costs €3.50 (or €4.50 including Metro line 2), and pays for itself quickly, but can be hard to find; many tobacco stores don't sell them. A weekly ticket (Mon-Sun) costs €12.50, or €16 including Metro line 2. Several versions of the Campania ArteCard (see sidebar on page 6) include free public transport in Naples.

By Metro (Metropolitana): Naples' subway has three main lines *(linea)*. Station entrances and signs to the Metro are marked by a red square with a white *M*.

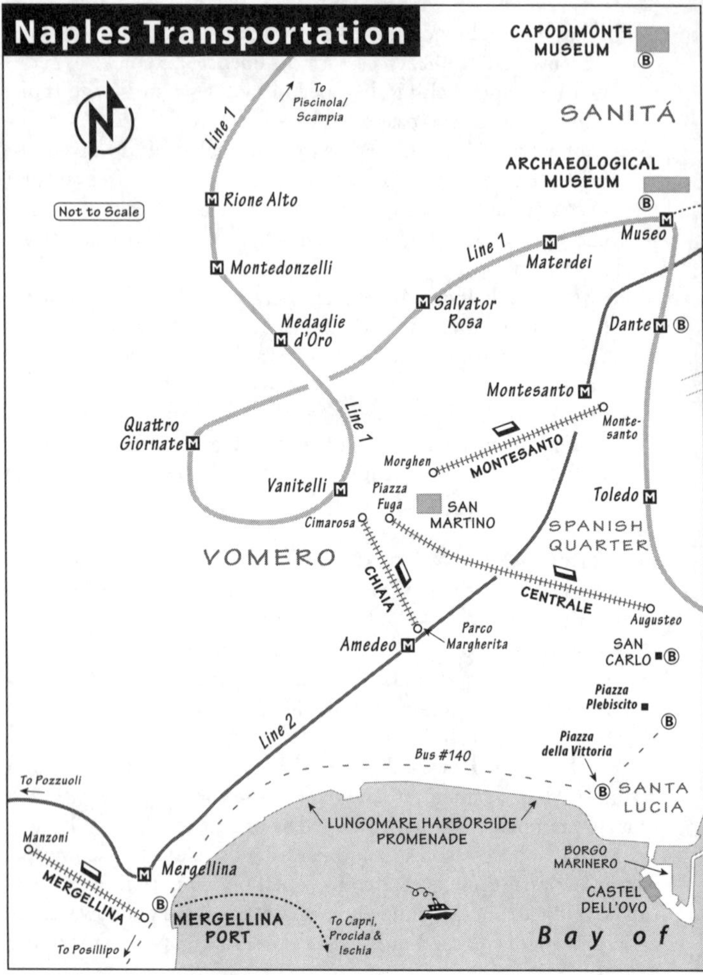

Line 1 is very useful for tourists. Starting from Centrale train station (stop name: Garibaldi), it heads to Università (the university), Municipio (at Piazza Municipio, just above the harbor and cruise terminal), Toledo (south end of Via Toledo, near Piazza del Plebiscito), Dante (Piazza Dante), and Museo (Archaeological Museum). Four stops beyond Museo is the Vanvitelli stop, near the hilltop San Martino sights; the end of the line is Piscinola. Many of line 1's stations are huge and elaborate, designed by prominent artists and architects; Naples is proud of them, and locals are excited to tell you about their favorite.

Line 2 (part of Trenitalia, the Italian national rail system) is most useful for getting quickly from the Centrale train station to Piazza Cavour (a 5-minute walk from the Archaeological Museum)

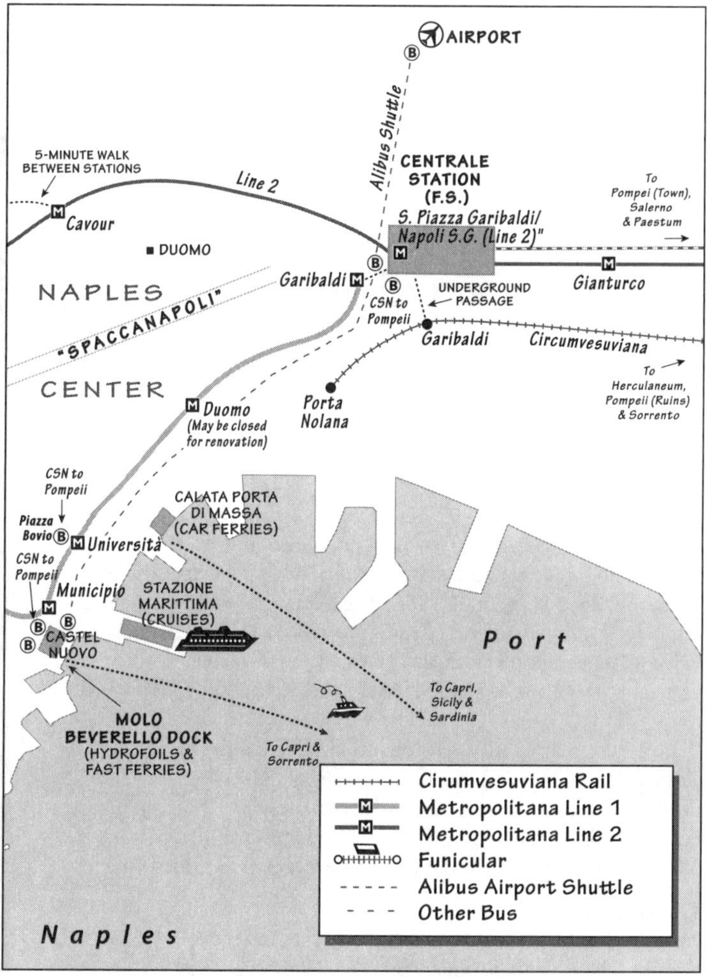

or Montesanto (the top of the Spanish Quarter and Spaccanapoli street, and base of one funicular up to San Martino). Note that the train station stop on this line is called "Napoli S.G." (for Stazione Piazza Garibaldi). Some trains on this line run all the way out into the suburbs (including to modern Pompei and Salerno).

By Funicular: Central Naples' three funiculars *(funicolare)* carry commuters and sightseers into the hilly San Martino neighborhood just west of downtown. All three converge near Piazza Fuga, a short walk from the hilltop fortress and monastery/museum. The Centrale line runs from the Spanish Quarter, just near Piazza del Plebiscito and the Toledo Metro stop; the Montesanto line from the Montesanto Metro stop and Via Pignasecca market zone; and the Chiaia line from near the Piazza Amadeo Metro stop.

By Taxi: A taxi lets you experience Naples traffic without actually driving in it—an experience worth at least ▲ (or more, when it's really chaotic). A short ride in town should cost €10-15. Always ask for the *tariffa predeterminata* (fixed rate), which should be prominently posted inside any legitimate taxi. Your hotel can call you a cab and make sure you know the appropriate rate. For metered rides, there are some legitimate extra charges (baggage fees, €2.50 supplement after 22:00 or all day Sun and holidays) but the destinations I recommend in this chapter are covered by the *tariffa predeterminata.* Radio Taxi 8888 is one reputable company (+39 081 8888).

Tours in Naples

🎧 To sightsee on your own, download my free Rick Steves audio tours of the Naples Archaeological Museum and my Naples Walk.

Local Guides

Pina Esposito has a Ph.D. in ancient archaeology and art and does fine private walking and driving tours of Naples and the region (Pompeii, Herculaneum, Capri, the Amalfi Coast, etc.), including Naples' Archaeological Museum (€60/hour, 2-hour minimum, RS%—10 percent off with this book, up to 20 percent off for full-day tours, mobile +39 338 763 4224, annamariaesposito1@virgilio.it).

The team at **Mondo Guide** offers private tours of the Archaeological Museum (€120/2 hours) and city (€240/4 hours) and can provide guides or drivers throughout the region. They can also arrange kayaking trips, boat trips, and whatever else you need (+39 081 751 3290, www.mondoguide.it, info@mondoguide.com).

Walking Tours

Mondo Guide offers my readers special shared tours of Naples and of Pompeii, as well as other trips. For details, see the sidebar.

Hop-On, Hop-Off Bus Tours

CitySightseeing Napoli tour buses make two different hop-on, hop-off loops through the city. Only the red line, which loops around the historical center and stops at the Archaeological Museum, is particularly helpful. It will also give you a sense of greater Naples that this chapter largely ignores (€23, ticket valid 24 hours, 2/hour, buy from driver or from kiosk at Piazza Municipio in front of Castel Nuovo near the port, scant recorded narration, +39 081 551 7279, www.napoli.city-sightseeing.it). The blue line takes you out along the seafront pedestrian promenade to Posillipo Hill—a more upscale part of the city that Neapolitans love.

Cruise-Ship Excursions

Convenient for cruise-ship passengers, the **Can't Be Missed** tour company takes you from the port of Naples on an all-day coach trip for up to 20 passengers along the Amalfi Coast that includes a stop in Sorrento and a guided tour of Pompeii (€89, meet at 8:00 in front of port, bus leaves at 8:30, returns at 15:45, Pompeii ticket extra, mobile +1 607 542 7981, www.cantbemissedtours.com, RS%—10 percent off when you use promo code "RICKSTEVES" on their website).

Archaeological Museum Tour

Naples' Archaeological Museum (Museo Archeologico), worth ▲▲▲, is one of the world's great museums of ancient art. It boasts supersized statues as well as art and decorations from Pompeii and Herculaneum, the two ancient burgs that were buried in ash by the eruption of Mount Vesuvius in AD 79. For lovers of antiquity, this museum alone makes Naples a worthwhile stop.

When Pompeii was excavated in the late 1700s, Naples' Bourbon king bellowed, "Bring me the best of what you find!" The finest art and artifacts ended up here, leaving the ancient sites themselves barren (though still impressive). It's here at the Archaeological Museum that you can get up close and personal with the ancient world.

ORIENTATION

Cost and Hours: €15, sometimes more for temporary exhibits; Wed-Mon 9:00-19:30, closed Tue. Avoid lines by purchasing your ticket online. Early and temporary closures are noted on a board near the ticket office: The Secret Room tends to have shorter hours (sometimes closing in the early afternoon), and additional rooms can be closed in July and August.

Information: +39 081 442 2149, www.museoarcheologiconapoli.it.

Getting There: From Centrale station, you can reach the museum by Metro or taxi. **Metro** line 2 is quickest: At the station, buy a single transit ticket at a newsstand or tobacco shop—specify you want line 2 since the price and ticket are different from line 1. Follow signs downstairs to *Metro Linea 2,* then fold and punch your ticket in the small blue boxes near the escala-

Mondo Guide Tours of Pompeii, Naples, the Amalfi Coast, and Capri for My Readers

Mondo Guide, a big Naples-based company, offers "shared tours" for Rick Steves readers. These allow you the luxury of a private, professional guide at a fraction of the usual cost, because you'll be sharing the expense with other travelers using this book. Tours run from April through October and include **Pompeii,** a walking tour of **Naples,** and two longer-distance trips from Sorrento: an **Amalfi Coast** van tour and a private boat to the **isle of Capri.** The Pompeii and Naples tours are timed so you can do both on the same day. Mondo also offers shore excursions for cruise passengers arriving in Naples or Salerno. I don't receive a cut from the tours; I set this up with Mondo Guide to help my readers have the most economical experience in this region.

Reservations are required. For specifics and to sign up, go to SharedTours.com (Mondo +39 081 751 3290, mobile +39 340 460 5254, www.mondoguide.it, sharedtours@mondoguide.com). On the website, use your credit-card number to reserve a spot. You'll then pay cash for the tour. If you must cancel, email more than three days in advance or you'll be billed.

Each tour requires a minimum of six participants. You'll be sent an email confirmation as soon as they're sure your tour will run. If there's not enough demand to justify the trip, they'll notify you three days before the departure date (giving you time to come up with alternative plan). Confirmed departures are continually updated on the website.

Pompeii Tour: This two-hour guided walk brings to life the ruins of the excavated city (€20, Pompeii entry extra—your guide will collect money and buy tickets, daily at 11:00; meet in Pompeii at Hotel/Ristorante Suisse, a 5-minute walk from the train station—exiting the station, turn right, pass the Porta Marina entrance, and continue down the hill to the restaurant, on the right).

Historic Naples Walk: Naples is a challenge to enjoy and understand; on this three-hour walk, a local Neapolitan guide helps you uncover the true character of the city (€30; daily at 15:00; meet at the steps of the Naples Archaeological Museum—you can

tor going down to the tracks. Take a train in the direction of Pozzuoli, Campi Flegrei, or Formina (attendants may ask and confirm which direction you're going). Ride one stop to Piazza Cavour. Exit and walk five minutes uphill through the park. Look for a grand old red building up a flight of stairs at the top of the block.

You can also take the Metro's slightly cheaper line 1 five stops from Centrale station to Museo—it's only a little slower, and drops you closer to the museum.

do the museum on your own before joining your guide).

Full-Day Amalfi Coast Minibus Tour from Sorrento: The Amalfi Coast can be complicated and time-consuming to visit on your own, making a shared minibus the simplest and most affordable way to enjoy the sights. (Small groups use an eight-seat minibus with only a driver; larger groups use a 19-seat minibus with a driver and a guide.) This nine-hour trip saves time and money and maximizes your experience. It begins in Sorrento and heads south for the breathtaking (and lightly narrated) drive, several photo stops, and an hour or two on your own in each of the three main towns—Positano, Amalfi, and Ravello—before returning to Sorrento. Lunch isn't included; to save time for exploring, grab a quick lunch in one of the towns (€65, daily at 9:00; meet in Sorrento in front of Hotel Antiche Mura, at Via Fuorimura 7, a block inland from Piazza Tasso).

Full-Day Capri Boat Trip from Sorrento: To sidestep the hassles of taking public boats from Sorrento for a Capri side trip, Mondo offers a trip to the island on a small private boat (12 people maximum), which includes an early visit to the Blue Grotto sea cave when conditions allow (€15, optional) and about four hours of free time to explore the island on your own. After your time on land, the boat takes you on a lightly narrated trip around the island with drinks, snacks, and a chance to swim if the weather cooperates (€120, daily at 8:00, pickup at Sorrento hotel, may be cancelled in bad weather).

Shore Excursions from Naples or Salerno: Mondo Guide offers all-day itineraries from the port of Naples or the port of Salerno that combine three big sights in the region and the scenic Amalfi Coast— from Naples, a guided visit to Pompeii with an hour of free time each in Sorrento and Positano; from Salerno, a guided visit to Pompeii with an hour of free time each in Sorrento and Amalfi town (€80, daily at 8:00-8:30 from the main exit of the Naples cruise terminal building or from your ship in Salerno).

Figure about €13 for a **taxi** from the train station to the museum.

Visitor Information: The shop (behind the ticket desk) sells a worthwhile *National Archaeological Museum of Naples* guidebook for €13.

Tours: The self-guided tour in this chapter covers all the basics. For more detail, the decent **audioguide** (€5, leave ID at ticket desk) focuses largely on the provenance of the artifacts and how they ended up here. For a **guided tour,** book Pina Esposito (see "Tours in Naples," earlier).

🎧 Download my free Archaeological Museum **audio tour.**

Baggage Check: Bag check is obligatory and free.

Eating: The museum's **$ Mann Caffè** has both a counter and table service, and a full menu. There are also a few good places to grab a meal within a 10-minute walk; see page 61.

➔ SELF-GUIDED TOUR

Entering the museum, cross the atrium, and stand at the base of the grand staircase. To your right, on the ground floor, are the larger-than-life statues of the Farnese Collection, starring the *Toro Farnese* and the *Farnese Hercules.* Up the stairs on the mezzanine level are mosaics and frescoes from Pompeii, including the Secret Room of erotic art. On the top floor are more artifacts from Pompeii, a scale model of the doomed city, and bronze statues from Herculaneum. WCs are behind the staircase.

• *From the base of the* ❶ ***grand staircase,*** *turn right through the door marked* Collezione Farnese *and head for the far end, walking through a rich collection of ancient portrait* ❷ ***busts.***

Pause at the busts of ***Caracalla*** *(a third of the way down, on the left), and marvel at how he evolved from idealistic youth to cruel tyrant (and nemesis of Russell Crowe in the movie* Gladiator*). Admire the* **Seated Agrippina** *(two-thirds of the way down) with her typical hairstyle, realistic face, and pensive look. Nearby, look in* ***Vespasian****'s right ear and see how the huge head was hollowed out in medieval times. Now, continue to the end and jog right, then left, entering Room 13.*

Ground Floor: The Farnese Collection

The Farnese Collection statues are not from Pompeii, but from Rome. Today they're displayed in this grand hall of huge, bright, and wonderfully restored statues excavated from Rome's Baths of Caracalla. Peruse the larger-than-life statues filling the hall. They were dug up in the 1540s at the behest of Alessandro Farnese (by then Pope Paul III) while he was building the family palace on the Campo de' Fiori in Rome. His main purpose in excavating the baths was to scavenge quality building stone. The sculptures were a nice extra and helped the palace come in under budget on decorations. In the 1700s, the collection ended up in the hands of Charles, the Bourbon king of Naples (whose mother was a Farnese). His son, the next king, had it brought to Naples.

• *Quick—look down to the left end of the hall. There's a woman being tied to a snorting bull.*

The tangled ❸ ***Toro Farnese*** tells a thrilling Greek myth. At 13 feet, it's the tallest ancient marble group ever found, and the

Naples Archaeological Museum

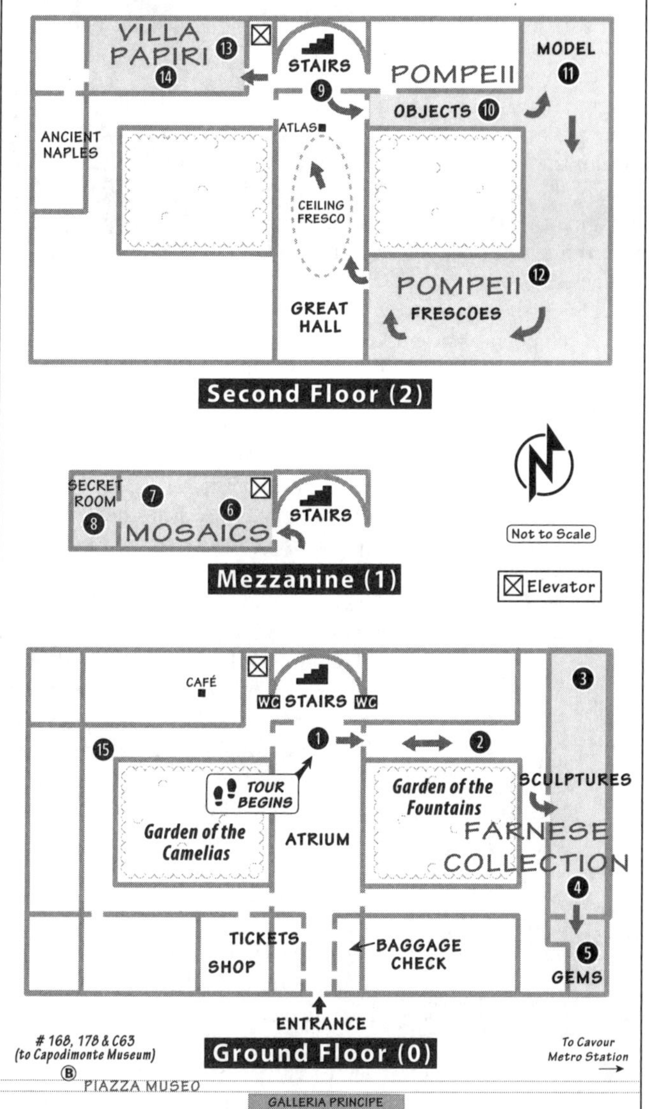

1. Grand Staircase
2. Hall of the Busts
3. Toro Farnese
4. Farnese Hercules
5. Farnese Cup
6. Various Mosaics
7. Dancing Faun & Battle of Alexander
8. Secret Room
9. Great Hall
10. Metal, Ivory & Glass Objects
11. Model of Pompeii
12. Frescoes
13. Papyrus Scrolls
14. Bronze Statues
15. Doriforo (might have moved)

largest intact statue from antiquity. A third-century AD copy of a lost bronze Hellenistic original, it was carved out of one piece of marble. Michelangelo and others "restored" it at the pope's request—meaning that they integrated surviving bits into a new work. Some pieces were actually carved by Michelangelo: the head of the woman in back, the torso of the aunt under the bull, and the dog. (Imagine how the statue would stand out if it were thoughtfully lit and not surrounded by white walls.)

Here's the tragic story behind the statue: Once upon an ancient Greek time, King Lycus was bewitched by Dirce. He abandoned his pregnant wife, Antiope (standing regally in the background). The single mom gave birth to twin boys. When they grew up, they killed their deadbeat dad and tied Dirce to the horns of a bull to be bashed against a mountain. Captured in marble, the action is thrilling: cape flailing, dog snarling, hooves in the air. You can almost hear the bull snorting. And in the back, Antiope oversees this harsh ancient justice with satisfaction.

At the opposite end of the hall stands the ❹ ***Farnese Hercules.*** The great Greek hero is exhausted. He leans wearily on his club (draped with his lion skin) and bows his head. He's just finished the daunting Eleventh Labor, having traveled the world, fought men and gods, freed Prometheus from his rock, and carried Atlas' weight of the world on his shoulders. Now he's returned with the prize: the golden apples of the gods, which he cups behind his back. But, after all that, he's just been told he has to return the apples and do one final labor: descend into hell itself. Oh, man.

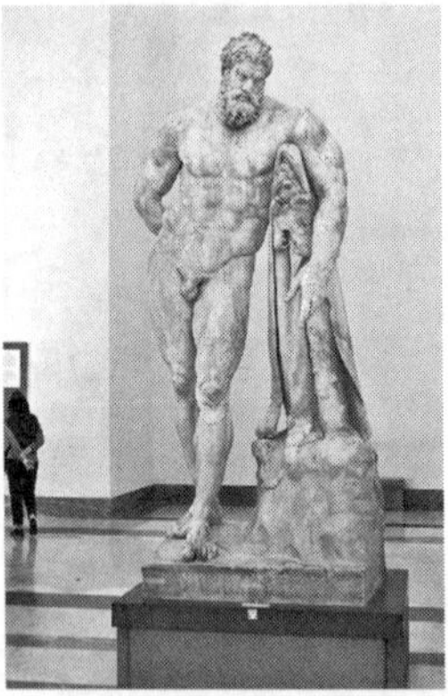

The 10-foot colossus is a third-century AD Roman marble copy (signed by "Glykon") of a fourth-century BC Greek bronze original (probably by Lysippos). The statue was enormously famous in its day. Dozens of copies—some marble, some bronze—have been found in Roman villas and baths. This version was unearthed in Rome's Baths of Caracalla in 1546, along with the *Toro Farnese.*

The *Farnese Hercules* was equally famous in the 16th-18th centuries. Tourists flocked to Rome to admire it, art students studied it from afar in prints, Louis XIV made a copy for Versailles, and petty nobles everywhere put small-scale knock-offs in their gardens. This curly-haired version of Hercules became the modern world's image of the Greek hero.

• *Behind Hercules is a doorway into the impressive Farnese gem collection (*Gemme Farnese, *Rooms 9 and 10). You'll see cameos and the ancient cereal bowl-shaped* ❺ **Farnese Cup,** *which features a portrait thought to be of Cleopatra. When you're ready to move on, backtrack to the main entry hall with its grand staircase—perhaps stopping briefly to admire the magnificent sarcophagi in adjacent rooms—then head up to the mezzanine level (turn left at the lion and go under the* Mosaici *sign), and enter Room 57.*

Mezzanine: Pompeiian Mosaics and the Secret Room

These ❻ **mosaics**—mostly of animals, battle scenes, and geometric designs—were excavated from the walls and floors of Pompeii's ritzy villas. The *Chained Dog* once graced a home's entryway. The colorful mosaic columns (to your right in adjoining Room 58) shaded a courtyard, part of an ensemble of wall mosaics and bubbling fountains. In Room 59, admire the realism of the tambourine-playing musicians, the drinking doves, and the skull—a reminder of impending death.

Continue a few steps into Room 60, with objects taken from one of Pompeii's greatest villas, the House of the Faun. The 20-inch-high statue was the house's delightful centerpiece, the ❼ ***Dancing Faun.*** This rare surviving Greek bronze statue (from the fourth century BC) is surrounded by some of the best mosaics of that age. (Find the wild-eyed little cat, who's caught a bird.)

A museum highlight, just beyond the statue, is the grand ***Battle of Alexander,*** a second-century-BC copy of the now-lost original Greek fresco, done a century earlier. It decorated a floor in the House of the Faun and was found intact. (The damage you see occurred as this treasure was moved from Pompeii to the king's collection here.) Alexander (left side of the scene, with curly hair and sideburns) is about to defeat the Persians under Darius (central figure, in chariot with turban and beard). This pivotal victory allowed Alexander to quickly overrun much of Asia (331 BC). Alexander is the only one without a helmet...a confident master of the battlefield while everyone else is fighting for their lives, eyes bulging with fear. Notice how the horses, already in retreat, add to

the scene's propaganda value. Notice also the shading and perspective, which Renaissance artists would later work so hard to accomplish. (A modern reproduction of the mosaic is now back in Pompeii, at the House of the Faun.)

Farther on, the ❽ **Secret Room** (*Gabinetto Segreto,* Room 65) contains a sizable assortment of erotic frescoes, well-hung pottery, and perky statues that once decorated bedrooms, meeting rooms, brothels, and even shops at Pompeii and Herculaneum. These bawdy statues and frescoes—many of them once displayed in Pompeii's grandest houses—were entertainment for guests. (By the time they made it to this museum, in 1819, the frescoes could be viewed only with permission from the king—see the letters in the glass case just outside the door.) The Roman nobles commissioned the wildest scenes imaginable. Think of them as ancient dirty jokes. If you're easily offended, or find scatological humor juvenile, skip this room.

At the entrance, you're enthusiastically greeted by big stone penises that once projected over Pompeii's doorways. A massive phallus was not necessarily a sexual symbol, but a magical amulet used against the "evil eye." It symbolized fertility, happiness, good luck, riches, straight A's, and general wellbeing.

Circulating counterclockwise through this section, look for the following: the fresco—high up—of a faun playfully pulling the sheet off a woman (#12), only to be surprised to find both sets of genitalia. A few steps farther, see horny "pygmies" from Africa in action (#27). There's a toga with an embarrassing bulge (#34). A particularly high-quality statue depicts a goat and a satyr engaging in a sex act (#36). And, watching over it all with remarkable aplomb, is Venus, the patron goddess of Pompeii (#39).

The back room is furnished and decorated the way an ancient brothel might have been. The 10 frescoes on the wall functioned as both a menu of services offered and as a kind of *Kama Sutra* of sex positions. The glass cases contain more phallic art, including dangling mobiles used as party favors at rowdy banquets.

• *So, now that your travel buddy is finally showing a little interest in art...finish up your visit by climbing the stairs to the top floor.*

At the top of the stairs, pause and get oriented to our final sights. Directly ahead is a doorway (marked Salone Meridiana*) that leads into a big, empty hall. To the left of this grand hall is a series of rooms with more artifacts from Pompeii. To the right are rooms of statues from Herculaneum. Keep this general layout in mind, because occasionally door-*

ways and routes are altered, and you may have to improvise a bit to find your way.

Top Floor: Frescoes, Statues, Artifacts, and a Model of Pompeii

First, step into the Salone Meridiana. This was the ❾ **great hall** of the university (17th and 18th centuries) until the building became the royal museum in 1777. Walk to the center. The sundial in the floor (angling off to the right, from 1791) still works. Look up to the far-right corner of the hall and find the tiny pinhole. At noon (13:00 in summer), a ray of sun enters the hall and strikes the sundial, showing the time of the year...if you know your zodiac.

Now, back where you entered, go into the series of rooms to the left of the grand hall, with ❿ **Metal, Ivory, and Glass Objects** found in Pompeii. You enter through a doorway marked *Vetri e Avori,* which leads into Room 89. Browse your way to the far end, with the stunning *Blue Vase* (Room 85), decorated with cameo Bacchuses harvesting grapes. Turn left, then right, to find the huge, room-filling ⓫ **model of Pompeii,** a 1:100 scale model of the ruins (Room 96). Face the model from the side labeled *plastico di Pompei.* This is how tourists enter today, up the street, and spilling into the large rectangular forum with the Temple of Jupiter at one end. Farther up in the model are the city's two amphitheater-shaped theaters. This was all that had been excavated when the model was made in 1879. Another model (displayed on the wall) shows the site in 2004, after more excavations, when they'd dug up as far as the huge oval-shaped arena. Video screens capture images from the 1879 model and reconstruct buildings in 3-D as they would have appeared before the eruption.

Continue on (through Rooms 83-80—turn right, then left) and enter Room 75 (marked *Affreschi*) to see the museum's impressive collection of (nonerotic) ⓬ **frescoes** taken from the walls of Pompeii villas. Pompeiians loved to decorate their homes with scenes from mythology (Hercules' labors, Venus and Mars in love), landscapes, everyday market scenes, and faux architecture. To the left (in Room 78), find the famous dual portrait of baker Terentius Neo and his wife—possibly two of the 2,000 victims when Vesuvius erupted.

• *Browse through more frescoes and objects from Pompeii in this labyrinth of rooms until, eventually, you end up back near the great hall. From here, facing the hall entrance, turn left and find the entrance to the wing labeled* La Villa dei Papiri.

These artifacts came from the Herculaneum holiday home of Julius Caesar's father-in-law. In Room 114, find the glass cases holding two blackened examples of the 2,000 ⓭ **papyrus scrolls** that gave the villa its name. The half-burned scrolls were unrolled and (with luck) read after excavation in the 1750s. Apparently Caesar's father-in-law was an educated man who appreciated everything from Greek philosophy to Latin history.

Continuing into Room 116, enjoy some of the villa's ⓮ **bronze statues.** Look into the lifelike blue eyes of the intense *Corridore* (runners), bent on doing their best. The *Five Dancers,* with their inlaid-ivory eyes and graceful poses, decorated a portico. The next room (117) has more fine works: *Resting Hermes* (with his tired little heel wings) is taking a break. Nearby, the *Drunken Faun* (singing and snapping his fingers to the beat, a wineskin at his side) is clearly living for today. This statue epitomizes the *carpe diem* lifestyle of the Epicurean philosophy followed by Caesar's father-in-law and so many other Romans living in Herculaneum and Pompeii on that fateful morning of August 24, AD 79, when Vesuvius changed everything.

• *Ka-pow. The artistic explosion you've just experienced in this mighty museum is now over. To exit, return to the ground floor. You may be able to leave the way you came in. Or you may be routed to another exit, past the café and around the museum courtyard to the gift shop. Either way, for extra credit, look for one more sight on your way out. (He tends to get moved around; if you can't find him ask a guard,* "Dov'è il Doriforo?"*)*

⓯ Doriforo

This seven-foot-tall "spear-carrier" (the literal translation of *doriforo*) just stands there, as if holding a spear. What's the big deal about this statue, which looks like so many others? It's a marble replica made by the Romans of one of the most-copied statues of antiquity, a fifth-century-BC bronze Greek original by Polyclitus. This copy once stood in a Pompeii gym, where it inspired ancient athletes by showing the ideal proportions of Greek beauty. So full of motion, and so realistic in its *contrapposto* pose (weight on one foot), the *Doriforo* would later inspire Donatello and Michelangelo, helping to trigger the Renaissance. And so the glories of ancient Pompeii, once buried and forgotten, live on today.

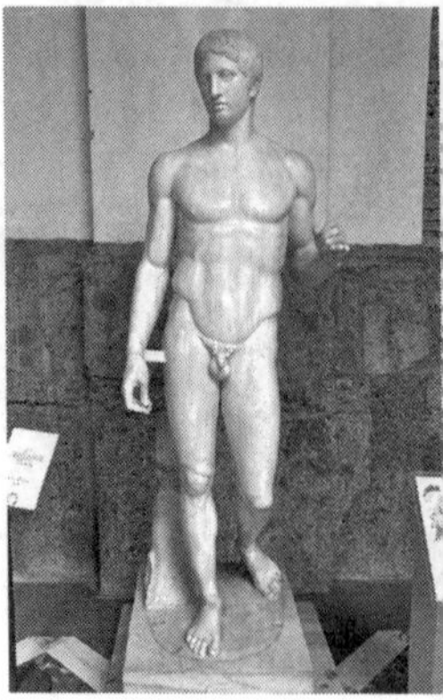

Naples Walk

Naples, a living medieval city, is its own best sight. Couples artfully make love on Vespas surrounded by more smiles per cobblestone than anywhere else in Italy. Sure, Naples has its important sights. But to capture its essence, take this walk through the core of the city.

A SLICE OF NEAPOLITAN LIFE

This self-guided walk, worth ▲▲▲, takes you from the Archaeological Museum through the heart of town. Allow at least two hours for the full two-part walk, plus time for pizza and sightseeing stops. If your time is short, from Piazza Carità—near the middle of the walk—you can head down Via Toledo to the Toledo Metro stop to zip back to the train station.

🎧 You can also download my free Naples City Walk audio tour.

Part 1: Archaeological Museum to Piazza Carità

Start at the Archaeological Museum, at the top of Piazza Cavour (Metro: Cavour or Museo; for directions on getting here, see page 15). From here, we'll ramble down a fine boulevard before cutting into the medieval heart of the city.

❶ **Archaeological Museum:** The palatial building, built in the mid-1700s, captures the glory of Naples at its peak, and is a great introduction to the Naples we'll see. Back then, the city was rich from sea trade and home to erudite nobles from abroad. They built a magnificent capital of buildings like this one. On this walk we'll see that grand city they built...and its remnants following centuries of decline.

• *From the door of the Archaeological Museum, cross the street, veer right, and enter the arched doorway of the beige-colored Galleria Principe di Napoli mall. (If the entrance is blocked, simply loop around the block to another entrance or pick up our walk behind the Galleria.)*

❷ **Galleria Principe di Napoli:** There's no better example of Naples' grandeur—and decline—than this elegant 19th-century shopping mall. You'll enjoy a soaring skylight, carved woodwork, ironwork lanterns, playful cupids, an elegant atmosphere...and empty shops. Built with great expectations, the galleria was named for the first male child of the royal Savoy family, the Prince of Naples. Malls like these were popular in Paris and London. In the US, we call this

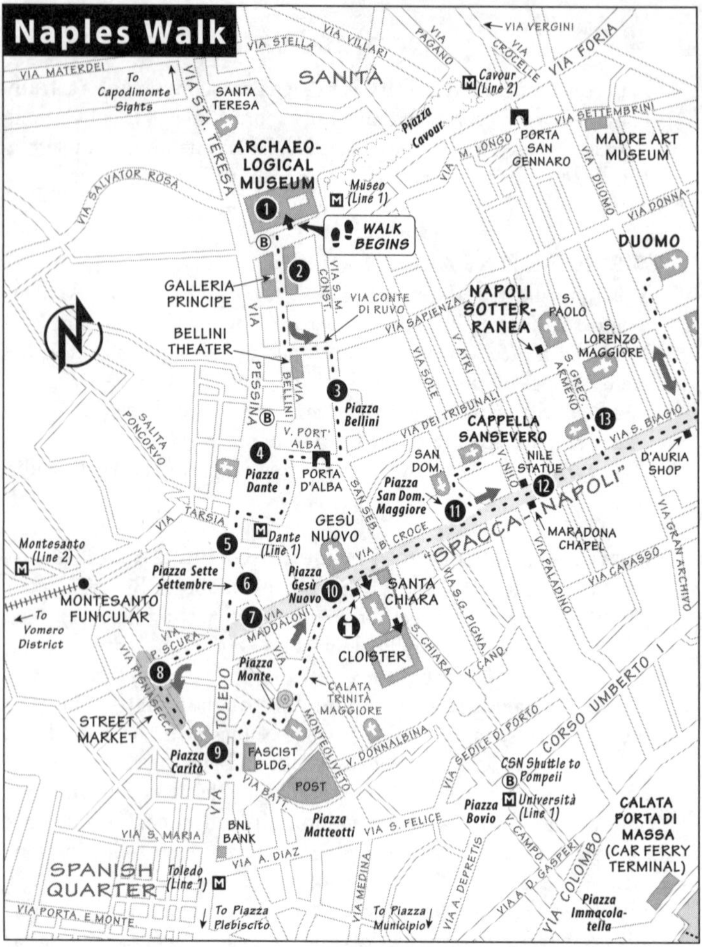

decorative style Art Nouveau; in Italy it's "Liberty Style," named for a British department store that was in vogue at a time when Naples was nicknamed the "Paris of the South." (Parisian artist Edgar Degas even left Paris to adopt Naples—which he considered more cosmopolitan and sophisticated—as his hometown.) Despite its grandeur, the mall never took off. Ambitious renovations in recent years have failed to attract much business, leaving the mall in a state of disrepair. Falling debris occasionally closes the entire structure.

• *Leaving the gallery through the opposite end, walk one block downhill on a pedestrian street. You'll pass alongside the palatial golden facade of the Academy of Fine Arts, fronted by tropical plants and (usually) busy with students at its outdoor cafés. At Via Conte di Ruvo, turn left, passing the fine* ***Bellini Theater*** *(also in Liberty Style). All along our walk,*

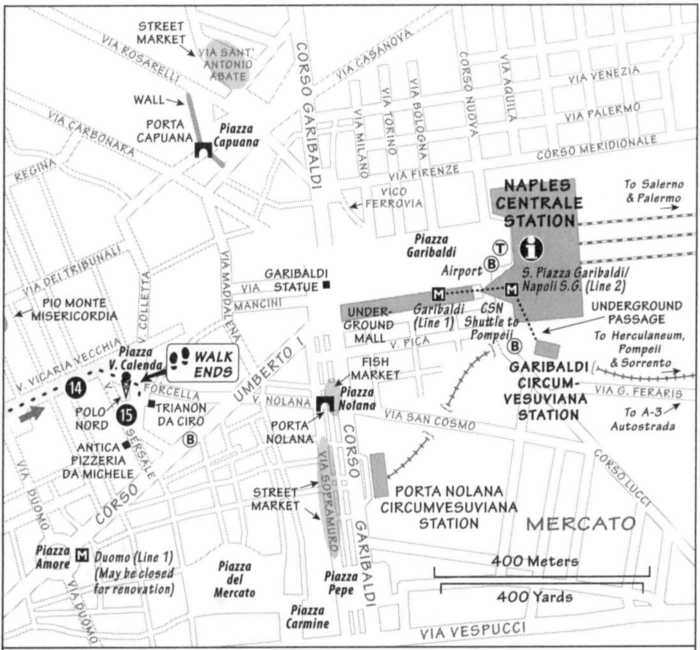

Part 1

1. Archaeological Museum
2. Galleria Principe di Napoli
3. Piazza Bellini
4. Piazza Dante
5. Via Toledo
6. Piazza Sette Settembre
7. Spaccanapoli
8. Via Pignasecca
9. Piazza Carità

Part 2

10. Piazza Gesù Nuovo
11. Piazza San Domenico Maggiore
12. Statue of the Nile
13. Via San Gregorio Armeno
14. Via Vicaria Vecchia
15. Eateries

be sure to enjoy the architecture of the late 19th century, when Naples was the last stop on Romantic Age travelers' Grand Tour of Europe. After one block, turn right on Via Santa Maria di Costantinopoli. Walking between two grand churches, continue directly downhill to a small park with a statue in the center called...

❸ **Piazza Bellini:** Suddenly you're in neighborhood Napoli. The statue honors the opera composer Vincenzo Bellini, whose career was launched in Naples in the early 1800s, when opera itself was being born. Just past the statue, peer down into the sunken area to see Naples' ancient origins as a fifth-century-BC Greek colony called Neapolis—literally, "the new city." These tuff blocks without mortar were part of a tower in the city wall. (And you're standing on land that, back then, was outside of the town.) You can see how the street level has risen from the rubble of centuries.

Now look around at the city of today. Survey the many balconies—and the people who use them as a "backyard" in this densely packed city. The apartment blocks were originally the palaces of noble families, as indicated by the stately family crests above grand doorways. For 2,500 years, laundry has blown in the breeze right here.

• *Walk 30 yards downhill on the right side. Stop at the horseshoe-shaped* ***Port'Alba gate*** *(just beyond the bottom of the square, on the right). Spin slowly 360 degrees and take in the scene. The proud tile across the street (upstairs, between the two balconies) shows Piazza Bellini circa 1890. Don't ignore the graffiti; try to figure out the issues that artists are calling attention to.*

Pass through the gate, down Via Port'Alba, and stroll through this pleasant passage lined with book stalls. You emerge into a big square called...

❹ **Piazza Dante:** This square is marked by a statue of Dante, the medieval poet. Fittingly, half the square is devoted to bookstores. Old Dante looks out over an urban area that was once grand, then chaotic, and is now slowly becoming grand again.

Along one side is a grandiose, orange-and-gray **pseudo-facade** of columns and statues designed by Luigi Vanvitelli, an architect who made his mark on the city in the late 1700s. Vanvitelli remade an existing Jesuit monastery into this new school, representing the power of the Bourbon monarchy when Naples was at its peak. Originally, a statue of the king stood in the square. But in 1799, the Bourbon monarchy was toppled when Napoleon invaded. The king's statue was removed and replaced with the generic figure of Dante. And note the name that was later added to the big facade—Victor Emmanuel (Vittorio Emanuele). These suggest the next phase of Naples' history—its decline—which we'll see in just a bit.

The Neapolitan people are survivors. A long history of corrupt and greedy colonial overlords (German, Norman, French, Austrian, Spanish, Napoleon, etc.) has taught Neapolitans to deal creatively with authority. Many credit this aspect of Naples' past for the strength of organized crime here.

• *Before moving on, note the red* "M" *that Dante seems to be gesturing to. This marks the* ***Dante Metro station,*** *the best of Napoli's art-splashed Metro stations. (To take a look, go down three flights of escalators and then back up; you'll need a ticket, unless you can sweet-talk a guard.) Then, exit Piazza Dante at the far (bottom) end, walking downhill on...*

❺ **Via Toledo:** The long, straight street heading downhill from Piazza Dante is Naples' principal shopping drag. It originated as a military road built by the Spanish viceroys (hence the name) who made Naples great in the 16th century. Back then, Via Toledo skirted the old town wall to connect the Spanish military headquarters (now the museum where you started this walk) with the Royal Palace (down by the bay). As you stroll, peek into the many lovely atriums, which provide a break from the big street.

After a couple hundred yards, you'll reach the triangular ❻ **Piazza Sette Settembre.** This public space recalls the event that precipitated Naples' swift decline. On September 7, 1860, from the white marble balcony of the Neoclassical building overlooking the square, the famous revolutionary Giuseppe Garibaldi celebrated his conquest of Naples. He declared Italy united and Victor Emmanuel II its first king. And a decade later, that declaration became reality when Rome also fell to unification forces. It was the start of a glorious new era for Italy, Rome, and the Italian people. But not for Naples.

Naples' treasury was confiscated to subsidize the industrial expansion of the north, and its bureaucrats were transferred to the new capital in Rome. Within a few decades, Naples went from being a thriving cultural and political capital to a provincial town, with its economy in shambles and its dialect considered backward.

• *Continue straight on Via Toledo. A block past Piazza Sette Settembre you'll come to Via Maddaloni, which marks the start of the long, straight, narrow street nicknamed...*

❼ **Spaccanapoli:** Via Maddaloni is the modern name for the beginning of this thin street that, since ancient times, has bisected the city. The name Spaccanapoli translates as "split Naples." Look left down the street (toward the train station), and right (toward San Martino hill), and you get a sense of how Spaccanapoli divides this urban jungle of buildings.

• *At this point in our walk, take a moment to plan your next move. From here, our walk loops to the right, through the edge of the intense residential Spanish Quarter neighborhood to Piazza Carità before cutting over to the Spaccanapoli district. (If you were to side-trip to the Royal Palace and Piazza del Plebiscito-area sights—described later in "Sights in Naples"—you'd do that from here...but that makes this walk very long.)*

At the Spaccanapoli intersection, go right (toward the church facade on the hill), heading up Via Pasquale Scura. After about 100 yards, you hit a busy intersection where the street begins to climb steeply uphill. Stop. You're on one of Naples' most colorful open-air market streets...

❽ **Via Pignasecca:** Take in the colorful scene at the intersection. Then, turn left down Via Pignasecca and stroll this colorful market strip. You'll pass fish stalls, tripe vendors, butchers, produce stands, cheap clothes stores, street-food vendors, and much more. There's more activity during the morning, but afternoon offers better light for photography.

This is a taste of Naples' famous **Spanish Quarter** (its center is farther down Via Toledo but this area provides a good sampling).

The Spanish Quarter is a classic world of *basso* (low) living. The streets—which were laid out in the 16th century for the Spanish military barracks outside the city walls—are unbelievably narrow (and cool in summer), and the buildings rise five stories high. In such tight quarters, life—flirting, fighting, playing, and loving—happens in the road. This is *the* cliché of life in Naples, as shown in so many movies. The Spanish Quarter is Naples at its most characteristic. The shopkeepers are friendly, and the mopeds are bold (watch out). Concerned locals will tug on their lower eyelids, warning you to be wary. Hungry? Pop into a grocery shop and ask the clerk to make you his best prosciutto-and-mozzarella sandwich (it should cost you about €4).

• *Turn left and follow Via Pignasecca as it leads back to Via Toledo at the square called...*

❾ **Piazza Carità:** This square, built for an official visit by Hitler to Mussolini in 1938, is full of stern, straight, obedient lines. The big building belonged to an insurance company. (For the best example of fascist architecture in town, take a slight detour from here: With your back to Via Toledo, leave Piazza Carità downhill on the right-hand corner and walk a block to the Poste e Telegrafi building. There you'll see several government buildings with stirring reliefs singing the praises of lobotomized workers and a totalitarian society.)

In Naples—long a poor and rough city—rather than being heroic, people learn from the cradle the art of survival. The modern memorial statue in the center of this square celebrates Salvo d'Acquisto, a rare hometown hero. In 1943, he was executed after falsely confessing to sabotage... saving 22 fellow Italian soldiers from a Nazi revenge massacre.

• *We're at the midpoint of this walk. Need a WC? Pop into the Burger King. Running out of time and energy? If you end the walk here, you'll find many cafés and wine bars nearby, and it's a short stroll down Via Toledo to the Toledo Metro station.*

To continue, face the fascist-style building and take the street on its left side. You'll angle through a downhill square called Piazza Monteoliveto. At the bottom of the square, cross the busy street, then angle up Calata Trinità Maggiore to the fancy column in the piazza at the top of the hill.

Part 2: Piazza Gesù Nuovo to Centrale Station

• *You're back on the straight-as-a-Greek-arrow Spaccanapoli, formerly the main thoroughfare of the Greek city of Neapolis. (Spaccanapoli changes names several times: Via Maddaloni, Via B. Croce, Via S. Biagio dei Librai, and Via Vicaria Vecchia.) Linger for a moment on...*

⑩ Piazza Gesù Nuovo: This square is marked by a towering 18th-century Baroque monument to the Counter-Reformation. Although the Jesuit order was powerful in Naples because of its Spanish heritage, locals never attacked Protestants here with the full fury of the Spanish Inquisition.

If you'd like, you can visit two bulky old churches, starting with the dark, fortress-like, 17th-century **Church of Gesù Nuovo,** followed by the simpler **Church of Santa Chiara** (in the courtyard across the street; both described under "Sights in Naples"). There's also a **TI** on this square.

• *Continue along the main drag for another 200 yards. Since this is a university district, you may see students and bookstores. As this neighborhood is also famously superstitious, look for incense-burning women with carts full of good-luck charms for sale.*

Passing Palazzo Venezia—the embassy of Venice to Naples when both were independent powers—you'll emerge into the next square...

⑪ Piazza San Domenico Maggiore: This square is marked by another ornate 17th-century monument built to thank God for ending the plague. From this square, you can detour left along the right side of the castle-like church, then follow yellow signs, taking the first right and walking one short block to the remark-

NAPLES

Still Naples After All These Years

For three centuries (1500-1800), Naples was one of the world's richest and most sophisticated cities. The remnants we see today are an elegant reminder of that golden age, and a fascinating case study in what went wrong.

500 BC-AD 500—Greek-Speaking Romans: Naples got its start as Neapolis ("new city"), a thriving Greek colony. Even when conquered by the Romans, the city never fully adopted the Latin language and Roman ways. Actually, those sophisticated Hellenist traditions were exactly what the Romans admired about Naples and made them want to vacation there. For the next 2,000 years, this pattern would repeat itself: The city, living under foreign rule, would evolve independently from the rest of the Italian peninsula.

500-1500—Independence Despite Foreign Rule: The city powered on relatively unchanged after the fall of Rome, ruled as the independent Duchy of Naples under Ostrogoths, Byzantines, and Lombards. Next, in late-medieval times, it was the Germans and French (or "Angevins") who possessed it as the Kingdom of Naples. As sea trade became more important to the European economy, Naples was suddenly smack-dab in the geographical heart of commerce—the Mediterranean.

1500-1800—Golden Age: In 1502, Spain conquered Naples, and their combined wealth made Naples one of the great cities on Earth. With a population of 300,000, Naples was eclipsed only by Paris. Deputies of the Spanish king called viceroys presided over the city, and proceeded to use Spain's New World wealth to beautify Naples.

When Spain's monarchy passed to the Austrian Habsburgs and Spanish Bourbons, the cosmopolitan nature of Naples was only enhanced. Naples was home to nobles and royalty from across Europe. Baroque culture thrived, with artists like Caravaggio and Bernini, thinkers like Giordano Bruno, composers like

able Baroque **Cappella Sansevero** (described under "Sights in Naples").

• *After touring the chapel, return to Via B. Croce (a.k.a. Spaccanapoli), turn left, and continue your cultural scavenger hunt. At the intersection of Via Nilo, find the...*

⓬ **Statue of the Nile** (on the left): A reminder of the multiethnic makeup of Greek Neapolis, this statue is in what was the Egyptian quarter. Locals like to call this statue *The Body of Naples,* with the overflowing cornucopia symbolizing the abundance of their fine city. (I once asked a Neapolitan man to describe the local women, who are famous for their beauty, in one word. He replied, simply, "Abundant.") This intersection is considered the center of old Naples.

Scarlatti, and a new art form called opera. Naples took on the "look" it retains today, with palatial Neoclassical buildings in pastel colors and lavishly ornamented churches.

Despite its veneer of sophistication, trouble was brewing. In 1656, a vicious bubonic plague (Europe's last) killed off half the population. Trade routes shifted west as Europe industrialized, but Naples languished, remaining feudal and agricultural, with the church owning much of the land. The gap between rich foreign elites and homegrown poor grew.

1800-2000: Napoleon conquered the city. Then the monarchy was restored under a medieval-era political arrangement called the Kingdom of the Two Sicilies (uniting Naples and Sicily). The city was still rich, thanks to its Spanish Bourbon rulers, but it was increasingly backward, left behind by a more industrialized and democratic Europe.

Meanwhile, sweeping down from the north, there was a movement for Italian nationhood. Naples—with its legacy of independence from the rest of the peninsula—resisted. But in 1860, Naples was forcefully united with the new nation-state of Italy. Its vast wealth was confiscated and taken to the capital in Rome.

This began a century-plus of decline. There was no foreign wealth and no local economy. An estimated four million southern Italians fled, emigrating to northern Italy and the US. During World War II, Naples suffered Italy's worst bombings. The postwar economic recovery in northern Italy never trickled south, which remained under the thumb of the feudal-style Camorra (the Naples-based Mafia).

Today: The lack of a postwar economic recovery is a boon to tourists. It preserved an independent way of life that dates back centuries. Visitors today enjoy a rare sight—a city that has been continuously inhabited, independent-minded, and self-sustaining for 2,500 years.

• Directly opposite the statue, inside of Bar Nilo, is the...

"Chapel of Maradona": The small "chapel" on the right wall is dedicated to Diego Maradona, an Argentinian soccer star who played for Naples in the 1980s—pushing the team to its greatest success. Locals consider soccer almost a religion, and this guy was practically a deity. You can even see a "hair of Diego" and a teardrop from the city when he went to another team for more money. Unfortunately, his reputation was later sullied by problems he'd had with organized crime, drugs, and police. However, when he passed away in 2020 (at age 60), Naples was overwhelmed with grief. New street-art murals of Maradona popped up all over the city—in many cases, alongside a portrait of a bishop. This is San Gennaro, the city's third-century patron saint—and his juxtaposition with Maradona indicates where the soccer star still ranks in the hearts of Neapolitans.

Meanwhile, the coffee bar has posted a quadrilingual sign (though, strangely, not in English) threatening that those who take a picture without buying a cup of coffee may find their camera damaged...*Capisce?*

• *Continue another 100 yards. You may pass gold and silver shops. Some say stolen jewelry ends up here, is melted down immediately, and gets resold in some other form as soon as it cools. Look for* compro oro ("I buy gold") *signs—a sign of Naples' economic woes. (Locals used to blame the 2008 economic crisis; now they blame Covid.) Continue to a tiny square at the intersection with...*

⓭ Via San Gregorio Armeno: Stroll up this tiny lane toward the fanciful tower that arches over the street. The street is lined with stalls selling lots of souvenir kitsch, as well as some of Naples' most distinctive local crafts. Among the many figurines on sale, find items relating to ***presepi*** (Nativity scenes). Just as many Americans keep an eye out year-round for Christmas-tree ornaments, Italians regularly add pieces to the family *presepe,* the centerpiece of their holiday decorations. You'll see elaborate manger scenes made of bark and moss, with niches to hold baby Jesus or mother Mary. You'll also see lots of jokey figurines caricaturing local politicians, soccer stars, and other celebrities. (Some of the highest-quality *presepi* pieces are sold at the D'Auria shop, a little farther down Spaccanapoli, on the right at #87. Expressive figures are made from terra-cotta, wood, and cloth, often fetching over €250. They even sell the classy *campane* version, under a glass bell.)

Another popular Naples souvenir sold here—and all over—is the ***corno,*** a skinny, twisted, red horn that resembles a chili pepper. The *corno* comes with a double symbolism for fertility: It's a horn of plenty, and it's also a phallic symbol turned upside-down. Neapolitans explain that fertility isn't sexual; it provides the greatest gift a person can give—life—and it ensures that one's soul will live on through the next generation. In today's Naples, just as in yesterday's Pompeii (where bulging erections greeted visitors at the entrance to a home), fertility is equated with good luck.

(By the way, a bit farther up Via San Gregorio Armeno, you'll find the underground **Napoli Sotterranea archaeological site,** along Via dei Tribunali, which also has some of the city's best **pizzerias**—both are described later.)

• *Continue down Spaccanapoli another 100 yards until you hit busy Via Duomo. Consider detouring five minutes north (left) up Via Duomo to visit Naples'* ***Duomo;*** *just around the corner from that is the* ***Pio Monte della Misericordia Church,*** *with a fine Caravaggio painting (both described later). But for now, continue straight, crossing Via Duomo. Here, Spaccanapoli is named...*

⓮ **Via Vicaria Vecchia:** Here along Via Vicaria Vecchia, the main "sight" is the vibrant street life. It's grittier and less touristy, but just as atmospheric as what we've been seeing. The street and side-street scenes intensify. The area is said to be a center of the Camorra (the Naples-based version of the Sicilian Mafia), but as a tourist, you won't notice. Paint a picture with these thoughts: Naples has the most intact street plan of any surviving ancient Greek or Roman city. Imagine this city during those times (and retain these images as you visit Pompeii), with streetside shop fronts that close up after dark, and private homes on upper floors. What you see today is just one more page in a 2,000-year-old story of a city: all kinds of meetings, beatings, and cheatings; kisses, near misses, and little-boy pisses.

You name it, it occurs right on the streets today, as it has since ancient times. People ooze from crusty corners. Black-and-white death announcements add to the clutter on the walls. Widows sell cigarettes from buckets. For a peek behind the scenes in the shade of wet laundry, venture down a few side streets. Buy two carrots as a gift for the woman on the fifth floor, if she'll lower her bucket to pick them up. The neighborhood action seems best at about 18:00.

At the tiny fenced-in triangle of greenery, hang out for a few minutes to just observe the crazy motorbike action and teen scene.

• *From here, veer right onto Via Forcella. You emerge into Piazza Vincenzo Calenda, where there's a round fence protecting another chunk of that ancient* ***Greek wall*** *of Neapolis. Hungry? Turn right here, on Via Pietro Colletta, and close out the walk with three typical Neapolitan...*

⓯ **Eateries:** Step into the North Pole at the recommended **Polo Nord Gelateria** (on the right, at #41). The oldest *gelateria* in Naples has had four generations of family working here since

1931. Before you order, sample a few flavors, including their *bacio,* or "kiss," flavor (named after the national chocolate-and-praline candy)—all are made fresh daily.

Two of Napoli's most competitive **pizzerias** are nearby. **Trianon da Ciro** (across the street from Polo Nord) has been serving them up hot and fast for almost a century. A half-block farther, on the right, is the place where some say pizza was born—at **Antica Pizzeria da Michele.** (For more on both, see "Eating in Naples," later.)

Return to Centrale Station: It's easy to return to Centrale station. Continue downhill on Via Pietro Colletta until you hit the grand boulevard, Corso Umberto I. Turn left and walk 15 minutes to the train station. Or cross the street and hop on any bus; they all go to the station.

Sights in Naples

Naples' best sights are the Archaeological Museum and my self-guided Naples Walk, both covered earlier. For extra credit, consider these sights.

ON OR NEAR SPACCANAPOLI

These sights are linked—in this order—on the second half of my Naples Walk.

▲Church of Gesù Nuovo

This church's unique pyramid-grill facade survives from a fortified 15th-century noble palace. Step inside for a brilliant Neapolitan Baroque interior. The second chapel on the right features a much-adored **statue of St. Giuseppe Moscati** (1880-1927), a Christian doctor famous for helping the poor. In 1987, Moscati became the first modern doctor to be canonized. Sit and watch a steady stream of Neapolitans taking turns to pay their respects.

Continue to the third chapel (past Moscati's vertical tombstone) and enter the **Sale Moscati.** Look high on the walls of this long room to see hundreds of ex-votos—tiny red-and-silver plaques of thanksgiving for prayers answered with the help of St. Moscati (each has a symbol of the ailment cured). Naples' practice of using ex-votos, while incorporated into its Catholic rituals, goes back to its pagan Greek roots. Rooms from Moscati's nearby apartment are on display, and a glass case shows possessions and photos of the great doctor.

Just before leaving the Sale Moscati, notice the big bomb casing that hangs high in the left corner. It fell through the church's dome in 1943, but caused almost no damage...yet another miracle.

Cost and Hours: Free, daily 6:45-13:00 & 16:00-19:30, Piazza del Gesù Nuovo, www.gesunuovo.it.

Church of Santa Chiara

Dating from the 14th century, this church is from a period of French royal rule under the Angevin dynasty. Consider the stark contrast between this church (Gothic) and the Gesù Nuovo (Baroque), across the street. Inside, look for the faded Trinity on the back wall (on the right as you face the door, under the stone canopy), which shows a dove representing the Holy Spirit between the heads of God the Father and Christ (c. 1414). This is an example of the fine frescoes that once covered the walls. Most were stuccoed over during Baroque times or destroyed in 1943 by Allied bombs. Continuing down the main aisle, you'll step over a huge inlaid-marble Angevin coat of arms on the floor. The altar is adorned with four finely carved Gothic tombs of Angevin kings. A chapel stacked with Bourbon royalty is just to the right.

Cost and Hours: Free, daily 7:30-13:00 & 16:30-20:00, Piazza del Gesù Nuovo, www.monasterodisantachiara.it. Its tranquil cloistered courtyard, around back, is not worth its €6 entry fee.

▲▲Cappella Sansevero

This small chapel is a Baroque explosion mourning the body of Christ, who lies on a soft pillow under an incredibly realistic veil.

It's also the personal chapel of Raimondo de Sangro, an eccentric Freemason, containing his tomb and the tombs of his family. Like other 18th-century Enlightenment figures, Raimondo was a wealthy man of letters, scientist and inventor, and patron of the arts—and he was also a grand master of the Freemasons of the Kingdom of Naples. His chapel—filled with Masonic symbolism—is a complex ensemble, with statues representing virtues such as self-control, religious zeal, and the Masonic philosophy of freedom through enlightenment.

Cost and Hours: €8, buy tickets at office at the corner—or reserve ahead online (€2 fee), open Wed-Mon 9:30-19:00, closed Tue, Via de Sanctis 19, +39 081 551 8470, www.museosansevero.it.

Crowd-Beating Tips: This popular sight often has a very long line and can sell out. To be on the safe side, it's best (and worth the extra fee) to prebook a timed entry. If you're just showing up, the least crowded time to visit is after 16:00—the later the better.

Visiting the Chapel: Pick up the free floor plan, which identifies each of the statues lining the nave. Once inside, study the incredible ***Veiled Christ*** in the center. Carved out of marble, it's like no other statue I've seen (by Giuseppe "Howdeedoodat" Sammartino, 1753). The Christian message (Jesus died for our salvation) is accompanied by a Masonic message (the veil represents how the body and ego are obstacles to real spiritual freedom). As you walk from Christ's feet to his head, notice how the expression on Jesus' face goes from suffering to peace.

Raimondo's mom and dad are buried on either side of the **main altar.** To the right of the altar, marking his father's tomb, a statue representing *Despair* or *Disillusion* struggles with a marble rope net (carved out of a single piece of stone), symbolic of a troubled mind. The flames on the head of the winged boy represent human intellect—more Masonic symbolism, showing how knowledge frees the human mind. To the left of the main altar is a statue of *Modesty,* marking the tomb of Raimondo's mother (who died after his birth, and was only 20). The veiled woman fingers a broken tablet, symbolizing an interrupted life.

Raimondo de Sangro himself lies buried in a side altar (on the right). Among his inventions was the deep-green pigment used on the ceiling fresco. The inlaid M. C. Escher-esque maze on the floor around de Sangro's tomb is another Masonic reminder of how the quest for knowledge gets you out of the maze of life. This tilework once covered the floor of the entire chapel.

Your Sansevero finale is downstairs: two mysterious...**skeletons.** Perhaps another of the mad inventor's fancies: Inject a corpse with a fluid to fossilize the veins so that they'll survive the body's decomposition. While that's the legend, investigations have shown that the veins were artificial, and the models were created to illustrate how the circulatory system works.

▲Napoli Sotterranea ("Underground Naples")

This archaeological site, a manmade underground maze of passageways and ruins from Greek and Roman times, can only be toured with a guide. You'll descend 121 steps under the modern city to explore two underground areas. One is the old Greek tuff quarry used to build the city of Neapolis, which was later converted into an immense cistern by the Romans. The other is an excavated portion of the Greco-Roman theater that once seated 6,000 people. The space has been encroached upon by modern development—some current residents' windows literally look down into the theater ruins. The tour involves a lot of stairs, as well as a long, narrow 20-inch-wide walkway—lit only by candlelight—that uses an ancient water channel (a heavyset person could not comfortably fit through this, and claustrophobes will be miserable). Although there's not much to see, the experience is fascinating and includes a little history from World War II—when the quarry/cistern was turned into a shelter to protect locals from American bombs.

Cost and Hours: €10, includes 1.5-hour tour, tours in English offered daily every two hours from 10:00 to 18:00. If the ticket-buying line is long, talk to an attendant: They *might* be able to move you into the next English-language tour. Bring a light sweater. +39 081 296 944, www.napolisotterranea.org.

Getting There: The site is at Piazza San Gaetano 68, along the lively Via dei Tribunali pizza zone, and just a couple of blocks uphill from Spaccanapoli's statue of the Nile. The entrance is immediately to the left of the Church of San Paolo Maggiore (look for the *Sotterranea* signs).

▲Duomo

Naples' historic cathedral, built by imported French Anjou kings in the 14th century, boasts a breathtaking Neo-Gothic facade. Step into the vast interior to see the mix of styles along the side chapels—from pointy Gothic arches to rounded Renaissance ones to gilded Baroque decor.

Cost and Hours: Free, Mon-Sat 8:30-13:30 & 14:30-20:00, Sun 8:30-13:30 & 16:30-19:30, Via Duomo.

Visiting the Church: The cathedral honors St. Gennaro, Naples' patron saint. The **main altar** at the front is ringed by carved wooden seats, filled three times a year by clergy to witness the Miracle of the Blood. Thousands of Neapolitans cram into this church for a peek at two tiny vials with the dried blood of St. Gennaro. As the clergy roots—or even jeers—for the miracle to occur, the blood temporarily liquefies. Neapolitans take this ritual with deadly seriousness, and believe that if the blood remains solid, it's terrible luck for the city. Sure enough, on the rare occasion that the miracle fails, locals can point to a terrible event soon after—such as an earthquake, an eruption of Mount Vesuvius, or an especially disappointing soccer loss.

The stairs beneath the altar take you to a **crypt** with the relics of St. Gennaro and a statue of the bishop who rescued the relics from a rival town and returned them to Naples. These relics are said to have stopped the lava from a 1631 Vesuvius eruption from destroying the city.

The cathedral has two large side chapels (flanking the nave, about halfway to the transept)—each practically a church in its own right. While interesting, they charge separate admissions and have shorter hours than the larger cathedral, and are skippable for most visitors. You can see most of the one on the left—the **Chapel of Santa Restituta**—for free. It stands on the site of the original, early Christian church that predated the cathedral. You'll find some 14th-century golden mosaics up at the front-left chapel-within-the-chapel. (I'd skip paying admission for the sixth-century baptismal font under mosaics.)

Pio Monte della Misericordia

This small church (near the Duomo, and run by a charitable foundation) displays one of the best works by Caravaggio, *The Seven Works of Mercy*. Upstairs is a ho-hum art gallery. The price is steep, but it may be worth it for Caravaggio fans.

Cost and Hours: €8 (ticket booth across the street), Mon-Sat 10:00-18:00, Sun 9:00-14:30, Via dei Tribunali 253, +39 081 446 944, www.piomontedellamisericordia.it.

Visiting the Church: Caravaggio's *The Seven Works of Mercy* hangs over the main altar in a darkened gray chapel. The painting is well-lit, allowing Caravaggio's characteristically dark canvas to really pop. In one crowded canvas, the great early-Baroque artist illustrates seven virtues: burying the dead (the man carrying a corpse by the ankles); visiting the imprisoned and feeding the hungry (Pero breastfeeding her starving father—a scene from a famous Roman story); sheltering the homeless (a pilgrim on the Camino de Santiago, with his floppy hat, negotiates with an innkeeper); caring for the sick and clothing the naked (St. Martin offers part of his cloak to the injured man in the foreground); and giving drink to the thirsty (Samson chugs from a jawbone in the background)—all of them set in a dark Neapolitan alley and watched over by Mary, Jesus, and a pair of angels.

Caravaggio painted this work in Naples in 1607 while in exile from Rome, where he had been sentenced to death for killing a man in a duel. Three years later Caravaggio died from an unknown illness on his way back to Rome to receive a pardon from the Pope.

MADRE

MADRE, a museum of contemporary art, displays works by Jeff Koons, Anish Kapoor, Francesco Clemente, and other big names in the art world. Aficionados of modern art consider it one of the better collections in the country. Some descriptions are in English—you'll need them.

Cost and Hours: €8; Wed-Mon 10:00-19:30—Sun until

20:00, closed Tue, last entry one hour before closing; Via Settembrini 79, +39 081 1973 7254, www.madrenapoli.it.

NEAR THE PORT

This cluster of important sights can be found between the big ceremonial square, Piazza del Plebiscito, and the cruise ship terminal. If touring the entire neighborhood, I'd see it in the order described here. For locations, see the map on page 8.

Getting There from Spaccanapoli: Walking down toward this area on Via Toledo (from the midpoint of my self-guided walk), you'll pass two more big, boxy, fascist-style banks: first, the chalky-white **BNL bank,** and then, past the Toledo Metro stop, the even more imposing **Banco di Napoli** at Via Toledo 178. A bit farther down is the **Banca Intesa Sanpaolo** (filling an older palace rather than a fascist-style building); it hosts Caravaggio's blood-spurting *The Martyrdom of Saint Ursula* in a small art gallery (see signs for entry details). Also along here, on a parklike little piazza on your right, is the easy-to-miss **Centrale funicular** up to the San Martino mountaintop. As you near Piazza del Plebiscito, you'll go through a congested area with popular bars and pizza windows. Push on until you reach the gigantic, semicircular square facing the orange-ish palace. To trace this route, see the map on page 56.

▲Piazza del Plebiscito

This square celebrates the 1860 vote (*plebiscito,* plebiscite) in which Naples became a part of a unified Italy. Dominating the top of the square is the Church of San Francesco di Paola, with its Pantheon-inspired dome and broad, arcing colonnades. If it's open, step inside to ogle the vast interior—a Neoclassical re-creation of one of ancient Rome's finest buildings.

• *Opposite is the...*

Royal Palace (Palazzo Reale)

Having housed Spanish, French, and even Italian royalty, this building displays statues of all those who stayed here. From the square in front of the palace, look for eight kings in the niches, each from a different dynasty (left to right): Norman, German, French, Spanish, Spanish, Spanish, French (Napoleon's brother-in-law), and, finally, Italian—Victor Emmanuel II, King of Savoy. The statues were done at the request of V. E. II's son, so his dad is the most dashing of the group. As far as palaces go, the interior is relatively unimpressive.

Cost and Hours: €10, skip the painfully dry €5 audioguide (each room has excellent panel descriptions in English; Thu-Tue 9:00-20:00, closed Wed, last entry one hour before closing; +39 848 082 408, www.coopculture.it).

Visiting the Palace: The palace's grand Neoclassical staircase leads up to a floor with 30 plush rooms. You'll follow a one-way route featuring the palace theater, paintings by "the Caravaggio Imitators," Neapolitan tapestries, fine inlaid-stone tabletops, chandeliers, gilded woodwork, and more. The rooms do feel quite grand, even if they lack the personality and sense of importance of Europe's better palaces. As a less-visited sight, wandering through the rooms at leisure makes you feel like royalty yourself. Don't miss the huge, tapestry-laden Hercules Hall or the chance to dance on the wooden floor of the wide-open ballroom. Ask a guard (nicely) to open the terrace garden balcony door to enjoy sweeping views of the Bay of Naples. On the way out, step into the royal chapel, with an altar made entirely of precious stones and a fantastic Nativity scene—a commotion of 18th-century ceramic figurines.

Hanging Gardens: This beautiful garden terrace, overlooking the Bay of Naples, costs extra and can be seen only a few times a day (with an attendant). If your visit happens to coincide with one of these times—and the weather's fine—it's worth adding on.

• *Continue 50 yards past the Royal Palace (toward the trees) to enjoy a...*

Fine Harbor View

While boats busily serve Capri and Sorrento, Mount Vesuvius smolders ominously in the distance. Look back to see the vast "Bourbon red" palace—its color inspired by Pompeii. The hilltop above Piazza del Plebiscito is San Martino, with its Carthusian monastery-turned-museum and the fortress called Castel Sant'Elmo (the Centrale funicular to the top is just across the square and up Via Toledo). The promenade you're on continues to Naples' romantic harborfront—the fishermen's quarter (Borgo Marinaro)—a fortified island connected to the mainland by a stout causeway, with its fanciful, ancient Castel dell'Ovo (Egg Castle) and trendy harborside restaurants. From there, the Lungomare harborside promenade—described later—continues past the Santa Lucia district, stretching out along the Bay of Naples. This long promenade, running along Via Francesco Caracciolo to the Mergellina district and beyond, is a delightful people-watching scene on balmy nights.

• *Head back through the piazza and pop into (on the left)...*

Gran Caffè Gambrinus

This coffeehouse, facing the piazza, takes you back to the elegance of 1860. It's a classic place to sample a crispy *sfogliatella* pastry, or perhaps the mushroom-shaped, rum-soaked bread-like cakes called *babà,* which come in a huge variety. Stand at the bar *(banco),* pay double to sit *(tavola),* or just wander around as you imagine the café buzzing with the ritzy intellectuals, journalists, and artsy bohemian types who munched on *babà* here during Naples' 19th-century heyday (daily 7:00-24:00, Piazza del Plebiscito 1, +39 081 417 582).

• *A block away, tucked behind the palace, you can peek inside the Neoclassical...*

Teatro di San Carlo

Built in 1737, 41 years before Milan's La Scala, this is Europe's oldest opera house and Italy's second-most-respected (after La Scala). The original theater burned down in 1816, and was rebuilt within the year. Guided 35-minute visits in English basically just show you the fine auditorium with its 184 boxes—each with a big mirror to reflect the candlelight (€9; tours in English usually run daily at 11:30 and 15:30, additional departures in Italian; schedule can change so check online or call to confirm; theater box office +39 081 797 2331, tour info +39 081 7972 412, www.teatrosancarlo.it).

• *Beyond Teatro di San Carlo and the Royal Palace is the huge, harborfront...*

Castel Nuovo

This imposing castle now houses government bureaucrats and the **Civic Museum.** It feels like a mostly empty shell, with a couple of dusty halls of Neapolitan art, but the views over the bay from the upper terraces are impressive (€6, Mon-Sat 9:00-18:00, closed Sun, last entry one hour before closing, +39 081 795 7722). The castle also hosts frequent special events and exhibits.

• *Head back to Teatro di San Carlo, cross the street, and go through the tall yellow arch into...*

▲Galleria Umberto I

This Victorian iron-and-glass shopping mall opened in 1890 to reinvigorate the district after a devastating cholera epidemic occurred here. Gawk up, then walk left to bring you back out on Via Toledo.

• *Just up the street and behind Piazza del Plebiscito is an interesting subterranean experience.*

▲Galleria Borbonica

Beneath Naples' Royal Palace was a vast underground network of caves, aqueducts, and cisterns that originated as a quarry in the 15th century. In the mid-1800s, when popular revolutions were threatening royalty across Europe, the understandably nervous king of Naples, Ferdinand II, had this underground world expanded to create an escape tunnel from the palace to his military barracks nearby. In World War II, it was used as an air-raid shelter; after the war, the police used it to store impounded cars and motorcycles. Today, enthusiastic guides take the curious on a fascinating 70-minute, 500-yard-long guided walk through this many-layered world littered with disintegrating 60-year-old vehicles upon which Naples sits.

Cost and Hours: €10 English-language tours leave Fri-Sun at 10:00, 12:00, 15:00, and 17:00; +39 081 764 5808, www.galleriaborbonica.com. The most convenient entry is just behind Piazza del Plebiscito—up Via Gennaro Serra and down Vico del Grottone to #4 (to avoid that entrance's 90 steep steps, enter at Via Morelli 61).

NORTH OF SPACCANAPOLI

▲▲Sanità District

While the characteristic Spaccanapoli and Spanish Quarter are being tamed, today's clear winner for wild-and-crazy Neapolitan life in the streets is the gritty Sanità District, north of the Archaeological Museum.

A big part of the attraction of Naples is its *basso* living (life in the streets). Many locals with enough money to move to the sanity of the suburbs choose instead to keep living where the action is—in a cauldron of flapping laundry, police sirens, broken cobblestone lanes, singing merchants, sidewalks clogged with makeshift markets, and walls crusted with ancient posters and graffiti.

One of Naples' most historic and colorful zones, Sanità is sometimes called "the living *presepe*" for the way people live stacked on top of each other in rustic conditions, as if in an elaborate manger scene. (Because organized crime is still strong in this quarter, development is slow.) Literally "the healthy place" (named for the freshness of the air, originally so high above the dense city), this is *the* place for a photo safari.

While the reason to visit Sanità is simply to swim through its amazing river of life, there are two remarkable burial sites in the district: the Catacombs of San Gaudioso (at the Basilica Santa Maria della Sanità) and the Cemetery of the Fountains.

Visiting the Sanità District: Check to be sure your valuables are zipped or buttoned safely away. From near the Porta San Gennaro gate (just west of Via Duomo, two blocks east of Metro: Cavour, six blocks east of Archaeological Museum), leave Via Foria and head up Via Crocelle. Venture a block up Via Crocelle and then three blocks up Via dei Vergini through a thriving daily market scene. Pop into the courtyard of the Palazzo dello Spagnuolo (#19 on the left) to peek at an extravagant 18th-century staircase.

Then dog-leg left on Via Arena della Sanità and continue uphill (past another massive staircase in the courtyard at #6) to Piazza Sanità, at the base of Capodimonte, where you'll stand before the Basilica Santa Maria della Sanità, which sits atop the **Catacombs of San Gaudioso.** Because this area was just outside the old city walls, the dead were buried here (entrance inside the church, €9 ticket also includes Catacombs of San Gennaro—described later, hourly English tours run daily 10:00-13:00, www.catacombedinapoli.it).

From here you have three options: Browse back down the way you just came; continue 10 minutes up Via Sanità and Via Fontanelle to the Cemetery of the Fountains (described next); or ride a free elevator (just past the church, under the high viaduct) up to the modern world and Capodimonte (described later).

▲Cemetery of the Fountains (Cimitero delle Fontanelle)

A thousand years ago, cut into the hills at the high end of Napoli was a quarry. Then, in the 16th century, churches with crowded cemeteries began moving the bones of their long dead here to make room for the newly dead. Later these caves housed the bones of plague victims and the city's paupers. In the 19th century, many churches again emptied their cemeteries and added even more skulls to this vast ossuary. Then a cult of people appeared whose members adopted the skulls. They named the skulls, put them in little houses, brought them flowers, and asked them to intervene with God for favors from the next life. Today, the quirky caves—stacked with human bones and dotted with chapels—are open to the public.

Cost and Hours: Free to enter but tips accepted, daily 10:00-17:00, Via Fontanelle 77, +39 081 795 6160.

Getting There: It's located in a sketchy-feeling neighborhood at the top end of Sanità. You can get here by hopping in a taxi; riding the Metro to the Materdei stop and following the brown signs for 10 minutes; or hiking 10 minutes from the Basilica Santa Maria della Sanità up Via Sanità and Via Fontanelle (described earlier).

ON CAPODIMONTE

Capodimonte, about a mile due north from the Archaeological Museum, is one of Naples' three hills. It's home to an excellent art museum (and its surrounding park) and, not far away, tourable catacombs.

Getting There: Reaching Capodimonte is easiest by taxi (figure €15 from the city center). Various public buses run from near Piazza Dante and the National Archaeological Museum up to Capodimonte, including #168, #178, and #C63—these stop near the catacombs (hop off when you get to the huge, domed church) before continuing up to the museum and park.

▲Capodimonte Museum (Museo di Capodimonte)

This hilltop is home to Naples' top art museum. Its pleasant collection has lesser-known (but still masterful) works by Michelangelo, Raphael, Titian, Caravaggio, and other huge names. It fills the Bourbons' cavernous summer palace, set in the midst of a sprawling hilltop park overlooking Naples, and part of the museum showcases the palace's history and furnishings. Most visitors to Naples understandably prefer to focus on the city's vibrant street life, characteristic churches, and ancient artifacts. But for art lovers and royalty buffs, Capodimonte rates ▲▲.

Cost and Hours: €12, Thu-Tue 8:30-19:30, closed Wed, last entry one hour before closing, avoid lines by purchasing your ticket online (additional fee possible), fine audioguide-€5, café, Via Miano 2, +39 081 749 9111, http://capodimonte.cultura.gov.it. Some rooms may close earlier, items can be out on loan, and special exhibits are frequent; for the latest, check the website.

Nearby: While people visiting the Capodimonte Museum are understandably focused on its paintings, don't overlook the expansive **Capodimonte Park** surrounding it. Once a hunting ground for royalty, the park is now a pleasure garden—beloved by Neapolitans—with elegant paths and lovely gardens sprouting trees and exotic plants from around the world. If you've planned ahead, this is a lovely spot for a picnic.

Visiting the Museum: The gigantic collection sprawls through the massive building, and the curator enjoys rearranging things, loaning and borrowing works, and so on—so it's hard to get a handle on exactly what's on view, and where. Room numbers—sometimes marked above doors—can be difficult to read and are often missing entirely, so they're of limited usefulness for navigating the collection. Still, here's an outline that should point you in the general direction of some interesting pieces.

• *After buying your ticket, pick up the free map and head up several flights of stairs (or ride the elevator) to the "first" floor. You'll step into a room marked...*

Tiziano (Room 2): The museum has a fine selection of works by Titian (1488-1576). At the far end, look for *Portrait of Pope Paul III.* It depicts Alessandro Farnese, the local bigwig whose family married into Bourbon royalty; later, as Pope Paul III, he was responsible for bringing great art to Naples. (Nearby, you'll see another—much younger—Titian portrait of Farnese, before he was pope.) Also in this room, look for one of many versions of Titian's *Danaë,* where—as told in the Greek myth—the sensuous central character looks up at a cloud containing the essence of Zeus (a shower of coins), about to impregnate her. Enjoy the cupid's surprised look at the action as the courtesan awaits her union. Finally, find Titian's poignant portrait of a penitent Mary Magdalene, with finely detailed tears running down her cheeks (1565).

• *Proceeding into the next room, turn left into the darkened...*

Room 4: The lights pop on as you enter, so you can see large charcoal drawings by Raphael (Moses shields his eyes from the burning bush, 1514) and Michelangelo (a group of soldiers, 1546; and *Venus and Love,* 1534).

• *Exiting this room back the way you came, look left down a very long hall of fancy weapons (marked* Armeria Borbonica*), but continue straight ahead, then turn left into a room labeled...*

Masaccio: Here you'll find works by this Renaissance pioneer. If it's not out on loan, you should see a section of his altarpiece (1426) showing a primitive attempt at 3-D: Masaccio has left out Jesus' neck to create the illusion that he's looking down on us.

In the next few rooms, look for some more interesting pieces: Mantegna's medallion-like *Portrait of Ludovico Gonzaga,* c. 1461, a very small but finely executed profile portrait; and Giovanni Bellini's *Circumcision of Christ.* (Bellini was Titian's master.)

• *Next you'll proceed into a section marked...*

Collezione Farnese: The core of the museum's collection sprawls through several rooms. As you explore this zone, keep an eye out for these highlights, which may appear in roughly this order:

You'll spot several works by **Raphael,** including a portrait of the man who will become Pope Paul III, back when he was "just" Alessandro Farnese. You may spot some pieces by **El Greco,** too.

Parmigianino's *Antea* (1531-1535)—one of the collection's highlights—addresses us with an unblinking, dilated gaze. She wears a mink stole (astonishingly lifelike, with disgusting little teeth), gold chain, and hair brooch—items commonly presented by a lover. By wearing the gifts, Antea signals her acceptance of her suitor's advances.

The Misanthrope (1568) is a remarkable work by **Pieter Bruegel the Elder.** The painting suggests the pointlessness of giving up on life and becoming a hermit; cut off from the world and lost in thought, the title figure doesn't even notice that he's about to step on a trail of thorns. Behind him, a wild-eyed young man is stealing the misanthrope's money pouch (Hey! I saw that guy on the Circumvesuviana!).

Annibale Carracci's *Hercules at the Crossroads* (1596) presents the hero with a choice: virtue (on the left, nature and letters, but a steep uphill climb) or vice (on the right, scantily clad women, music, theater masks, and an easy, flat path). While his foot points one way, he looks the other...his mind not yet made up.

• *At the end of the Collezione Farnese, turn left to enter the...*

Royal Apartments: It's easy to forget that this museum is set in a royal palace. Originally a simple hunting lodge, in the 18th century the king decided it could be a grand palace. Several dynasties enjoyed its regal ballrooms and imposing reception rooms while amassing their impressive collections of art. From here on out, you'll pass through some of the opulent apartments of this building, decorated with stunning period details and furniture.

The **grand hall** in the corner (Room 31) comes with a massive bronze chandelier hanging over an ancient Roman inlaid-marble floor, which originally decorated the palace of Roman Emperor Tiberius on Capri (installed here in 1877).

The following rooms tell stories of three Bourbon kings with portraits and objects from their reign. At the opposite corner of this wing, imagine attending a regal ball in the grand ***Salone delle Feste*** (Room 42).

Branching off from here (Rooms 38-40), look for the **Collezione delle Ciccio,** which is filled with royal porcelain—considered white gold—from all corners of Europe: Naples, Vienna, Paris (Sèvres), and Meissen (Germany).

From here, depending on which areas are open, you may circle through even more apartments (perhaps seeing several rooms decorated in the Napoleon-pleasing Neoclassical style—a reminder that Napoleon's older brother once ruled the Kingdom of Napoli). Or you may be routed back to the Collezione Farnese.

• *Either way, when done at this level, head back to where you entered and climb up four flights of stairs (or take the elevator) to the...*

Second Floor: Here you'll find art from private collections and paintings mostly from local churches. First you'll see a cycle of **Flemish tapestries** (depicting the Battle of Pavia). Then, as you pass through a few halls of Gothic altarpieces, watch out for a few highlights:

Near the end of the **altarpiece corridor,** in Room 65, on the right is a fine altarpiece from Nottingham, England. Carved out of alabaster in the 15th century, it shows expressive scenes from the Passion of Christ.

At the far end of this corridor (just past Nottingham) is a darkened room (Room 66) with **Simone Martini**'s lavish and delicate portrait from 1317 of San Ludovico di Tolosa crowning Roberto king of Naples.

Now proceed down a long line of adjoining rooms. In Room 67, find Colantonio's painting ***San Girolamo nello Studio*** (c. 1445), in which the astonishing level of detail—from the words on the page of the open book, to the balled-up pages tucked away at the bottom of the frame—drives home the message: Only through complete devotion and meticulous dedication can you hope to accomplish great things...like pulling a thorn out of a lion's paw.

Finally, near the end of this wing, watch for another of the museum's top pieces, **Caravaggio's *The Flagellation*.** Typical of his *chiaroscuro* (light/dark) style, Caravaggio uses a ribbon of light to show us only what he wants us to see: a broken Christ about to be whipped, and the manic fury of the man (on his left) who will do the whipping. This scene could be set in a Naples alley. Compare this with most of the paintings we've seen so far—of popes, saints, and aristocrats. Caravaggio was given refuge in Naples while fleeing a murder trial in Rome. (They put him to work painting. Of the eight canvases he painted during this period, three remain in Naples.) Caravaggio was revolutionary in showing real life rather than idealized scenes—helping common people to better relate to these stories.

The Rest of the Museum: There's so much more to see, including many temporary exhibits. Elsewhere on the second floor, you'll find both Baroque and contemporary works. As in all great collections, more works of art are in storage than can be displayed at any given moment—and the curator enjoys surprising visitors by pulling items out from time to time, hoping to encourage dialogue about lesser-known artists, and get you thinking about what might be hiding in other museum storerooms.

▲▲Catacombs of San Gennaro

Behind the towering modern church of Madre del Buon Consiglio (Mother of Good Counsel) are tucked the most impressive ancient catacombs south of Rome. It started as a pagan tomb of little consequence, but then St. Agrippino, the local bishop, was buried here in the third century. Later, in the fifth century, the bones of St. Gennaro (patron of Naples) were moved here. Suddenly a site of special reverence—complete with miracles—it became a place where Neapolitans wanted to be buried as well. Today, the catacombs are run by a nonprofit organization of earnest young people who conduct walking tours. These half-mile walks survey more than a thousand burial niches on two levels that date from the second to sixth centuries (many with frescoes surviving...barely).

Cost and Hours: €9 ticket includes Catacombs of San

Gaudioso—described earlier, at busy times it's wise to prebook online, included English-language tours depart on the hour daily 10:00-17:00, Via di Capodimonte 13, +39 081 744 3714, www.catacombedinapoli.it.

SOUTH OF SPACCANAPOLI

Porta Nolana Open-Air Fish Market

Naples' fish market squirts and stinks as it has for centuries under the darkened Porta Nolana (gate in the city wall), four long blocks down from Centrale station. Of the town's many boisterous outdoor markets, this will net you the most photos and memories. From Piazza Nolana, wander under the medieval gate and take your first left down Via Sopramuro, enjoying this wild and entirely edible cultural scavenger hunt (Tue-Sun 8:00-14:00, closed Mon). Stalls display the best catch of the day as water jets caress mounds of mussels and clams.

Two other markets with more clothing and fewer fish are at Piazza Capuana (several blocks northwest of Centrale station and tumbling down Via Sant'Antonio Abate, Mon-Sat 8:00-18:00, Sun 9:00-13:00) and a similar cobbled shopping zone along Via Pignasecca (just off Via Toledo, west of Piazza Carità, described on page 30).

▲▲Harborside Promenade: The Lungomare *Passeggiata*

Each evening, relaxed and romantic Neapolitans in the mood for a scenic harborside stroll do their *vasche* (laps) along the inviting Lungomare harborside promenade and beyond. To join in this elegant people-watching scene (best after 19:00), stroll down to the waterfront from Piazza del Plebiscito and then along Via Nazario Sauro to the beginning of a delightful series of harborside promenades that stretch romantically all the way out of the city. Along the way, you'll enjoy views of Mount Vesuvius and the Bay of Naples. The entire route is crowded on weekends and lively any good-weather evening of the week with families, amorous couples, and friends hanging out. Here's a brief rundown of its three sections:

Santa Lucia and Borgo Marinaro: Via Nazario Sauro passes the Santa Lucia district, so called because this is where the song "Santa Lucia" was first performed. (The song is probably so famous in America because immigrants from Naples sang it to remember the old country.) At the fortified causeway, make a short detour out to Borgo Marinaro ("Fisherman's Quarter"), and poke around this fabled island neighborhood. With its striking Castel dell'Ovo and a trendy restaurant scene, you can dine here amid yachts with a view of Vesuvius. From here, follow Via Partenope to Piazza Vittoria.

Piazza Vittoria and Via Francesco Caracciolo: From Piazza Vittoria the strolling action stretches along the Lungomare on Via Francesco Caracciolo all the way to the Mergellina district. The convenient bus #140 starts at Piazza Vittoria, making stops all along the promenade to Posillipo (at the end of the nice strolling stretch). Walk as far as you like away from the city center and, when you're ready to return, just hop on the bus or grab a cab. (From Piazza Vittoria you can shortcut scenically directly back to Piazza del Plebiscito by heading inland through Piazza dei Martiri and down Via Chiaia.)

Mergellina and Via Posillipo: The promenade continues past yacht harbors and rocks popular for swimming and sunbathing, under lavish Liberty Style villas, to tiny coves and inviting fish restaurants. Perched on the hillside at Posillipo (the end of the nice stretch) awaits the delightful **$$$ Ristorante Reginella,** with majestic views (closed Tue, Via Posillipo 45a, +39 081 240 3220)...and the bus #140 stop for your quick return.

Posillipo Hill

More a very long, tree-covered, villa-slathered peninsula than a "hill," this promontory helps define the southern boundary of the Bay of Naples. Only conquered by road-building engineers in the early 19th century, Posillipo's hallmark are its many waterfront villas. While these come in a dizzying array of architectural styles, most Posillipo villas have certain features in common: huge cellars (for protection against both sea storms and invaders); decorative fringes on top (often castle-like crenellations); and watchtowers. These are best seen from the water—giving a look at the spacious, green, and colorful Naples in contrast to the congested, tight lanes of the historical center. Italians, who romanticize Posillipo, recognize many of these villas from their favorite movies and TV shows. Out at the tip of Posillipo is a fine, sprawling park called Parco Virgiliano, which locals call "Lovers' Park" for its restful trails and gorgeous views over the Bay of Naples, with Vesuvius looming on the horizon.

ON SAN MARTINO

The ultimate view overlooking Naples, its bay, and the volcano is from San Martino hill, just above (and west of) the city center. Up top you'll find a mighty fortress, Castel Sant'Elmo (which charges for entry but offers the best views from its ramparts) and the adjacent Baroque San Martino monastery-turned-museum. The surrounding neighborhood (especially Piazza Fuga) has a classy "uptown" vibe compared to the gritty city-center streets below. Cheapskates can enjoy the views for free from the benches on the square in front of the monastery.

Getting There: From Via Toledo, the Spanish Quarter gradually climbs up San Martino's lower slopes, before steep paths take you up the rest of the way. But the easiest way to ascend San Martino is by **funicular.** Three different funicular lines with departures every 10 minutes lead from lower Naples to the hilltop: the Centrale line from near the bottom of Via Toledo; the Montesanto line from the Metro stop of the same name (near the top end of Via Toledo); and the Chiaia line from farther out, near Piazza Amadeo. All three are covered by any regular local transit ticket. Ride any of these three up to the end of the line. All lines converge within a few blocks at the top of the hill—Centrale and Chiaia wind up at opposite ends of the charming Piazza Fuga, while Montesanto terminates a bit closer to the fortress and museum.

Leaving any of the funiculars, head uphill, carefully seeking out the brown signs for *Castel S. Elmo* and *Museo di San Martino* (a few strategically placed escalators make the climb easier). Regardless of where you come up, you'll pass the Montesanto funicular station—angle left (as you face the station) past the municipal police station, and then continue following the signs. You'll reach the castle with its bronze plaque first, and then the monastery/museum (both about a 10-minute walk from Piazza Fuga).

Another convenient—if less scenic—approach is via the Metro's line 1 to the Vanvitelli stop, which is near the upper funicular terminals.

Castel Sant'Elmo

While little more than an empty husk with a decent modern art museum, this 16th-century, Spanish-built, star-shaped fortress boasts commanding views over the city and the entire Bay of Naples. Buy your ticket at the booth, then ride the elevator near the entrance to the upper courtyard and climb up to the ramparts for a slow circle to enjoy the 360-degree views. In the middle of the yard is the likeable little Museo del Novecento, a gallery of works by 20th-century Neapolitan artists (covered by same ticket); the castle also hosts temporary exhibits.

Cost and Hours: €5, half-price after 16:15; open daily 8:30-19:30, last entry one hour before closing; museum closes at 17:00

and is closed Tue; Via Tito Angelini 22, +39 081 229 4401, www.polomusealecampania.beniculturali.it.

▲▲San Martino Carthusian Monastery and Museum (Certosa e Museo di San Martino)

The monastery, founded in 1325 and dissolved in the early 1800s, is now a sprawling museum with several parts. The square out front has city views nearly as good as the ones you'll pay to see from inside, and a few cafés angling for your business.

Cost and Hours: €6, Thu-Tue 8:30-17:00, may be open later in summer, closed Wed, last entry one hour before closing, some rooms (such as the Naval Museum) open at 9:30—don't arrive too early, audioguide-€5, Largo San Martino 5, +39 081 229 4502.

Visiting the Monastery and Museum: After purchasing your ticket, step into the **church** across the courtyard. First built in the mid-1300s, this church (as well as the entire complex) received a makeover by master Baroque architect Cosimo Fanzago—responsible for most of the big Baroque you've already seen in the city center. To protect the inlaid marble floor, you're not allowed into the nave; instead you can enjoy this Baroque explosion with beautifully decorated **chapels** from its main entryway. (The space behind the altar is accessible later in your visit.)

A variety of museum exhibits, art, and sculpture are housed in the rest of the complex. The **Naval Museum** has nautical paintings, model boats, and giant ceremonial gondolas that were used by various royalty. In a series of rooms opposite the Naval Museum is an excellent collection of *presepi* (Nativity scenes), both life-size and miniature, including a spectacular one by Michele Cucinello—the best I've seen in this *presepi*-crazy city. Beyond the *presepi* is the larger **garden cloister,** where monks would eventually rest in peace (look for the carved skulls).

Follow *chiesa* signs to access the back of the church and the **sacristy.** Cherub-covered ceilings painted by Naples favorite Luca Giordano and intricate, inlaid wood cabinets compete for your attention. Return to the cloister and find the terra-cotta-tiled floor to enter a **painting gallery** (with lots of antique maps and artifacts of old Naples). Finally, step into the massive **Prior's Quarters** with its private corner terrace and privileged views of the bay. Another view terrace is just outside, but the prior had the power view.

Sleeping in Naples

As an alternative to intense Naples, most travelers prefer to sleep in mellow Sorrento, just over an hour away (see the Sorrento chapter). But, if needed, here are a few good options. High season in Naples is spring and late fall. Prices are soft during the hot, slow summer months (July-Sept) and plunge during the pleasantly cool winters.

ON AND AROUND VIA TOLEDO

To see the city's best face, stay in the area that stretches between the Archaeological Museum and the port.

$$$$ Decumani Hotel de Charme is a classy oasis tucked away on a residential lane in the very heart of the city, just off Spaccanapoli. While the street is Naples-dingy, the hotel is an inviting retreat, filling an elegant 17th-century palace with 39 rooms and a stunning breakfast room (air-con, elevator, Via San Giovanni Maggiore Pignatelli 15, Metro: Università; if coming from Spaccanapoli, this lane is one street toward the train station from Via Santa Chiara, +39 081 551 8188, www.decumani.com, info@decumani.com).

$$$ Hotel Piazza Bellini is an artistically decorated hotel with 48 minimalist but solid and comfortable rooms surrounding a peaceful, inviting courtyard. Two blocks below the Archaeological Museum, just off the lively Piazza Bellini, and close to the great pizzerias and restaurants on Via dei Tribunali, it offers modern sanity in a strategic city-center location (air-con, elevator, Via Santa Maria di Constantinopoli 101, Metro: Dante, +39 081 451 732, www.hotelpiazzabellini.com, info@hotelpiazzabellini.com).

$$$ Art Resort Galleria Umberto has 25 rooms in two buildings inside the Umberto I shopping gallery at the bottom of Via Toledo, just off Piazza del Plebiscito. This genteel-feeling place gilds the lily, with an aristocratic setting and decor but older bathrooms. Consider paying about €30 extra for a room overlooking the gallery (air-con, elevator, Galleria Umberto 83, fourth floor—ask at booth for coin to operate elevator if needed, Metro: Toledo, +39 081 497 6224, www.artresortgalleriaumberto.com, booking@hotelgalleriaumberto.com).

$$$ Hotel Il Convento is a good choice for those who want to sleep in the tight tangle of lanes called the Spanish Quarter—quintessential Naples. You're only a couple of short blocks off the main Via Toledo drag, and heavy-duty windows help block out some (if not all) of the scooter noise and church bells. A rare haven of calm in this characteristic corner of town, it has 14 small but comfortable rooms—all with teensy balconies—as well as top-floor rooms with a private garden terrace (family rooms, air-con, elevator; Via Speranzella 137A, Metro: Toledo—from just below Banco di Napoli entrance, walk two blocks up Vico Tre Re a Toledo; +39 081 403 977, www.hotelilconvento.com, info@hotelilconvento.com).

$$ Chiaja Hotel de Charme, with the same owner as the Decumani (listed earlier), rents 33 rooms on the Via Chiaia pedestrian shopping drag near Piazza del Plebiscito. The building has a fascinating history: Part of it was the residence of a marquis, and the rest was one of Naples' most famous brothels (some view rooms, air-con, elevator, Via Chiaia 216, first floor, Metro: Toledo, +39 081 415 555, www.hotelchiaia.it, info@hotelchiaia.it).

AT THE TRAIN STATION

These hotels are less convenient for sightseeing and dining, and the neighborhood gets dodgy as you move away from the station. But they're handy for train travelers, practical for a quick stay, and less expensive.

$$ Hotel Stelle has 38 sterile, identical, newly remodeled rooms with modern furnishings. It feels sane compared to its hectic surroundings, and a back entrance leads directly into the train station (air-con, elevator, Corso Meridionale 60, exit station near track 5, +39 081 1889 3090, www.stellehotel.com, info@stellehotel.com).

$$ Ibis Styles Napoli Garibaldi, with 88 rooms, offers chain predictability and a bright, youthful color scheme a five-minute walk from the station (air-con, elevator, pay parking; Via Giuseppe Ricciardi 33, exit station onto Piazza Garibaldi, then take second left onto Via G. Ricciardi; +39 081 690 8111, www.ibis.com, h3243@accor.com).

$ Grand Hotel Europa, across the seedy street right next to the station, has 89 decent rooms and hallways whimsically decorated with not-quite-right reproductions of famous paintings. The hotel is a decent value, and its 1970s-era vibe (including the Kool-Aid and canned fruit at breakfast) makes for fun memories (RS%, family rooms, air-con, elevator, restaurant, Corso Meridionale 14, across street from station's north exit near track 5, +39 081 267 511, www.grandhoteleuropa.com, info@grandhoteleuropa.com).

Eating in Naples

Yes, Naples is (justifiably) famous for pizza. But the Campania region has other delicious tastes, as well. The abundant sunshine and volcanic soil produce excellent fruits and vegetables; the famous San Marzano tomatoes come from just outside Naples; and Italy's best mozzarella (*di bufala,* from water buffalo milk) also originates in Campania. Pastas with bright, flavorful tomato and other sauces

Naples Hotels & Restaurants

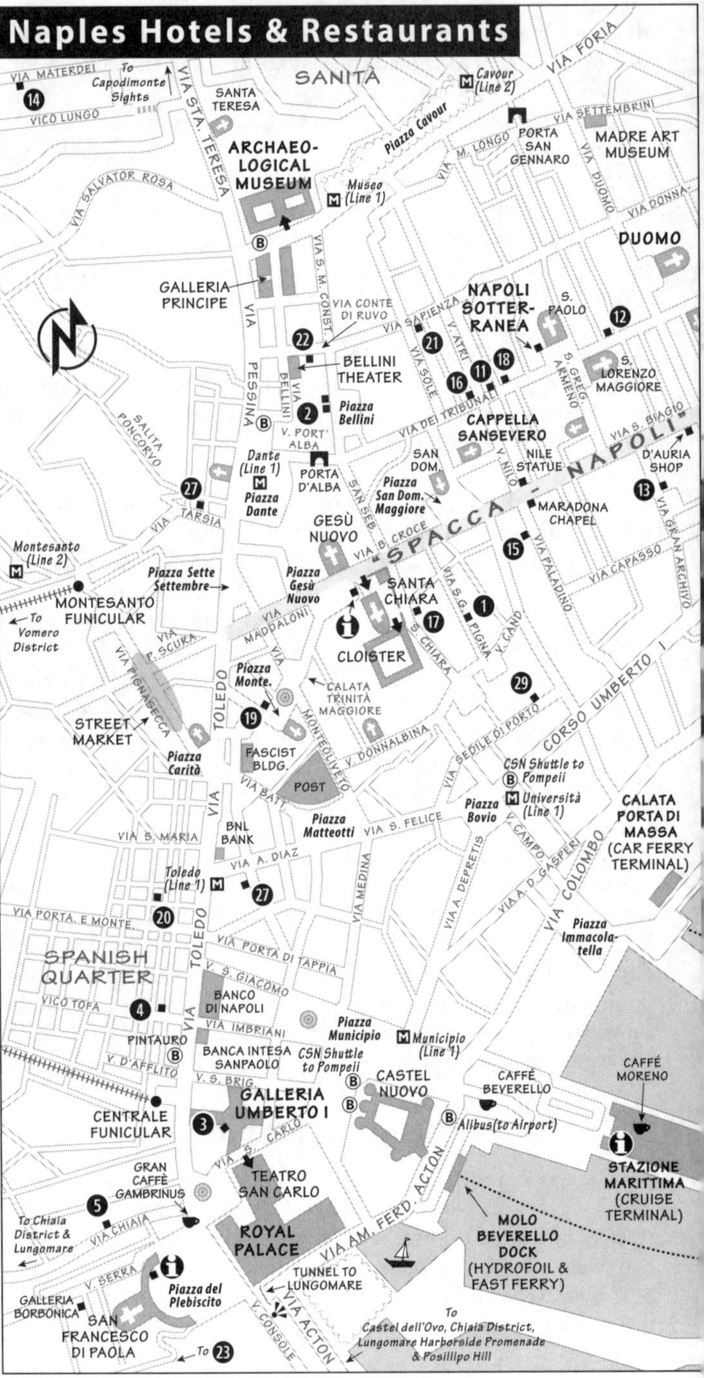

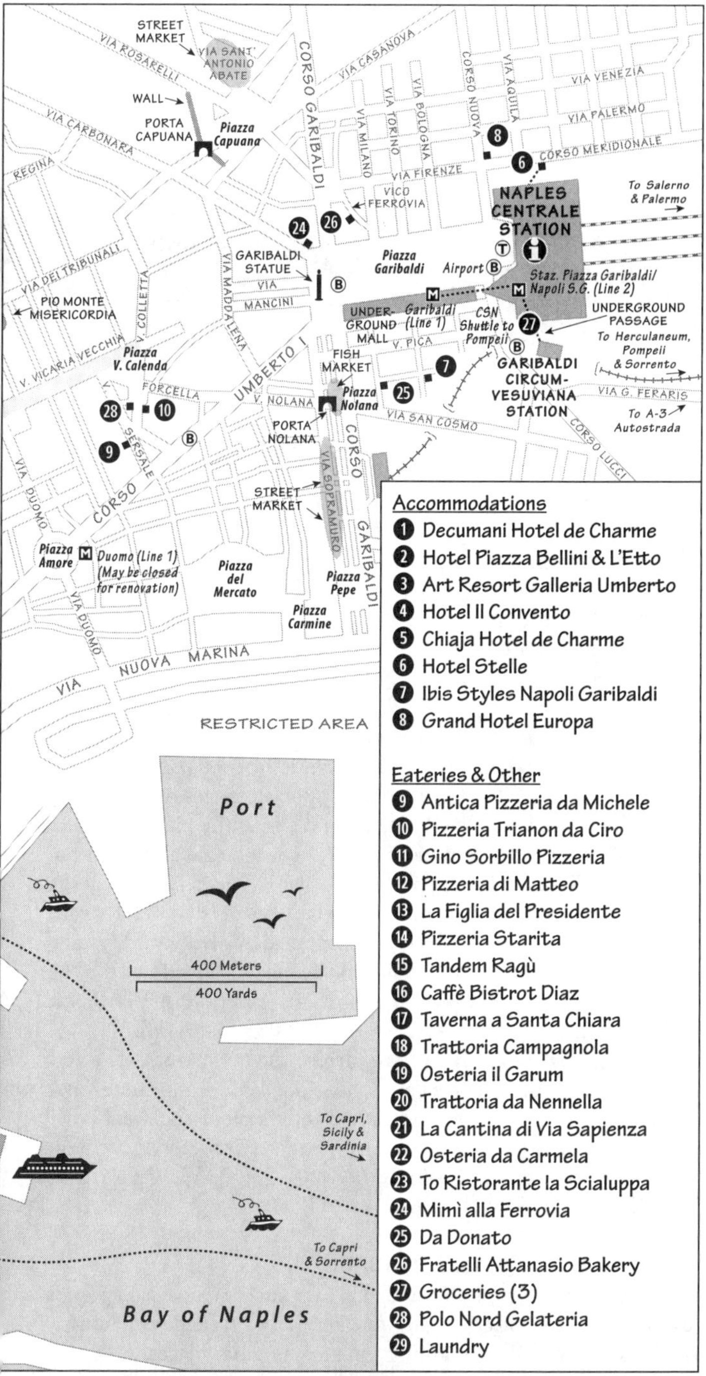
STREET MARKET
VIA SANT' ANTONIO ABATE
VIA ROSARELLI
WALL
PORTA CAPUANA
Piazza Capuana
VIA CARBONARA
REGINA
CORSO GARIBALDI
VIA CASANOVA
VIA MILANO
VIA TORINO
VIA BOLOGNA
CORSO NUOVA
VIA AQUILA
VIA VENEZIA
VIA PALERMO
CORSO MERIDIONALE
VIA FIRENZE
VICO FERROVIA
NAPLES CENTRALE STATION
To Salerno & Palermo
Piazza Garibaldi
Airport
Staz. Piazza Garibaldi/ Napoli S.G. (Line 2)
GARIBALDI STATUE
VIA MANCINI
VIA DEI TRIBUNALI
PIO MONTE MISERICORDIA
VIA COLLETTA
VIA MADDALENA
UNDER-GROUND MALL
Garibaldi (Line 1)
CSN Shuttle to Pompeii
UNDERGROUND PASSAGE
To Herculaneum, Pompeii & Sorrento
V. PICA
V. VICARIA VECCHIA
Piazza V. Calendà
FISH MARKET
UMBERTO I
GARIBALDI CIRCUM-VESUVIANA STATION
VIA G. FERRARIS
FORCELLA
V. NOLANA
Piazza Nolana
PORTA NOLANA
VIA SAN COSMO
To A-3 Autostrada
CORSO LUCCI
SERSALE
VIA DUOMO
CORSO
STREET MARKET
VIA SOPRAMURO
CORSO GARIBALDI
Piazza Amore
Duomo (Line 1) (May be closed for renovation)
Piazza del Mercato
Piazza Pepe
Piazza Carmine
VIA NUOVA MARINA
RESTRICTED AREA
Port
400 Meters
400 Yards
To Capri, Sicily & Sardinia
To Capri & Sorrento
Bay of Naples
Accommodations
1 Decumani Hotel de Charme
2 Hotel Piazza Bellini & L'Etto
3 Art Resort Galleria Umberto
4 Hotel Il Convento
5 Chiaja Hotel de Charme
6 Hotel Stelle
7 Ibis Styles Napoli Garibaldi
8 Grand Hotel Europa
Eateries & Other
9 Antica Pizzeria da Michele
10 Pizzeria Trianon da Ciro
11 Gino Sorbillo Pizzeria
12 Pizzeria di Matteo
13 La Figlia del Presidente
14 Pizzeria Starita
15 Tandem Ragù
16 Caffè Bistrot Diaz
17 Taverna a Santa Chiara
18 Trattoria Campagnola
19 Osteria il Garum
20 Trattoria da Nennella
21 La Cantina di Via Sapienza
22 Osteria da Carmela
23 To Ristorante la Scialuppa
24 Mimì alla Ferrovia
25 Da Donato
26 Fratelli Attanasio Bakery
27 Groceries (3)
28 Polo Nord Gelateria
29 Laundry

are a highlight here. And don't miss the classic dessert, the delicate, super-crunchy, ricotta-filled *sfogliatella*.

FANTASTIC, FAMOUS PIZZA

Naples is the birthplace of pizza. Its pizzerias bake just the right combination of fresh dough (soft and chewy, as opposed to Roman-style, which is thin and crispy), mozzarella, and tomatoes in traditional wood-burning ovens. You can head for the famous, venerable places, but these can have long lines stretching out the door, and half-hour waits for a table. If you want to skip the hassle, just ask your hotel for directions to the neighborhood pizzeria. An average one-person pie (usually the only size available) costs €6-9; most places offer both takeout and eat-in, and pizza is often the only thing on the menu.

Near the Station

These two pizzerias—the most famous—are both a few long blocks from the train station, and near the end of my self-guided Naples Walk.

$ Antica Pizzeria da Michele is for pizza purists. Filled with locals (and tourists), it serves just two varieties: *margherita* (tomato sauce and mozzarella) and *marinara* (tomato sauce, oregano, and garlic, no cheese). Come early to sit and watch the pizza artists in action. A pizza with beer costs around €8. As this place is often jammed with a long line, arrive early or late to get a seat. If there's a mob, head inside to get a number. If it's just too crowded to wait, try the less-exceptional Pizzeria Trianon (described next), which often has room (Mon-Sat 10:30-24:00, closed Sun; look for the vertical red *Antica Pizzeria* sign at the intersection of Via Pietro Colletta and Via Cesare Sersale at #1; +39 081 553 9204).

$ Pizzeria Trianon da Ciro, across the street and left a few doors, has been da Michele's archrival since 1923—and these days, it survives mainly on their overflow. It offers more choices, higher prices, air-conditioning, and a cozier atmosphere; for less chaos, head upstairs (daily 11:00-15:30 & 19:00-23:00, Via Pietro Colletta 42, +39 081 553 9426).

On and near Via dei Tribunali

This street, which runs a couple of blocks north of Spaccanapoli, is legendary for its pizzerias and fun eateries. It's packed with hungry strollers and long lines marking the most popular places.

$ Gino Sorbillo is on all the "best pizza in Naples" lists...as you'll learn the hard way if you show up at peak mealtimes, when huge mobs crowd outside the front door waiting for a table. While many locals believe it doesn't warrant the hype, don't tell the happy travelers eating here (Mon-Sat 12:00-15:30 & 19:00-24:00, closed Sun, Via dei Tribunali 32, +39 081 446 643). Relatives run similarly named places on the same street at #35 (a good option for its specialty: fried pizza) and #37.

$ Pizzeria di Matteo is popular for its fried takeout treats. People waiting out front line up at the little window to snack on deep-fried goodies—*arancini* (with rice, gooey cheese, peas, and sausage), *melanzane* (eggplant), *frittatine* (balls of mac and cheese plus sausage), and *crocché* (croquettes)—for €1-2 apiece (sometimes closed Sun, Via dei Tribunali 94, +39 081 455 262).

Nearby: $ La Figlia del Presidente is a short walk south from the two legendary joints listed above, and is quickly establishing its own loyal clientele. Push your way through the locals gathered around the door and get a number, then patiently wait for a slice of heaven. Or you can dine in the big, plain, high-ceilinged cellar (Tue-Sat 12:00-15:30 & 19:00-23:30, Mon 12:00-15:30, closed Sun, Via Grande Archivio 24, +39 081 286 738).

Near the Archaeological Museum

If you've had enough of crowds at the museum, head a few blocks north for world-class pizza without the throngs of people.

$ Pizzeria Starita has been in business for over 100 years, first as a cantina (featured in a Sophia Loren flick) then offering pizza since the 1950s. The fourth generation currently runs this bustling, friendly eatery just off the normal tourist circuit. Neapolitans think less is more with regard to pizza, but Starita offers both modern and traditional toppings (Tue-Sun 12:00-15:30 & 19:00 until late, closed Mon, no reservations—just show up and add your name to the wait list, from the museum walk 10 minutes up Via Santa Teresa degli Scalzi to the intersection with Via Materdei—the pizzeria is a few steps down on the left at #27, Metro: Museo, +39 081 557 3682).

OTHER RESTAURANTS

If you want a full meal rather than a pizza, consider these options.

Between Spaccanapoli and Via Toledo

$$ Tandem Ragù Restaurant, tiny with a few charming tables inside and out, features a fun menu specializing in Neapolitan *ragù* (beef, pork, or vegetarian options). The *scarpetta* (little shoe) dishes are simply various *ragù*s with baskets of bread for dunking (Tue-

Sun 12:00-23:00, closed Mon, Via Giovanni Paladino 51, 50 yards off Spaccanapoli, below the statue of the Nile, +39 081 1900 2468).

$$ Caffè Bistrot Diaz, close to the famous pizzerias on atmospheric Via dei Tribunali, has a short menu of Neapolitan classics that are executed very well. Locals say it's so tasty because *mamma* is cooking in the kitchen. The indoor seating is modern and nondescript; outdoor tables squeeze into a tight piazza in front of a church (Mon-Sat 7:00-22:00, closed Sun, Via dei Tribunali 25, +39 081 292 383).

$$ Taverna a Santa Chiara is your classic little eatery buried deep in the old center of Naples. It's convivial, warmly run, and simple. Just 100 yards from the tourist commotion of Spaccanapoli, it provides a fun and easygoing break (daily 12:00-16:00 & 19:00-24:00, closed Sun at dinner, Via Santa Chiara 6, +39 081 048 4908).

$$ Trattoria Campagnola is a classic family place with a daily home cooking-style chalkboard menu on the back wall, mamma busy cooking in the back, and wine on tap. Here you can venture away from pastas, be experimental with a series of local dishes, and not go wrong (daily 12:30-16:00 & 19:30-23:00, opposite the famous pizzerias at Via Tribunali 47, +39 081 459 034 but no reservations).

$$ Osteria il Garum is great if you'd like to eat on a classic Neapolitan square. It's named for the ancient fish sauce that was widely used in Roman cooking. These days, mild-mannered Luigi and his staff inject their pricey local cuisine with centuries of tradition, served in a cozy split-level cellar or outside on a covered terrace facing a neighborhood church. It's just between Via Toledo and Spaccanapoli, a short walk from the Church of Gesù Nuovo (Wed-Mon 12:00-15:30 & 19:00-23:30, closed Tue, Piazza Monteoliveto 2A, +39 081 542 3228).

$$ Trattoria da Nennella is fun-loving chaos buried in the Spanish Quarter, with red-shirted waiters barking orders, a small festival anytime someone puts a tip in the bucket, and the fruit course served in plastic bidets. There's one price—€15 per person—and you choose three courses plus a fruit. House wine and water is served in tiny plastic cups, the crowd is ready for fun, and the food's good. You can sit indoors or on a cobbled terrace under a trellis. No reservations are taken, so put your name on the list when you arrive—the line moves pretty fast (Mon-Sat 12:00-15:00 & 19:00-23:00, closed Sun, leave Via Toledo a block down from the BNL bank and walk up Vico del Teatro Nuovo three short blocks to the corner, Vico Lungo del Teatro Nuovo 103, +39 081 414 338).

$ La Cantina di Via Sapienza is a lunch-only hole-in-the-wall, serving up traditional Neapolitan fare in an interior that feels like a neighborhood joint (but has also been discovered by tourists).

It's a block north of the congested, pizzeria-packed Via dei Tribunali, and a good alternative if those places are just too crowded and your heart isn't set on pizza (Mon-Sat for lunch only, closed Sun, Via Sapienza 40, +39 081 459 078).

Near the Archaeological Museum

$$ Osteria da Carmela serves up traditional Neapolitan classics only mama could make—like *ragù, polpetti,* and tasty fried fish—with a dash of Old World charm, as well as a sprinkle of modern class. Affordable house wine and fine cheeses complete the meal. Tables are limited, so reservations are smart (Mon-Sat 12:00-15:30 & 19:00-24:00, closed Sun, Via Conte di Ruvo 11, +39 081 549 9738, www.osteriadacarmela.it).

$$ L'Etto is *not* the place to go for traditional Neapolitan cooking. This stylish restaurant, with a whisper of pretense in its white-minimalist interior and outside at its long row of sidewalk tables, focuses on a wide variety of creatively assembled, nutritious bowls, plus some trendy cocktails (daily 12:30-15:30 & 19:30-22:30, longer hours on weekends, facing Piazza Bellini at Via S. Maria di Costantinopoli 102, +39 081 1932 0967).

A Romantic Splurge on the Harbor

$$$$ Ristorante la Scialuppa ("The Rowboat") is a great bet for a fine local meal on the harbor. Located in the romantic Santa Lucia district, you'll walk across the causeway to the Castel dell'Ovo in the fisherman's quarter (the castle on the island) just off Via Partenope. They boast fine indoor and outdoor seating facing the marina, attentive waitstaff, a wonderful assortment of *antipasti,* great seafood, and predictably high prices. Reservations are smart (Tue-Sun 12:30-15:00 & 19:30-23:30, closed Mon, Piazzetta Marinari 5, +39 081 764 5333, www.ristorantelascialuppa.net).

Near the Station

$$ Mimì alla Ferrovia is a classic neighborhood *trattoria;* stepping inside, surrounded by well-dressed, in-the-know-locals, you know you're in for a good meal. The menu consists of well-executed Neapolitan classics. It's run by a father-and-son team, who combine a passion for tradition with a willingness to innovate. Their ricotta is heavenly (Mon-Sat 12:00-15:30 & 19:00-23:00, closed Sun, Via Alfonso d'Aragona 19, +39 081 553 8525).

$$ Da Donato, a traditional, family-run *trattoria* on a glum street near the station, serves delicious food in an unpretentious atmosphere. The best approach is for two people to share the astonishing *antipasti* sampler—*degustazione "fantasia" della Casa Terra e Mare.* You'll get more than a dozen small portions, each more delicious than the last. A version without seafood is cheaper (Tue-Sun

Getting Around the Region

For specifics, check the "Connections" sections of each chapter. Confirm times and prices locally.

By Bus: CitySightseeing's fleet of bright red buses with audio commentary offer easy trips from Naples to the ruins at Pompeii (see page 69), along the popular Amalfi Coast (see page 135), and even up to the town of Ravello (see page 161). Crowded SITA buses also traverse the Amalfi Coast; see page 134.

By Train: The dingy, crowded **Circumvesuviana** commuter train—popular with locals, tourists, and pickpockets—links Naples, Herculaneum, the Pompeii ruins, and Sorrento. The most important Circumvesuviana station in Naples (called "Garibaldi") is underneath Naples' Centrale station; follow the signs downstairs to *Stazione Garibaldi* and then *Circumvesuviana* and/or *Linee Vesuviane* signs to the Circumvesuviana ticket windows and turnstiles (stand in line or get your ticket at a newsstand). Buy your ticket, confirm the time and track, insert your ticket at the turnstiles, and head down another level to the platforms.

The Circumvesuviana is covered by the Campania ArteCard (see page 6), but not by rail passes. For Pompeii or Herculaneum, take any Circumvesuviana train marked *Sorrento*—they all stop at both (usually depart from platform 3). Sorrento-bound trains depart twice hourly and take about 15 minutes to reach Ercolano Scavi (for the Herculaneum ruins, €2.20 one-way), 35 minutes to reach Pompei Scavi-Villa dei Misteri (for the Pompeii ruins, €2.90 one-way), and 60 minutes to reach Sorrento, the end of the line (€3.90 one-way). Express trains to Sorrento marked *DD* (6/day) reach Sorrento 15 minutes sooner (and stop at Herculaneum and Pompeii). For schedules, see the Italian-only website www.eavsrl.it.

On the platform, double-check with a local that the train goes to Sorrento (avoid lines that branch out to other destinations). When returning to Naples on the Circumvesuviana, validate your ticket before boarding and get off at the next-to-the-last station, Garibaldi (Centrale station is just up the escalator).

Pricier **Campania Express trains,** operated by Circumvesuviana, use the same tracks and stops. They run only four times a day, but are less crowded and have air-conditioning (€15 one-way in high season to any destination: Herculaneum, 10 minutes; Pompeii, 30 minutes; Sorrento, 1 hour; mid-March-Oct only, not covered by Campania ArteCard, buy tickets at http://ots.eavsrl.it or at the station).

Trenitalia (Italy's national railway) runs **Metropolitana** trains—part of Naples' Metro line 2—to Pompei town, from which it's a short shuttle bus ride or long walk to the ruins (trains run 1-2/hour, 45 minutes, covered by Campania ArteCard; see details on page 6). Metropolitana trains stop downstairs in Naples' Centrale station (near the center of the station—look for *Metro linea 2*) and conveniently also link to the Naples Archaeological Museum (Piazza Cavour stop). After Pompei town, these continue to Salerno (for boats and buses to Amalfi), though there are faster options. Note that the Metropoli-

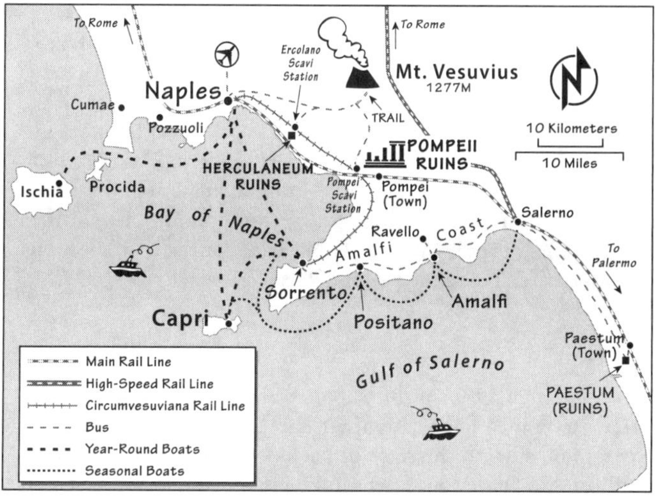

tana is *not* convenient for reaching Herculaneum or Sorrento.

By Taxi: The 30-mile taxi ride from Naples directly to your Sorrento hotel costs about €110 (ask the driver for the nonmetered *tariffa predeterminata*). A cab on Capri runs about €70/hour. Taxis on the Amalfi Coast are generally expensive, and often overcharge, but can be convenient, especially with a larger group. See "Getting Around the Amalfi Coast—By Taxi" on page 136.

By Boat: Major companies include Caremar (www.caremar.it), SNAV (www.snav.it), Gescab (a.k.a. NLG Jet, www.gescab.it), Navigazione Libera del Golfo (www.navlib.it), Alilauro (www.alilauro.it), Travelmar (www.travelmar.it), and Alicost (www.alicost.it). Each company has different destinations and prices; some compete for the same trips. Some lines (like Sorrento-Capri) run all year; others (on the Amalfi Coast, for example) only in summer. Trips can be cancelled in bad weather. Faster watercraft cost a little more than slow car ferries. A hydrofoil, sometimes called a "jet boat," skims between Naples and Sorrento—it's swifter, safer from pickpockets, more scenic, and more expensive than the Circumvesuviana train.

For schedules, check online (www.capritourism.com; click "Shipping Timetable"), or ask at any TI or at Naples' Molo Beverello boat dock. (The handy departure board on the rooftop of the Molo Beverello terminal shows all the upcoming departures.) Most boats charge €2 or so for luggage. When you arrive, note the return times—the last boat usually leaves before 19:00. The preset price for a taxi between Naples' Centrale train station and its port (Molo Beverello) is €11, or you can take Metro line 1 to the Municipio stop and walk to the port.

By Shared Trips: Mondo Guide is sometimes able to play "matchmaker" between travelers looking for an efficient, direct car connection instead of a complicated train or bus connection. By splitting the cost with others headed the same way, this can become reasonable. For details, see www.sharedtrips.com.

12:30-14:30 & 19:30-22:00, closed Mon, two blocks from Piazza Garibaldi—turn down Via Silvio Spaventa to #39, +39 081 287 828).

PASTRY

To get the full overview of Neapolitan pastries at good prices, visit the bakery outlet of **Fratelli Attanasio** on a small alley near the train station—with your back to the station building, it's off the far-right corner of the big square. Come early for the best selection (Tue-Sun 6:30-19:30, closed Mon, Vico Ferrovia 1, +39 081 285 675).

PICNICS

A good supermarket for picnic supplies is **Sapori & Dintorni,** in the train-station complex (Mon-Sat 8:00-20:30, Sun 8:00-15:00, enter from outside, to the right of bookstore). By Piazza Dante is a small **Superò** that's convenient to hotels near this stretch of Via Toledo (Mon-Sat 8:30-20:30, Sun 8:30-14:00, at corner of Via Tarsia and Vico San Domenico Soriano). By the Toledo Metro stop a small **Conad** is handy to hotels near Galleria Umberto I and the Spanish Quarter (daily 8:00-21:00, Via Roberto Bracco 4).

Naples Connections

BY TRAIN

See the "Getting Around the Region" sidebar for information on getting to **Herculaneum,** the ruins at **Pompeii, Pompei Town,** and **Sorrento** by train.

By Train to: Rome (Trenitalia: 1-5/hour, 70 minutes on Frecciarossa, 2 hours on Intercity, 2.5 hours and much cheaper on regional trains; Italo: hourly, 70 minutes), **Civitavecchia** (at least hourly, 3 hours, most change in Rome), **Florence** (Trenitalia: at least hourly, 3 hours, most change in Pisa or Rome; Italo: hourly, 3 hours), **Salerno** (Trenitalia: at least hourly, 35-45 minutes, change in Salerno for bus or boat to Amalfi; *regionale* trains are cheaper but Intercity and Freccia express trains have a first class section for a little extra; avoid slower Metropolitana trains that leave from the same platforms as Metro's line 2; Italo: 4/day, 45 minutes), **Paestum** (12/day, 1.25 hours, direction: Sapri or Reggio), **Brindisi** (4/day, 5-6 hours, change in Caserta; from Brindisi, ferries sail to Greece), **Milan** (Trenitalia: 2/hour, 5 hours; Italo: 1-2/hour), **Venice** (Trenitalia: almost hourly, 5.5 hours, some change in Bologna or Rome; Italo: 3/day, 5.5 hours, reservations required), **Palermo** (2/day direct, 9.5 hours, also an overnight train). Any train listed on the schedule as leaving Napoli PG or Napoli-Garibaldi departs not from Napoli Centrale, but from the adjacent Garibaldi station.

BY BOAT

Ferries and cruise ships dock next to each other in the shadow of the old fortress (Castel Nuovo), a short walk from the old town sightseeing action. Naples has great ferry connections to Sorrento, Capri, and other nearby destinations. Cruise ships use the giant Stazione Marittima cruise terminal, hydrofoils and faster ferries use the Molo Beverello dock (to the west of the terminal), and slower car ferries leave from Calata Porta di Massa, east of the terminal. The entire port area is currently a big construction zone, and has been torn up for years; hopefully it will be tidied up in time for your visit.

Whether arriving by ferry or cruise ship, you can get to the city center by taxi, Metro, or on foot; the Alibus shuttle bus runs to the airport (see "By Plane," next).

A **taxi** stand is in front of the port area. Expect to pay €12-15 to connect the port to the train station or the Archaeological Museum.

Straight ahead across the road from the cruise terminal (on the right side of the big fortress) is Piazza Municipio, with the handy Municipio **Metro** stop. From here, line 1 zips you right to the Archaeological Museum (Museo stop) or, in the opposite direction, to the train station (Garibaldi stop). A €1.10 single ticket *(corsa singola)* covers rides on line 1. You can buy tickets at any tobacco shop or some cafés: Caffè Moreno is between the two buildings of the cruise terminal, and Caffè Beverello is along the busy street on the waterfront. Remember to validate your ticket as you enter the Metro station.

On foot, it's a seven-minute **walk**—past the gigantic Castel Nuovo, then to the left—to Piazza del Plebiscito and the old city center.

From Naples by Boat to: Sorrento (6/day, more in summer, departs roughly every 2 hours starting at 9:00, few or no boats on winter weekends, leaves from Molo Beverello, 40 minutes), **Capri** (roughly hourly, more in summer, hydrofoil: 45 minutes from Molo Beverello; ferries: 60-90 minutes from Calata Porta di Massa). Sometimes seasonal boats go to **Positano** and **Amalfi,** on the Amalfi Coast—ask. For a map showing boat connections, see page 95. For timetables, visit www.capritourism.com and click "Shipping Timetable."

BY PLANE

Naples International Airport (Aeroporto Internazionale di Napoli, a.k.a. Capodichino, code: NAP) is close to town (+39 081 789 6767, www.aeroportodinapoli.it). In summer, you may find a TI here. Alibus **shuttle buses** zip you in 10 minutes from the airport to Naples' Centrale train station, and then head to the port/Piazza

Municipio for boats to Capri and Sorrento (buses run daily 6:00-23:00, 4/hour, 20-30 minutes to the port, €5 on board). The shuttle bus departs from a stop located straight out the airport exit, past the rental car lots. If you take a **taxi** to or from the airport, ask the driver for the fixed price (€18 to the train station, €21 to the port, €25 to the Chiaia district near the waterfront).

To reach **Sorrento** from Naples Airport, take the direct Curreri bus (see page 116). A taxi to Sorrento costs about €110.

POMPEII & NEARBY

Pompeii • Herculaneum • Vesuvius

Stopped in their tracks by the eruption of Mount Vesuvius in AD 79, Pompeii and Herculaneum offer the best look anywhere at what life in Rome must have been like around 2,000 years ago. These two cities of well-preserved ruins are yours to explore. Of the two sites, Pompeii is grander, while Herculaneum is smaller, more intimate, and more intact. Pompeii is easily reached from Naples on the CitySightseeing bus or by either the Circumvesuviana commuter, Campania Express, or Trenitalia Metropolitana trains; Herculaneum is best reached by train. Vesuvius, still smoldering ominously, rises up on the horizon. It last erupted in 1944, and is still an active volcano. Buses from the train stations at Herculaneum or Pompeii drop you a half-hour hike below its crater rim.

Pompeii

A once-thriving commercial port of 20,000, Pompeii (worth ▲▲▲) grew from Greek and Etruscan roots to become an important Roman city. Then, on August 24, AD 79, everything changed. Vesuvius erupted and began to bury the city under 20 feet of hot volcanic ash. For the archaeolo-

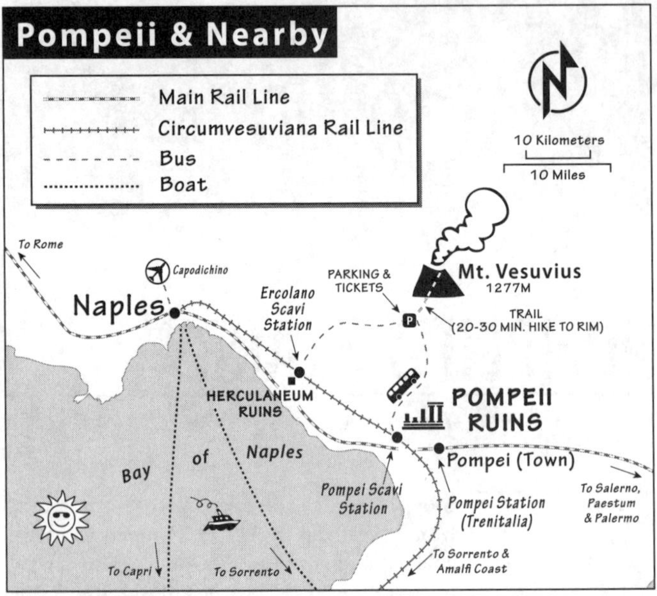

gists who excavated it centuries later, this was a shake-and-bake windfall, teaching them volumes about daily Roman life. Pompeii was accidentally rediscovered in 1599; excavations began in 1748.

GETTING TO POMPEII

By Train from Naples or Sorrento Directly to the Ruins: Pompeii is roughly midway between Naples and Sorrento on the crowded, run-down **Circumvesuviana commuter train** line (2/hour, 35 minutes from Naples, 30 minutes from Sorrento, either trip costs €2.90 one-way, not covered by rail passes, no air-con, Italian-only website: www.eavsrl.it). In the Naples station, you'll find these downstairs (follow signs for *Circumvesuviana* as well as for *Linee Vesuviane*—both lead to the same tracks). Get off at the **Pompei Scavi-Villa dei Misteri** stop; from Naples, it's the stop after Villa Regina. DD express trains (6/day) bypass several stations but do stop at Pompei Scavi, shaving 10 minutes off the trip from Naples.

Less-frequent **Campania Express trains** use the same tracks and stops, but are less crowded and have air-conditioning (4/day, 30 minutes from Naples, 25 minutes from Sorrento, either trip costs €8 one-way, mid-March-Oct only, http://ots.eavsrl.it). Due to return times, it may work best to take the Campania Express *to* Pompeii and a different train back to Naples. For train details, see page 62.

From the Pompei Scavi train station, it's just a two-minute

walk to the ruin's Porta Marina entrance: Leaving the station, turn right and walk down the road about a block (entrance on left).

By Train from Naples to Pompei Town (with Bus Transfer to Pompeii Ruins): Trenitalia (Italy's national railway) operates the **Metropolitana** train from Naples to the town center of Pompei (with one "i"), which is a short bus ride (or long walk) from the Pompeii archaeological site. This train is part of Naples' Metro line 2, which stops under Centrale station (at the stop called Stazione Piazza Garibaldi, or "Napoli S.G." for short). It also reaches the Piazza Cavour stop near the Archaeological Museum—handy for those who want to directly connect Pompeii to its greatest artifacts.

In Pompei town, the Metropolitana is coordinated with a **BusLink shuttle bus** that runs to the ruins. The bus is also operated by Trenitalia, so the entire train-bus trip shows up on their online schedules (1-2/hour, 70 minutes, €4.10, search for "Pompei Scavi"; train to Pompei town only: 1-2/hour, 45 minutes, €2.90, search for "Pompei"; www.trenitalia.com).

If you decide to **walk** to the archaeological site, it's actually quite pleasant (allow 25-30 minutes to the main Porta Marina entrance, or 15-20 minutes to the Anfiteatro entrance): Head straight out from the train station to the big church tower, which marks the tidy main piazza of modern Pompei. From there, turn left and you'll soon be walking along the outer gate of the Pompeii site, passing various entrances along the way (see map).

By Shuttle Bus from Naples: CitySightseeing Italy offers a convenient, clean, and stress-free shuttle bus from Naples to Pompeii. The bus departs from three pick-up points in Naples: At the Piazza Municipio end of the Castel Nuovo, at Piazza Bovio near the Università Metro stop, and at Centrale station (stop located across the street and left when exiting, near the Hotel D'Anna). Tickets can be purchased online, but be aware that each bus has a specific return time about 4.5 hours after arrival; no return-trip changes are allowed. Early morning departures beat the heat at Pompeii, but traffic congestion can delay your arrival and cut into your sightseeing time. Check the most recent details on their website (generally 3/day in summer, 2/day off-season, 30-minute ride from the train station when traffic is light, €10 one-way, €18 round-trip, +39 081 551 7279, www.city-sightseeing.it). Skip the option to purchase your Pompeii entrance ticket through CitySightseeing—you'll pay more than buying it yourself online (details later).

By Car: Parking is available at Camping Zeus, next to the Pompei Scavi train station (€3/hour, €20/day); several other campgrounds/parking lots are nearby.

Day-Tripping from Rome: It's possible to day-trip to Pompeii from Rome, if you start early and plan on a long day. Figure about 2.5-3 hours for transportation each way, plus time at the site.

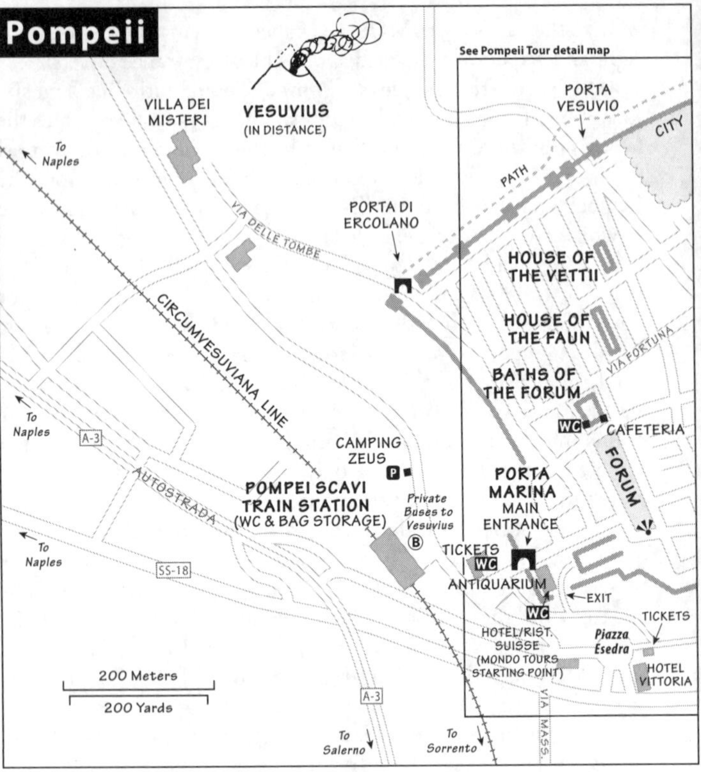

First, take the express train to Naples. In Naples, transfer either to the Circumvesuviana or Campania Express train (which drops you directly at the ruins) or to the Trenitalia Metropolitana train (which takes you to the modern town of Pompei, where you'll board a shuttle bus to the site). Or, time your train trip from Rome to catch the CitySightseeing shuttle bus from Naples to Pompeii. All of these options are outlined above.

ORIENTATION TO POMPEII

Cost: €16, includes special exhibits. Consider the Campania ArteCard (see page 6) if visiting other sights in the region. Avoid crowded free entry days (usually once a month on a Sunday).

Hours: Daily 9:00-19:30, Nov-March until 17:00, last entry 1.5 hours before closing.

Information: +39 081 857 5347, general info at www.pompeiisites.org, tickets at www.ticketone.it.

Crowd-Beating Tips: To skip ahead of everyone, purchase your ticket online at www.ticketone.it (€1.50 surcharge). If you're buying onsite and there's a very long ticket line at the Porta Marina entrance, continue walking three minutes to the ticket

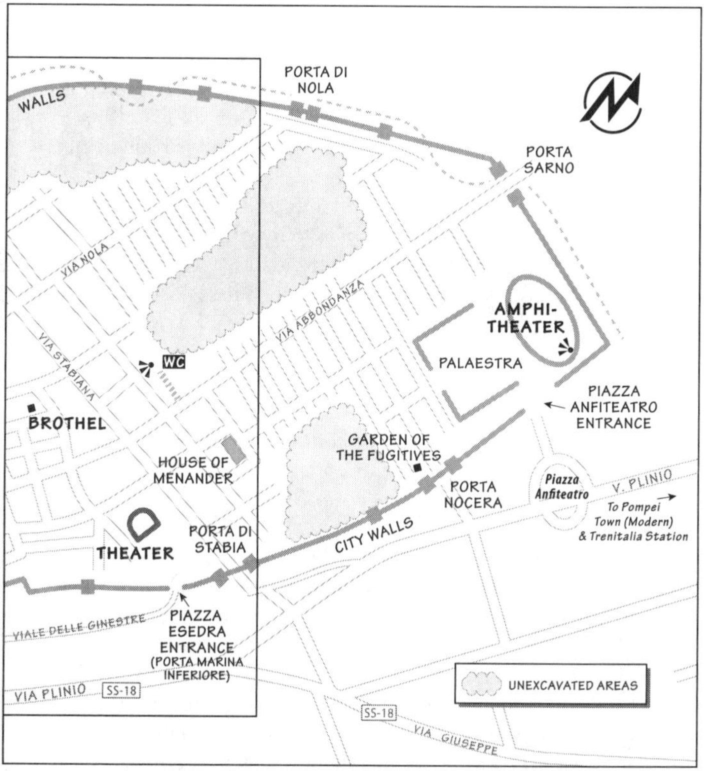

booth near Hotel Vittoria (called Piazza Esedra or Porta Marina Inferiore; there's rarely a line). Buy your ticket, then either enter here or—to start my tour directly—return to Porta Marina, and walk right in.

Visitor Information: You may get a flimsy map of the site with your ticket, and you'll see QR codes here and there encouraging you to access online maps. But this book's map should suit your needs.

Some buildings and streets are bound to be closed for restoration when you visit. Use your map to find your way. Street names and building numbers are clearly marked throughout the site.

The bookshop sells a couple of books with plastic overlays that allow you to re-create Pompeii from the ruins (€18; if you buy from a street vendor, pay no more than that). Another good book is the €6 *Pompeii (Brief) Guide,* with excellent photos and additional walking routes.

Ignore the "info point" kiosk at the train station, which is a private agency selling tours.

Tours: Here are several ways to enjoy an organized and educational visit to Pompeii.

Simply follow the **self-guided** tour in this chapter (or, better, enjoy the audio version with my free Rick Steves Audio Europe app). Both cover the basics and provide plenty of information for do-it-yourselfers.

Join a **Mondo Guide shared tour** for Rick Steves readers. This is your best budget bet for a tour with an actual guide (€20, doesn't include Pompeii entry, daily at 11:00, reservations required; meet at Hotel/Ristorante Suisse, just down the hill from the Porta Marina entrance; for details, see page 16).

Hire guide **Antonio Somma** for a private or shared tour. Antonio and his team of guides offer good two-hour tours of Pompeii for €120 (mobile +39 393 406 3824, +39 081 850 1992, www.tourspompeiiguide.com, info@pompeitour.com).

Other Options: Audioguides are available from a kiosk near the ticket booth at the Porta Marina entrance (€8, €13 for 2, ID required).

When you step off the train, you'll likely be accosted by touts for the "info point" kiosk, which sells €15 tours that depart whenever enough people sign up. Private guides (around €120/2 hours) of varying quality cluster near the ticket booth and may try to herd you into a group with other travelers, which is fine if it makes the price more reasonable. It's unethical for a guide to double charge by combining two groups into one tour. Instead, tourists should enjoy the savings and tip higher.

Rated Risqué: Parents, note that the ancient brothel and its sexually explicit frescoes are included on tours; let your guide know if you'd rather skip that stop.

Length of This Tour: Allow two hours, or three if you visit the theater and amphitheater. With less time, focus on the Forum, Baths of the Forum, House of the Vettii, House of the Faun, and brothel.

Baggage Check: Use the free baggage check near the turnstiles at the site entrance (just yards from the station). The train station also offers pay luggage storage (downstairs, by the WC).

Services: There's a pay WC at the train station. The Pompeii site has four free WCs—at the entrance, in the cafeteria, in the Antiquarium museum, and near the end of this tour, uphill from the theaters.

Eating: These **$** eateries offer reasonably priced meals (though your cheapest bet may be to bring your own food for a discreet picnic).

The **Ciao cafeteria,** within the site, serves good sandwiches, pizza, and pasta. You're welcome to picnic here if you buy a drink. **Bar Sgambati,** the café/restaurant at the train station, has air-conditioning, Wi-Fi, sandwiches to go, and pastas and pizzas. **Marius Juice Shop** (run by local guide Antonio Somma's family) sells sandwiches to go, and is located between Bar Sgambati and the Porta Marina entrance.

A second cluster of eateries around the ticket booth near Hotel Vittoria dishes out handy slices of pizza, salads, and pasta.

Starring: Roofless (collapsed) but otherwise intact Roman buildings, plaster casts of hapless victims, some erotic frescoes, and the dawning realization that these ancient people were not that different from us.

BACKGROUND

Pompeii, founded in 600 BC, eventually became a booming Roman trading city. Not rich, not poor, it was middle class—a perfect example of typical Roman life. Most streets would have been lined with stalls and jammed with customers from sunup to sundown. Chariots vied with shoppers for street space. Two thousand years ago, Rome controlled the entire Mediterranean—making it a kind of free-trade zone—and Pompeii was a central and bustling port.

There were no posh neighborhoods in Pompeii. Rich and poor mixed it up as elegant houses existed side by side with simple homes. While nearby Herculaneum would have been a classier place to live (a smaller, seaside resort with traffic-free streets, fancier houses, and far better drainage), Pompeii was the place for action and shopping. It served an estimated 20,000 residents with more than 40 bakeries, 130 bars, restaurants and hotels, and 30 brothels. With most of its buildings covered by brilliant white ground-marble stucco, Pompeii in AD 79 was an impressive town.

As you tour Pompeii, remember that its best art is safeguarded in the Archaeological Museum in Naples (described in the Naples chapter). Visiting the museum before or after going to Pompeii will help put this fascinating sight into context.

➲ SELF-GUIDED TOUR

• *Just past the ticket-taker, start your approach up to the...*

❶ Porta Marina

The city of Pompeii was born on the hill ahead of you. This was the original town gate. Before Vesuvius blew and filled in the harbor, the sea came nearly to here. Notice the two openings in the gate (ahead, up the ramp). Both were left open by day to admit major traffic. At night, the larger one was closed for better security.

• *Pass through the Porta Marina and continue up to the top of the street, pausing at the three large stepping-stones in the middle.*

❷ Pompeii's Streets

Every day, Pompeiians flooded the streets with gushing water to clean them. These stepping-stones let pedestrians cross without getting their sandals wet. Chariots traveling in either direction could straddle the stones (all had standard-size axles). A single stepping-stone in a road means it was a one-way street, a pair indicates an ordinary two-way, and three (like this) signifies a major thoroughfare. The basalt stones are the original Roman pavement. The sidewalks (elevated to hide the plumbing—you'll see ancient plumbing revealed throughout the site) were paved with bits of broken pots (an ancient form of recycling) and studded with reflective bits of white marble. These "cats' eyes" helped people get around after dark, either by moonlight or with the help of lamps.

• *Continue straight ahead, don your mental toga, and enter the city as the Romans once did. The road opens up into the spacious main square: the Forum. Stand at the right end of this rectangular space (near the centaur statue) and look toward Mount Vesuvius.*

❸ The Forum (Foro)

Pompeii's commercial, religious, and political center stands at the intersection of the city's two main streets. While it's the most ruined part of Pompeii, it's grand nonetheless. Picture the piazza surrounded by two-story buildings on all sides. The pedestals that line the square once held statues of VIPs and various gods (now safely displayed in the museum in Naples). In Pompeii's heyday, its citizens gathered here in the main square to shop, talk politics,

Pompeii Tour

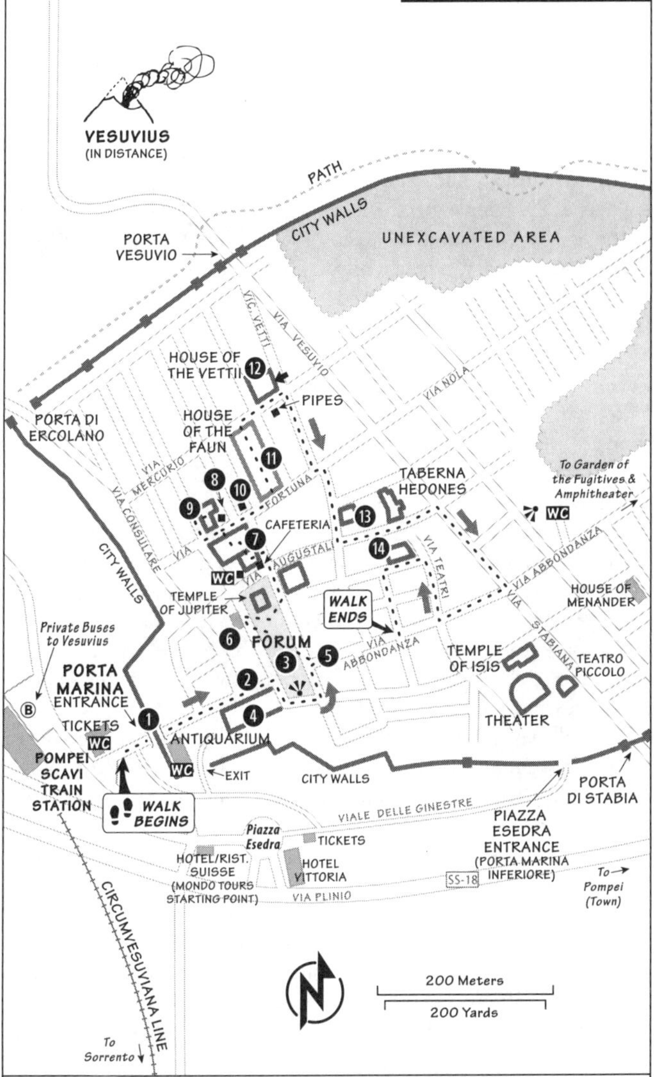

1. Porta Marina
2. Pompeii's Streets
3. Forum
4. Basilica
5. Via Abbondanza
6. Forum Granary; Plaster Casts of Victims
7. Baths of the Forum
8. Fast-Food Joint
9. House of the Tragic Poet
10. Aqueduct Arch
11. House of the Faun
12. House of the Vettii
13. Bakery & Mill
14. Brothel

and socialize. Business took place in the important buildings that lined the piazza.

The Forum was dominated by the **Temple of Jupiter,** at the far end (marked by a half-dozen ruined columns atop a stair-step base). Jupiter was the supreme god of the Roman pantheon—you might be able to make out his little white marble head at the center-rear of the temple. To the left of the temple is a fenced-off area, the **Forum granary,** where many artifacts from Pompeii are stored (and which we'll visit later).

At the near end of the Forum (behind where you're standing) is the **curia,** or City Hall. Like many Roman buildings, it was built with brick and mortar, then covered with marble walls and floors. To your left (as you face Vesuvius and the Temple of Jupiter) is the **basilica,** or courthouse.

Since Pompeii was a pretty typical Roman town, it has the same layout and components that you'll find in any Roman city—main square, curia, basilica, temples, axis of roads, and so on. All power converged at the Forum: religious (the temple), political (the curia), judicial (the basilica), and commercial (this piazza was the main marketplace). Even the power of the people was expressed here, since this is where they gathered to vote. Imagine the hubbub of this town square in its heyday.

Look beyond the Temple of Jupiter. Five miles to the north looms the ominous backstory to this site: **Mount Vesuvius.** Mentally draw a triangle up from the two remaining peaks to reconstruct the mountain before the eruption. When it blew, Pompeiians had no idea that they were living under a volcano, as Vesuvius hadn't erupted for 1,200 years. Imagine the wonder—then the horror—as a column of pulverized rock roared upward, and then ash began to fall. The weight of the ash and small rocks collapsed Pompeii's roofs later that day, crushing people who had taken refuge inside buildings instead of fleeing the city.

• *As you face Vesuvius, the basilica is to your left, lined with stumps of columns. Step inside.*

❹ Basilica

Pompeii's basilica was a first-century palace of justice. This ancient law court has the same floor plan later adopted by many Christian churches (which are also called basilicas). The big central hall (or nave) is flanked by rows of columns marking off narrower side aisles. Along the side walls are traces of the original stucco imitating marble.

The columns—now stumps all about the same height—were not ruined by the volcano. Rather, they were left unfinished when Vesuvius blew. Pompeii had been devastated by an earthquake in AD 62, and was just in the process of rebuilding the basilica when Vesuvius erupted, 17 years later. The half-built columns show off the technology of the day. Uniform bricks were stacked around a cylindrical core. Once finished, they would have been coated with marble-dust stucco to simulate marble columns—an economical construction method found throughout Pompeii (and the Roman Empire).

Besides the earthquake and the eruption, Pompeii's buildings have suffered other ravages over the years, including Spanish plunderers (c. 1800), 19th-century souvenir hunters, WWII bombs, creeping and destructive vegetation, another earthquake in 1980, and modern neglect. The fact that the entire city was covered by the eruption of AD 79 actually helped preserve it, saving it from the sixth-century barbarians who plundered many other towns into oblivion.

• *Exit the basilica and cross the short side of the square to where the city's main street hits the Forum. Stop at the three white stones that stick up from the cobbles.*

❺ Via Abbondanza

Glance down Via Abbondanza, Pompeii's main street. Lined with shops, bars, and restaurants, it was a lively, pedestrian-only zone. The three "beaver-teeth" stones are traffic barriers that kept chariots out. On the corner at the start of the street (just to the left), take a close look at the dark travertine column standing next to the white one. Notice that the marble drums of the white column are not chiseled entirely round—another construction project left unfinished when Vesuvius erupted.

• *Our tour will eventually end a few blocks down Via Abbondanza after making a big loop. But now, head toward Vesuvius, cutting across the Forum. To the left of the Temple of Jupiter is the...*

The Eruption of Vesuvius

At about 1:00 in the afternoon on August 24, AD 79, Mount Vesuvius erupted, sending a mushroom cloud of ash, dust, and rocks 12 miles into the air. It spewed for 18 hours straight, as winds blew the cloud southward. The white-gray ash settled like a heavy snow on Pompeii, its weight eventually collapsing roofs and floors, but leaving the walls intact. And though most of Pompeii's 20,000 residents fled that day, about 2,000 stayed behind.

Although the city of Herculaneum was closer to the volcano—about four miles away—at first it largely escaped the rain of ash, due to the direction of the wind. However, 12 hours after Vesuvius awoke, the type of eruption suddenly changed. The mountain let loose a superheated avalanche of ash, pumice, and gas. This red-hot "pyroclastic flow" sped down the side of the mountain at nearly 100 miles per hour, engulfing Herculaneum and cooking its residents alive. Several more flows over the next few hours further entombed Herculaneum, burying it in nearly 60 feet of hot material that later cooled into rock, freezing the city in time. Then, at around 7:30 in the morning, another pyroclastic flow headed south and struck Pompeii, dealing a fatal blow to those who'd remained behind.

❻ Forum Granary

A substantial stretch of the west side of the Forum was the granary and ancient produce market. Today, it houses thousands of artifacts excavated from Pompeii. You'll see lots of crockery, pots, pans, jugs, and containers used for transporting oil and wine. You'll also see casts of a couple of victims (and a dog) of the eruption. These casts show Pompeiians eerily captured in their last moments, hands covering their mouths as they gasped

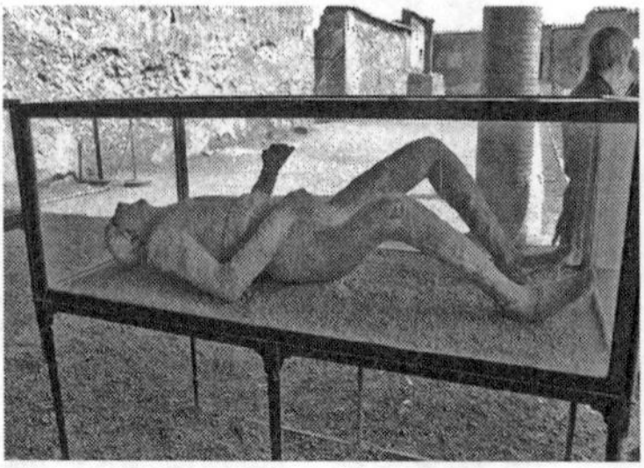

for air. They were quickly suffocated by a superheated avalanche of gas and ash, and their bodies were encased in volcanic debris. While excavating, modern archaeologists detected hollow spaces underfoot, created when the victims' bodies decomposed. By gently filling the holes with plaster, the archaeologists created molds of the Pompeiians who were caught in the disaster.

A few steps to the left of the granary is a tiny alcove that contained the **Mensa Ponderaria,** a counter where standard units (such as today's liter or gallon) were used to measure the quantities of liquid and solid food that were sold. And just to the right of the granary is the remains of a public toilet. You can imagine the many seats, lack of privacy, and constantly flushing stream running through the room.

• *Exit the Forum by crossing it again in front of the Temple of Jupiter and turning left. Go under the arch. In the road are more "beaver-teeth" traffic blocks. On the pillar to the right, look for the pedestrian-only road sign (two guys carrying an amphora, or ancient jug; it's above the* REG VII INS IV *sign). The modern cafeteria (on the left) is the only eatery inside the archaeological site. Twenty yards past the cafeteria, on the left-hand side at #24, is the entrance to the...*

❼ Baths of the Forum (Terme del Foro)

Pompeii had six public baths, each with a men's and a women's section. You're in the men's zone. The leafy courtyard at the entrance was the gymnasium. After working out, clients could relax with a hot bath *(caldarium),* warm bath *(tepidarium),* or cold plunge *(frigidarium).*

The first big, plain room you enter served as the **dressing room.** Holes on the walls were for pegs to hang clothing. High up, the window (with a faded Neptune underneath) was originally covered with a less-translucent Roman glass. Walk over the nonslip mosaics into the next room.

The ***tepidarium*** is ringed by mini statues or *telamones* (male caryatids, figures used as supporting pillars), which divided the lockers. Clients would undress and warm up here, perhaps relaxing on one of the bronze cow-footed benches near the bronze heater while waiting for a massage. Look at the ceiling—half crushed by the eruption and half intact, with its fine blue-and-white stucco work.

Next, admire the engineering in the steam-bath room, or ***caldarium.*** The double floor was heated from below—so it was nice for bare feet (look into the grate across from where you entered to see the brick support towers). The double walls with brown terracotta tiles held the heat. Romans soaked in the big tub, which was filled with hot water. Opposite the big tub is a fountain, which spouted water onto the hot floor, creating steam. The lettering on the fountain reminded those enjoying the room which two politicians paid for it...and how much it cost them. (On the far right, the Roman numerals indicate they paid 5,250 *sestertii*). To keep condensation from dripping annoyingly from the ceiling, fluting (ribbing) was added to carry water down the walls.

• *Today's visitors exit the baths through the original entry (at the far end of the dressing room). Hungry? Immediately across the street (at #8) is an ancient...*

❽ Fast-Food Joint

After a bath, it was only natural to want a little snack. So, just across the street is a fast-food joint, marked by a series of rectangular marble counters. Most ancient Romans didn't cook for themselves in their tiny apartments, so to-go places like this were commonplace. The holes in the counters held the pots for food. Each container was like a thermos, with a wooden lid to keep the soup hot, the wine cool, and so on. You could dine in the back or get your food to go. Notice the groove in the front doorstep and the holes out on the curb. The holes likely accommodated cords for stretching awnings over the sidewalk to shield the clientele from the hot sun, while the grooves were for the shop's folding accordion doors. Look at the wheel grooves in the pavement, worn down through centuries of use. Nearby are more stepping-stones for pedestrians to cross the flooded streets.

• *Just a few steps uphill from the fast-food joint, at #5 (behind a glass wall), is the...*

❾ House of the Tragic Poet (Casa del Poeta Tragico)

This house is typical Roman style. The entry is flanked by two family-owned shops (each with a track for a collapsing accordion door). The home is like a train running straight away from the street: atrium (with skylight and pool to catch the rain), den (where deals were made by the shopkeeper), and garden (with rooms facing it and a shrine to remember both the gods and family ancestors). In the entryway is the famous "Beware of Dog" *(Cave Canem)* mosaic.

When it's open, today's visitors enter the home by the back door (circle around to the left). On your way there, look for the modern exposed pipe on the left side of the lane; this is the same as ones used in the ancient plumbing system, hidden beneath the raised sidewalk. The richly frescoed dining room is off the garden. Diners lounged on their couches (the Roman custom) and enjoyed frescoes with fake "windows," giving the illusion of a bigger and airier room. Next to the dining room is a humble BBQ-style kitchen with a little closet for the toilet (the kitchen and bathroom shared the same plumbing).

• *Return to the fast-food place and continue about 10 yards downhill to the big intersection. From the center of the intersection, look left to see a giant arch, framing a nice view of Mount Vesuvius.*

⑩ Aqueduct Arch—Running Water

Water was critical for this city of 20,000 people, and this arch was part of Pompeii's water-delivery system. A 100-mile-long aqueduct carried fresh water down from the hillsides to a big reservoir perched at the highest point of the city wall. Since overall water pressure was disappointing, Pompeiians built arches like the brick one you see here (originally covered in marble) with hidden water tanks at the top. Located just below the altitude of the main tank, these smaller tanks were filled by gravity and provided each neighborhood with reliable pressure. Look closely at the arch and you'll see 2,000-year-old pipes (made of lead imported all the way from Cornwall in Britannia) embedded deep in the brick.

If there was a water shortage, democratic priorities prevailed: First the baths were cut off, then the private homes. The last to go were the public fountains, where all citizens could get drinking and cooking water.

• *If you're thirsty, fill your water bottle from the modern fountain. Then turn right and continue straight downhill one block (50 yards), to #2 on the left.*

⑪ House of the Faun (Casa del Fauno)

Stand across the street and marvel at the grand entry with *"HAVE"* (hail to you) as a welcome mat. Go in. Notice the two shrines above the entryway—one dedicated to the gods, the other to this wealthy family's ancestors. (Contemporary Neapolitans still carry on this practice; you'll notice little shrines embedded in walls all over Naples.)

You are standing in Pompeii's largest home, where you're greeted by the delightful small bronze **statue of**

the *Dancing Faun,* famed for its realistic movement and fine proportion. (The original is in Naples' Archaeological Museum.) With 40 rooms and 27,000 square feet, the House of the Faun covers an entire city block. Just think of how vibrant and luxurious this house would have seemed before the eruption.

At the far end of the first garden is the famous floor mosaic of the ***Battle of Alexander.*** (The original is also at the museum in Naples.) In 333 BC, Alexander the Great beat Darius and the Persians. Romans had much respect for Alexander, the first great emperor before Rome's. While most of Pompeii's nouveau riche had notoriously bad taste and stuffed their palaces with over-the-top, mismatched decor, this guy had class. Both the faun (an ancient copy of a famous Greek statue) and the Alexander mosaic show an appreciation for history.

The house's back courtyard is lined with pillars rebuilt after the AD 62 earthquake. Take a close look at the brick, mortar, and fake-marble stucco veneer.

• *Leave the House of the Faun through its back door in the far-right corner, past a tiny guard's station. (If closed, exit out the front and walk around to the back.) Turn right and walk about a block until you see metal cages over the sidewalk protecting exposed stretches of ancient lead water pipes. Continue east and take your first left, walking about 20 yards to the entrance (on your left) to the...*

⓬ House of the Vettii

This is Pompeii's best-preserved home, retaining many of its mosaics and frescoes. The House of the Vettii was the bachelor pad of two wealthy merchant brothers. In the entryway, it's hard to miss the huge erection. This was not pornography. This was a symbol of success: The penis and sack of money balance each other on the goldsmith scale above a fine bowl of fruit. Translation? Only with a balance of fertility and money can you enjoy true abundance.

Step into the atrium with its replica wooden ceiling open to the sky and a lead pipe to collect water for the house cistern. The pool was flanked by two large moneyboxes (one survives, the footprint of the other shows how it was secured to the ground). The brothers wanted all who entered to know how successful they were. A variety of rooms give an intimate peek at elegant Pompeiian life. The dark room to the right of the entrance (as you face out) is filled with exquisite frescoes. Notice more white "cat's eye" stones embedded in the floor. Imagine these glinting like little eyes as the brothers and their friends wandered around by oil lamp late at night, with their sacks of gold, bowls of fruit, and enormous...egos.

• *Our next stop, the Bakery, is located about 150 yards south (downhill) from here. To get there, return to the street in front of the House of the Vettii. Walk downhill along Vicolo dei Vetti. Go one block, to where you dead-end at a T-intersection with Via della Fortuna. Go a few steps left and then right at the first corner. Continue down this gently curving road to #22 (on the left).*

⓭ Bakery and Mill

The stubby stone towers are flour grinders. Grain was poured into the top and donkeys or slaves, treading in a circle, pushed wooden bars that turned the stones that ground the grain. The powdered grain dropped out the bottom as flour—flavored with tiny bits of rock. Nearby, the thing that looks like a modern-day pizza oven was...a brick oven. Each neighborhood had a bakery just like this.

• *Continue down the curvy road to the next intersection. As you walk consider the destructive power of all the plants and vines that you see around. Also, notice the chariot grooves worn into the pavement. When the curvy road reaches the intersection with Via degli Augustali, turn left. Ahead, in 50 yards, at #44 (on the left), is the* ***Taberna Hedones,*** *an ancient tavern with an original floor mosaic still intact.*

Our next stop is the site's most popular attraction. (Consequently, even though it's just 50 yards from here, we'll have to circle all the way around to reach it from the other side.) Proceed beyond the Taberna Hedones and turn right at the next big street. Follow it downhill, turning right when you reach the wide Via Abbondanza (this is the "main drag" we saw higher up, earlier). Walk along here, passing the entrance to #8 (Terme Stabiane) and carrying on a bit farther. Eventually you'll come to a narrow lane on the right where there's usually a big commotion of visitors. Head up here and get in line to enter #18—one of many Pompeii brothels.

⓮ Brothel (Lupanare)

You'll find the biggest crowds in Pompeii at a place that was likely also quite popular 2,000 years ago—the brothel. Prostitutes were nicknamed *lupe* (she-wolves), alluding to the call they made when attracting business. The brothel was a simple place, with beds and pillows made of stone and then covered with mattresses. The ancient graffiti includes tallies and exotic names of the sex workers, indicating how they came from all corners of the Mediterranean (it also served as feedback from satisfied customers). The faded frescoes above the cells may have been a kind of menu for services offered. Note the idealized women (white, which was considered beautiful; one wears an early bra) and the rougher men (dark, considered horny). The bed legs came with little disk-like barriers to keep critters from crawling up, the tiny rooms had curtains for doors, and the prostitutes provided sheepskin condoms.

• *Leaving the brothel, go right, then take the first left, and continue going downhill two blocks to return to Via Abbondanza. This walk is over.*

The ***Forum****—and exit—are to the right. If you exit now, you'll be* *routed through the shop and the **Antiquarium**—a fine museum with a variety of artifacts, on three floors, from ancient Pompeii. While all the best stuff is in Naples' Archaeological Museum, here you can see a few frescoes, pottery, statues, and other decor. The most interesting things here are several more casts of Pompeiians frozen in time (plus a horse).*

The Rest of the Archaeological Site

These extra stops are worth the time and energy (if you have any left). To locate them, refer to your map. You can weave them together easily, starting by heading left down Via Abbondanza.

Temple of Isis

This temple served Pompeii's Egyptian community. The little white stucco shrine with the modern plastic roof housed holy water from the Nile. Isis, from Egyptian myth, was one of many foreign gods adopted by the eclectic Romans. Pompeii must have had a synagogue, too, but it has yet to be excavated.

Theater

Originally a Greek theater (Greeks built theirs with the help of a hillside), this was the birthplace of the Greek port here in 470 BC. During Roman times, the theater sat 5,000 people in three sets of seats, all with different prices: the five marble terraces up close (filled with romantic wooden seats for two), the main section, and the cheap nosebleed section (surviving only on the high end, near the trees). The square stones above the cheap seats once supported a canvas rooftop. The high-profile boxes, flanking the stage, were for guests of honor. From this perch, you can see the gladiator barracks—the colonnaded courtyard beyond the theater. They lived in tiny rooms, trained in the courtyard, and fought in the nearby amphitheater. Check out the adjacent and well-preserved smaller Teatro Piccolo.

House of Menander (Casa di Menandro)

Once owned by a wealthy Pompeiian, this house takes its current name from a fresco of the Greek playwright Menander on one of the walls. Admire the grand atrium (with frescoes depicting scenes from Homer's *Iliad* and *Odyssey*, and an altar to the family gods), the wall frescoes, and the mosaics. The cloister-like back courtyard leads to a room with skeletons (not plaster casts) of eruption victims from this house. Farther back, a passage leads to the servants' quarters.

Viewpoint

You're at ground level—post eruption. To the right (inland), the farmland shows how locals lived on top of the ruins for centuries without knowing what was underneath. To the left, you can see the entire ancient city of Pompeii spread out in front of you and appreciate the magnitude of the excavations.

Garden of the Fugitives

There's no better reminder in Pompeii of the horror caused by a volcanic eruption (and how we all might act given the same circumstances) than this "garden." Archaeologists identified this house as belonging to a middle-class merchant family. Plaster casts of this fleeing ("fugitive") family are placed exactly as the bodies were found after the eruption: lined up in single file as they attempted to escape several cubic feet of already fallen ash. Their exit was stopped by a sudden wave of hot gas and volcanic material, likely traveling over 100 miles per hour. Frozen in time, servants cannot be distinguished from their masters.

Amphitheater

If you can, climb to the upper level of the amphitheater (though the stairs are often blocked). With Vesuvius looming in the background, mentally replace the tourists below with gladiators and wild animals locked in combat. Walk along the top of the amphitheater and look down into the grassy rectangular area surrounded by columns. This is the **Palaestra,** an area once used for athletic training. (If you can't get to the top of the amphitheater, you can see the Palaestra from outside—in fact, you can't miss it, as it's right next door.) Facing the other way, look for the bell tower that tops the roofline of the modern city of Pompei, where locals go about their daily lives in the shadow of the volcano, just as their ancestors did 2,000 years ago.

• *If it's too crowded to bear hiking back along uneven lanes to the entrance, you can slip out the site's "back door," next to the amphitheater. Exiting, turn right and follow the site's wall all the way back to the entrance (see map on page 70).*

Or, to head directly to the Archaeological Museum in Naples, consider this alternative: Exit here, turn left, walk to the big church tower in the center of modern Pompei, turn right, and carry on down to the train station. Here you can catch a Trenitalia Metropolitana train (described earlier) that will take you, in about 50 minutes, directly to the Piazza Cavour Metro stop in downtown Naples—just a five-minute walk from the museum.

Herculaneum

Smaller, less crowded, and not as ruined as its famous big sister, Herculaneum (worth ▲▲, Ercolano in Italian—also the name of the modern town) offers a closer, more intimate peek into ancient Roman life. It lacks the grandeur of Pompeii (there's barely a colonnade), but it's a refreshingly uncrowded "Back Door" alternative to its more famous sibling.

GETTING TO HERCULANEUM

Ercolano Scavi, the nearest train station to Herculaneum, is about 20 minutes from Naples and 50 minutes from Sorrento on the same Circumvesuviana train that goes to Pompeii (for details on the Circumvesuviana, see page 62; Trenitalia trains stop in Ercolano at a station that's farther from the site, and isn't recommended).

Walking from the Ercolano Scavi train station to the ruins takes 10 minutes: Leave the station and turn right, then left down the main drag; continue straight, eight blocks gradually downhill to the end of the road, where you'll run right into the grand arch that marks the entrance to the ruins. (Skip Museo MAV.) Pass through the arch and continue 200 yards down the path—taking in the bird's-eye first impression of the site to your right—to the ticket office in the modern building.

ORIENTATION TO HERCULANEUM

Cost: €13, covered by the Campania ArteCard (see page 6). Avoid crowded free entry days (usually once a month on a Sunday).

Hours: Daily mid-March-mid-Oct 9:30-19:30, off-season 8:30-17:00, ticket office closes 1.5 hours earlier.

Information: +39 081 777 7008, http://ercolano.beniculturali.it.

Closures: Like Pompeii, various sections of Herculaneum can be closed unexpectedly.

Tours: The audioguide provides more information, but it's pricey (€10, €16 for 2, ID required); this book's tour covers the basics for a targeted visit.

Length of This Tour: Allow two hours, including time to visit the Antiquarium museum.

Baggage Storage: Herculaneum is harder than Pompeii for those with luggage, but not impossible. Herculaneum's train station has lots of stairs and no baggage storage, but you can roll wheeled luggage down to the ruins and store it for free in a locked area in the ticket office building (pick up bags at least 30 minutes prior to site closing). To get back to the station, consider splurging on a €5 taxi (ask the staff to call one for you).

Services: There's a free WC in the ticket office building, and others near the site entry.

Eating: Vending machines and café tables are near the entry to the site. There are also several eateries on the way from the train station.

➲ SELF-GUIDED TOUR

Caked and baked by the same AD 79 eruption that pummeled Pompeii (see sidebar on page 78), Herculaneum is a small community of intact buildings with plenty of surviving detail. While Pompeii was initially smothered in ash, Herculaneum was spared at first—due to the direction of the wind—but got slammed about 12 hours after the eruption started by a superheated avalanche of ash and hot gases roaring off the volcano. The city was eventually buried under nearly 60 feet of ash, which hardened into tuff, perfectly preserving the city until excavations began in 1748.

After leaving the ticket building, go through the turnstiles and walk the path below the site to the entry point. Look seaward and note where the shoreline is today; before the eruption, it was where you are standing, a quarter-mile inland. This gives you a sense of how much volcanic material piled up. The present-day city of Ercolano looms just above the ruins. The modern buildings don't look much different from their ancient counterparts.

• *Before entering the site, watch on your left for two buildings that house worthwhile museums. The bigger one (farther along) is the most worthwhile.*

Antiquarium: This houses some stunning original pieces from Herculaneum (you'll see replicas of some of these as we tour the site), as well as several slice-of-life items that help capture what ordinary life might have been like here 2,000 years ago. The exhibit ("Splendori da Ercolano") was intended to be temporary, but it appears to be semi-permanent—so hopefully you'll find these items:

As you enter, you face the **Hydra of Lerna,** a sculpted bronze fountain that features the seven-headed monster defeated by Her-

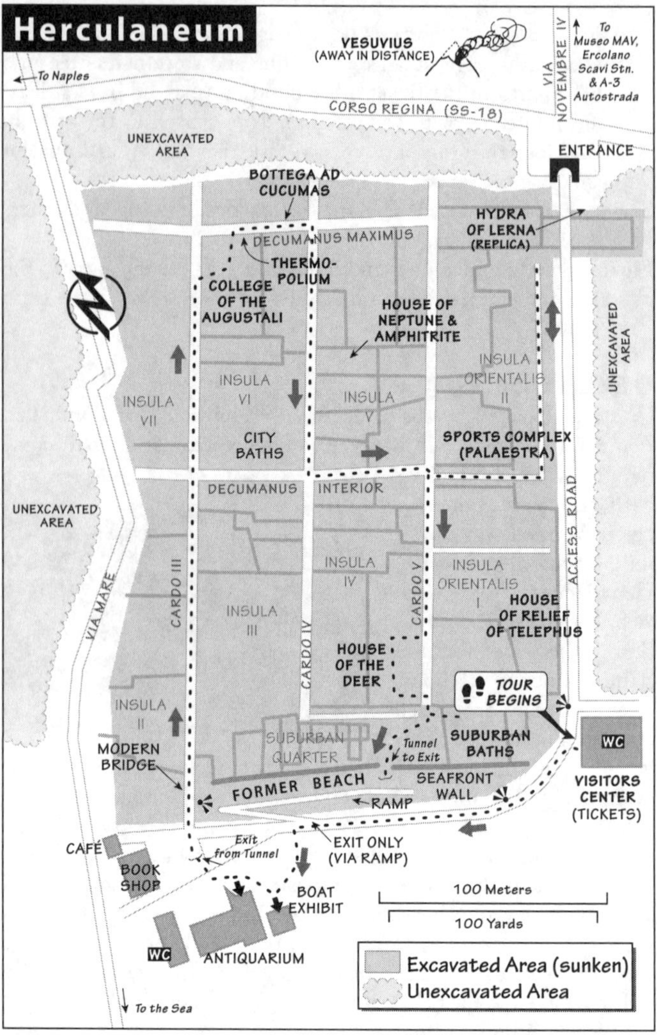

cules—the city's namesake—as one of his 12 labors. Beyond that, **Room 1** displays the original marble deer from the House of the Deer; a marble statue of Demeter; a detailed statue of Bacchus from the blacksmith's shop; and several small everyday items. Circling into **Room 2,** you see even more items that help resurrect life at ancient Herculaneum. Look for the tiny, precise surgeon's tools (a row of scalpels); a very rusty key; and a carbonized rope and wicker basket. You'll also find jewelry, including golden snake bracelets, amulets, and combs. Finally, in **Room 3,** you'll see a carbonized wooden table, juxtaposed with a (replica) fresco showing a very similar table in an ancient home. Another fresco shows a wealthy woman being dressed for the day, displayed with actual pieces of jewelry and perfume bottles.

• *There's one more, very compact museum (the small, red-brick building just before the Antiquarium), the...*

Boat Exhibit (Padiglione Barca): In this space you'll find an ancient, 30-foot, wooden fishing boat (with three sets of oars on each side) that was found on the beach in front of Herculaneum in 1982.

• *Now let's head into Herculaneum itself.*

Herculaneum Excavation Site: Go down the stairs and cross the modern bridge into the site, looking down into the moat-like **ditch.** On one side, you see Herculaneum's seafront wall. On the other is the wall that you just walked on, a solidified ash layer from the volcano that shows how deeply the town was buried.

After crossing the bridge, stroll straight up the **street.** As at Pompeii, Herculaneum's streets were ruts that sat well below the sidewalk level, so they could be flushed easily with water for quick cleaning. You can duck into any number of houses along here, but I've called out some of the more interesting.

At the end of the street find the **College of the Augustali** (Sede degli Augustali, #24). Decorated with frescoes of Hercules (for whom this city was named), it belonged to an association of freed slaves working together to climb their way up the ladder of Roman society. Here and farther on, look around doorways and ceilings to spot ancient wood charred by the pyroclastic flows. Most buildings were made of stone, with wooden floors and beams (which were preserved here by the ash but rarely survive at ancient sites).

Leave the building through the back and go to the right, down the lane. The adjacent ***thermopolium*** (#19) was the Roman equivalent of a lunch counter or fast-food joint, with giant jars for wine, oil, and snacks. Most of the buildings along here were shops, with apartments above.

A few steps on, the **Bottega ad Cucumas** wine shop (#14, on the right) still has charred remains of beams, and its drink list remains frescoed on the outside wall (under glass).

Take the next right, go halfway down the street, and on the left find the **House of Neptune and Amphitrite** (Casa di Nettuno e Anfitrite, #7). Outside, notice the intact upper floor and imagine it going even higher. Inside, you'll see vivid, intact mosaics and a unique "frame" made of shells.

Back outside, continue downhill to the intersection, then head left for a block and proceed straight across the street into the don't-miss-it **sports complex** (*palaestra;* #4). First you'll see a row of "marble" columns, which (look closer) are actually made of rounded bricks covered with a thick layer of plaster, shaped to look like carved marble. While important buildings in Rome had solid marble columns, these imitations are typical of ordinary buildings.

Continuing deeper into the complex, look for the hole in the hillside and walk through one of the triangular-shaped entrances to find a replica of the **Hydra of Lerna** (the original is in the Antiquarium).

Return through the sports complex and turn downhill. Just before the path goes underground, on the right, is the **House of the Deer** (Casa dei Cervi, #21). It's named for the statues of deer being attacked by dogs in the garden courtyard (these are copies; the originals are in the Antiquarium). As you wander through the rooms, notice the colorfully frescoed walls. Ancient Herculaneum, like all Roman cities of that age, was filled with color, rather than the stark white we often imagine (even the statues were painted).

You can see more of these colors, this time bright orange, across the street in the **House of Relief of Telephus** (Casa del Rilievo del Telefo, #2).

Continue downhill through the archway. The **Suburban Baths** illustrate the city's devastation (Terme Suburbane, #3; enter near the side of the statue on the terrace, sometimes closed). After you descend into the baths, look back at the steps. You'll see the original wood charred in the disaster, protected by the wooden planks you just walked on. At the bottom of the stairs, in the waiting room to the right, notice where the floor collapsed under the sheer weight of the volcanic debris. (The sunken pavement reveals the baths' heating system: hot air generated by wood-burning furnaces and circulated between the different levels of the floor.) A doorway in front of the stairs is still filled with solidified ash. Despite the damage, elements of refinement remain intact, such as the delicate stuccoes in the *caldarium* (hot bath).

Back outside, make your way down the steps to the sunken area just below. As you descend, you're walking across what was formerly Herculaneum's beach. Looking back, you'll see **arches** that were part of boat storage areas. Archaeologists used to wonder why so few victims were found in Herculaneum. But during excavations in 1981, hundreds of skeletons were discovered here, between the wall of volcanic stone behind you and the city in front of you. Some of Herculaneum's 4,000 citizens tried to escape by sea, but were overtaken by the pyroclastic flows.

• *Thankfully, your escape is easier. Either follow the sound of water and continue through the tunnel (you'll climb up and pop out near the site entry), or, more scenically, backtrack and exit the same way you entered.*

Vesuvius

The 4,000-foot-high Vesuvius, mainland Europe's only active volcano, has been sleeping restlessly since 1944. While Europe has other dangerous volcanoes, only Vesuvius sits in the middle of a three-million-person metropolitan area that would be impossible to evacuate quickly.

Many tourists don't know that you can easily visit the summit. Up top, it's desolate and lunar-like, and the rocks are newly born. Walk the entire accessible part of the crater lip for the most interesting views; the far end overlooks Pompeii. Be still. Listen to the wind and the occasional cascades of rocks tumbling into the crater. Any steam? Vesuvius could blow again. (Don't worry—there'd likely be at least a few hours or days of warning.)

Note: You may need to **reserve a time slot** in advance via www.vivaticket.it (search for "Vesuvio"). If you're considering an ascent, check before you go to ensure you have the proper access.

GETTING TO VESUVIUS

By Car or Taxi: Drivers take the exit *Torre del Greco* and follow signs to *Vesuvio.* Just drive to the end of the road and pay to park. A taxi costs €90 round-trip from Naples, including a 2-hour wait; it's about €70 from Pompeii.

By Bus from Pompeii: From near the Pompei Scavi train station on the Circumvesuviana line (just outside the main entrance to the Pompeii ruins), you have three bus services to choose from, each taking about three hours (40 minutes up, 40 minutes down, and about 1.5 hours at the summit).

The cheapest option is the **public bus** operated by EAV (€3.10 each way, pay on board, 8/day, blue bus departs from in front of train station).

The old-fashioned **Vesuvius Trolley Tram** (Tramvia del Vesuvio) uses the main road up (€25 round-trip plus €12 summit admission, 6/day, tickets sold at and tram departs from Pompei Scavi train station, +39 081 777 3247, www.tramvianapoli.com).

Busvia del Vesuvio winds you up a bumpy back road to the crater rim (Via Boscotrecase) in a cross between a shuttle bus and a monster truck. The walk up to the rim at the end is about the same, but you approach it from the other direction. It's a fun, more scenic way to go, but not for the easily queasy (€22 includes summit admission, hourly April-Oct Mon-Sat 9:00-15:00, until later June-Aug, buy tickets at "info point" at Pompei Scavi train station, www.busviadelvesuvio.com).

By Bus from Herculaneum: The quickest trip up is on the **Vesuvio Express.** These small buses leave from the Ercolano Scavi train station (on the Circumvesuviana line, where you get off for the Herculaneum ruins; €10 round-trip plus €12 summit admission, daily from 9:30, runs every 45 minutes based on demand, 20 minutes each way—about 2.5 hours total, office on square in front of train station, +39 081 777 76 52, www.vesuvioexpress.it).

ORIENTATION TO VESUVIUS

Cost and Hours: €12 covers national park entry and the park guide's orientation; may need to prebook at www.vivaticket.it (search for "Vesuvio")—arrive within 30 minutes before or after your appointed time or you won't be let in; ticket office open daily July-Aug 9:00-18:00, April-June and Sept until 17:00, closes earlier off-season. Bad weather can occasionally close the trail.

Information: The ticket office is 200 yards downhill from the parking lot. +39 081 865 3911, www.vesuviopark.it (official site) or www.guidevesuvio.it (more helpful site run by guides).

When to Go: Early morning visitors enjoy the freshest air and snare the best parking spots. The mountain is open all year, but spring and fall are the most comfortable times to visit. Yellow broom flowers blossom in May and June.

VISITING VESUVIUS

Bring sunscreen, water, a light jacket in summer, and a hat and warm coat in winter. By bus, taxi, or private car, you'll reach the volcano crater up a good but windy road from Torre del Greco (between Herculaneum and Pompeii). As you drive up, you'll pass the remnants of the pre-AD 79 mountain (on your left, now called Monte Somma) and lava flows from the most recent 1944 eruption. No matter how you travel up, you'll land at the parking lot.

Backtrack 200 yards downhill to enter the site. Use the pay WC, as there's none at the summit. From the parking lot, it's a moderately steep half-mile, 25-minute hike (with a 600-foot elevation gain) up a dirt access road to the top. Say "no thank you" to the gentleman passing out walking sticks in return for a tip—you don't need one.

At the rim, a sweeping view of the Bay of Naples is on your right; on your left, fenced off, there's a fearsome drop into the crater. Mountain guides orient you and then set you free.

SORRENTO & CAPRI

Just an hour south of Naples, serene Sorrento makes an ideal home base for exploring this fascinating region. From this easy-to-enjoy town, you can take day trips to Naples, Pompeii, the Amalfi Coast, the Greek temples at Paestum, and the romantic island of Capri. And every night you can return "home" to Sorrento, to enjoy its elegant strolling scene and sort through its many fine restaurant options.

Sorrento

Wedged on a ledge under the mountains and over the Mediterranean, spritzed by lemon and olive groves, Sorrento is an attractive resort of 20,000 residents and, in summer, just as many tourists. It's as well located for regional sightseeing as it is a fine place to stay and stroll. The Sorrentines have gone out of their way to create a relaxed place for tourists to come and spend money. As 90 percent of the town's economy is tourism, everyone seems to speak fluent English and work for the Chamber of Commerce. This gateway to the Amalfi Coast has a pedestrianized old quarter, lively shopping streets, and a spectacular cliffside setting. Residents are proud of the many world-class romantics who've vacationed here, such as famed tenor Enrico Caruso, who chose Sorrento as the place to spend his last months.

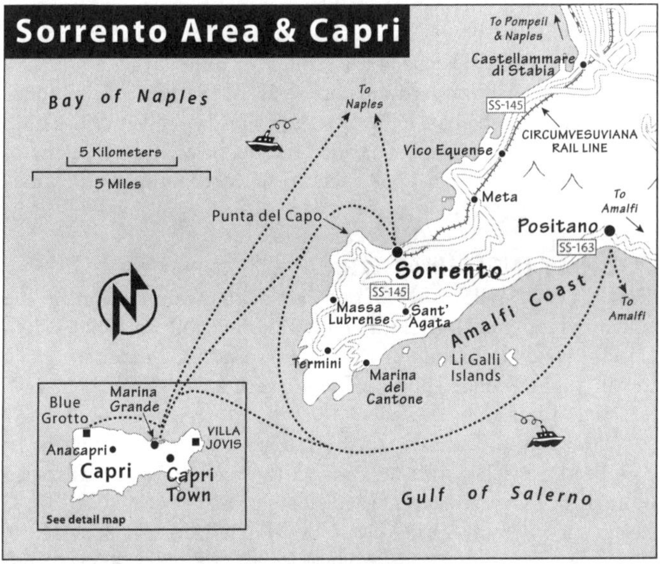

PLANNING YOUR TIME

Sorrento itself has no world-class sights, but it can easily give you a few pleasant hours. More importantly, Sorrento is a fine base for visiting nearby destinations, all reachable within an hour or so: Naples (by boat or train); Pompeii, Herculaneum, and Mount Vesuvius (by train, plus a bus for Vesuvius); the Amalfi Coast (by bus or boat); and the island of Capri (just 30 minutes by boat).

Sorrento hibernates in winter. Many places close down in November—others after the New Year—and stay closed until the town reawakens in March.

Orientation to Sorrento

Downtown Sorrento is long and narrow. Piazza Tasso marks the town's center. The main drag, Corso Italia, runs parallel to the sea through Piazza Tasso and then out toward the cape, where the road's name becomes Via Capo. Nearly everything mentioned here (except Marina Grande and the hotels on Via Capo) is within a 10-minute walk of the station. The town is perched

on a cliff (some hotels have elevators down to sundecks on the water); the best real beaches are a couple of miles away.

Sorrento has two separate port areas. Marina Piccola is a functional harbor with boats to Naples and Capri, as well as cruise-ship tenders. Despite its name, Marina Grande, below the other end of downtown is a little fishing enclave, with recommended restaurants and more charm.

TOURIST INFORMATION

The TI's two "Ask Me" InfoPoints are at the **train station** (in the converted caboose out front; daily 10:00-13:00 & 16:00-19:00, closed Nov-March) and on **Piazza Tasso** at #25, under the clock tower (slightly longer hours). They have maps and can help with basic questions.

Unless it's off-season, there's rarely any reason to trek to the TI's head office, in the entryway to the recommended **Terrazza delle Sirene** view restaurant (Mon-Sat 9:00-19:00, Sun until 18:00 except closed Sun April-May; Nov-March Mon-Fri 8:30-16:00, closed Sat-Sun; Via Luigi de Maio 35, +39 081 807 4033, http://incampania.com).

The privately run website SorrentoInsider.com also has lots of good practical information.

ARRIVAL IN SORRENTO

By Train or Bus: Sorrento is the last stop on the Circumvesuviana train line from Naples. In front of the train station is the town's main bus stop, as well as taxis waiting to overcharge you (€15 minimum). All recommended hotels—except those on Via Capo—are within a 10-minute walk. (For details on taking the bus to Via Capo, see "Sleeping in Sorrento," later.) As you exit the station, the huge mural to your left, at the end of the street, shows beloved Italian singer-songwriter Lucio Dalla, who died in 2012.

By Boat: Passenger boats and cruise-ship tenders dock at Marina Piccola. From there it's a short, steep walk up to the town center. I like to ride the elevator up; it's to the right, about a five-minute walk along the base of the cliff (follow *lift/acensore* signs, €1.10, www.sorrentolift.it; faster, cheaper, and more predictable than a bus). The elevator takes you to the Villa Comunale city park. Exit through the park's iron gate and bear left; Piazza Tasso is about four blocks away. With a bit more bother, minibuses from the port can take you up to town (buy €1.30 ticket at newsstand or tobacco shop, look for stop marked *Fermata Riservata/EAV Bus*, ask driver to drop you at or near Piazza Tasso); for more on buses, see "Getting Around Sorrento," later. You can also climb the stairs from the port.

By Car: The public Achille Lauro underground parking garage is centrally located, just a couple of blocks in front of the train station, and good for a short stay (€2/hour for first 3 hours, then €3/hour, €51/24 hours, on Via Correale). Overnight rates are lower at other garages (around €30), such as the Autoparco Vallone dei Mulini, across from the recommended Hotel Antiche Mura.

HELPFUL HINTS

Church Services: At Santa Maria delle Grazie (perhaps the most beautiful Baroque church in town), cloistered nuns sing from above and out of sight during a Mass each morning at 7:30 (on Via Santa Maria delle Grazie at Piazza Sant'Antonino).

Baggage Storage: The underground parking lot Parcheggio de Curtis, just downhill from the train station, moonlights as a convenient place to store luggage (daily 7:30-23:30, shorter hours off-season, Via E. de Curtis 5, just before Corsa Italia).

Laundry: A handy 24-hour self-service launderette, **Rosy Laundry,** is a 10-minute walk past the train station (daily, Corso Italia 321g, across from Esso gas station, +39 331 912 1122).

Haircuts: A fun hair salon for men, **Satisfhair,** is run by hairless Luca and Tony and makes for a happy memory (€19 for a good cut, closed Sun-Mon, Via S. Maria della Pieta 17, +39 081 878 3476).

Guided Tours of Pompeii, Naples, the Amalfi Coast, and Capri: Naples-based **Mondo Guide** offers affordable tours of these destinations, including an Amalfi Coast drive that starts from Sorrento (meet in front of the Hotel Antiche Mura; kindly do not use hotel facilities if you are not a guest). You'll team up with fellow Rick Steves readers to split the cost. For details, see page 16.

Local Guides: For excursions around Sorrento and to Amalfi, **Giovanna Donadio** is a knowledgeable, upbeat guide (€120/half-day, €180/day, same price for any size group, +39 338 466 0114, giovanna_dona@hotmail.com). She does a food-themed walk, and can also escort six to eight people from Sorrento on a well-organized full day of fun on Capri (€200 plus public transportation expenses and admissions).

GETTING AROUND SORRENTO

Distances are short in Sorrento. If taking a bus seems too complicated, use the elevator, stairs, and your feet.

By Bus: Local EAV buses run from the train station (bays 7-8) to the port (Marina Piccola), the fishing village (Marina Grande), Via Capo, and Meta beach until at least 20:00 (1-3/hour, buy €1.30 ticket from tobacco shop or newsstand and stamp it on bus, drivers reluctantly sell tickets for €1.60, www.eavsrl.it). Stops are usually marked by a blue sign saying *Fermata a Richiesta* with a stylized

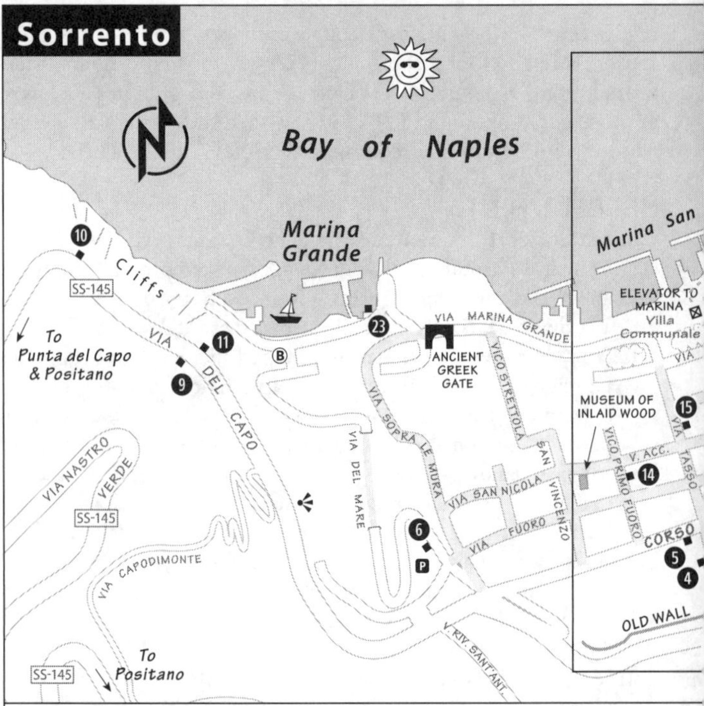

Accommodations
1 Hotel Antiche Mura ("Mondo Guide" meeting point) & Plaza Sorrento
2 Palazzo Tasso
3 Il Palazzo Starace B&B
4 Hotel Mignon & Supermarket
5 Casa Astarita B&B
6 Ulisse Deluxe Hostel
7 Hotel Nice
8 Grand Hotel Ambasciatori
9 Hotel Minerva
10 Hotel la Tonnarella & Hotel Désirée
11 Albergo Settimo Cielo

Eateries
12 Ristorante il Buco
13 L'Antica Trattoria
14 Inn Bufalito
15 Donna Sofia

EAV. Check the destination display on the front of the bus (*Porto* for Marina Piccola, *Stazione* for the train station, *Massa Lubrense* for Via Capo hotels), wave to flag down the driver, and let them know where you are going.

By Scooter: Several places near the station rent motor scooters for about €35 per day, including **Europcar** (Corso Italia 210p, +39 081 878 1386, www.sorrento.it) and **Penisola Rent** (Piazza Lauro 44, +39 081 362 2189, www.penisolarent.com). Don't rent a vehicle in summer unless you enjoy traffic jams.

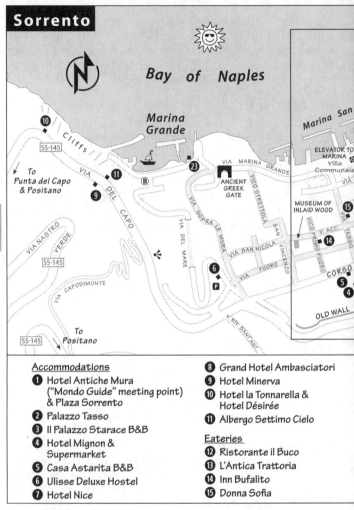

By Taxi: Taxis line up at the station and Piazza Tasso, but even short rides in town will cost at least €15-20. Thanks to traffic and one-way roads, you'll get to most central locations faster by

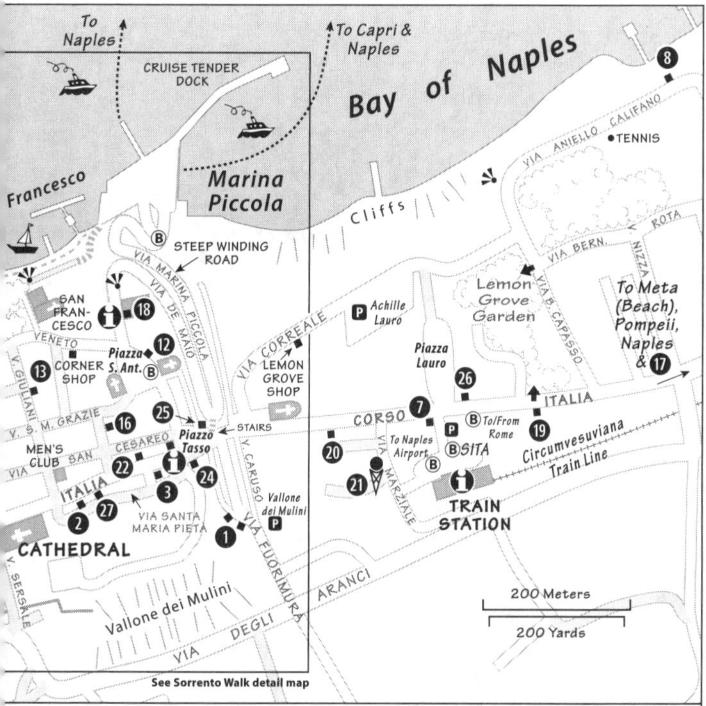

⓰ Ristorante Pizzeria da Gigino
⓱ To La Cantinaccia del Popolo & Launderette
⓲ Terrazza delle Sirene
⓳ Pizzeria da Franco
⓴ Supermarket
㉑ Gelateria David
㉒ Gelateria Primavera
㉓ Trattoria da Emilia & Porta Marina

Nightlife & Other
㉔ Fauno Bar
㉕ Daniele's Club
㉖ Europcar & Scooter Rental
㉗ Satisfhair Salon & Kebab Ciampa

walking. If you do use a taxi, don't ask the price, just be sure it has a meter (all official taxis do).

Sorrento Walk

Get to know Sorrento with this lazy self-guided town stroll that ends down by the waterside at the small-boat harbor, Marina Grande.

• *Begin on the main square. Stand under the flags between the sea and the town's main square...*

❶ **Piazza Tasso:** As in any southern Italian town, this piazza is Sorrento's living room. It may be noisy and congested, but lo-

cals want to be where the action is...and be part of the scene. The most expensive apartments and top cafés are on or near this square.

Look out at the Bay of Naples. You can see the city of Naples in the distance. From here, it's a five-minute walk—including 130 stairs—to Marina Piccola, the harbor for cruise-ship tenders and boats to Capri and Naples. On the right side of the gorge, overlooking the bay, is Hotel Excelsior Vittoria. This elegant, 19th-century Grand Tour hotel is where tenor Enrico Caruso (who died in 1921) spent his last months.

Turn to face the square. A statue of St. Anthony the Abbot, patron of Sorrento, is surrounded by traffic. He faces north as if greeting those coming from Naples (on festival days, he's equipped with an armload of fresh lemons and oranges).

This square bridges the gorge that divides downtown Sorrento. The newer section (to your left) was farm country just two centuries ago. The older part (to your right) retains its ancient Greek gridded street plan. (Like much of southern Italy, Sorrento was Greek-speaking for centuries before it was Romanized.)

For a better glimpse of the city's gorge-gouged landscape, take this quick detour: With the water to your back, cross through the square and walk straight ahead a block inland, under a canopy of trees and past a long taxi queue. Belly up to the railing in front of Hotel Antiche Mura and look down into the deep **Vallone dei Mulini** ("Valley of the Mills"). It's named after the sawmills and flour mills whose remains you see, next to the stream that powered them (along with a public laundry) until well into the 19th century.

The combination of the gorge and the seaside cliffs made Sorrento easy to defend. A small section of wall closed the landward gap in the city's defenses (you can still see a surviving piece of it a few blocks away, near Hotel Mignon).

Sorrento's name may come from the Greek word for "siren," the legendary half-bird, half-woman that sang an intoxicating lullaby. According to Homer, the sirens lived on an island near here. All those who sailed by the sirens succumbed to their incredible musical charms...and to death when they shipwrecked on the island. But Homer's hero Ulysses was determined to hear the song and restrain his manhood. He put wax in his oarsmen's ears and had himself lashed to the mast of his ship and survived their song. The sirens, thinking they had lost their powers, threw themselves into the sea, and the place became safe to inhabit. Ulysses' odyssey was all about the westward expansion of Greek culture, and to the ancient Greeks, places like Sorrento were the wild, wild west.

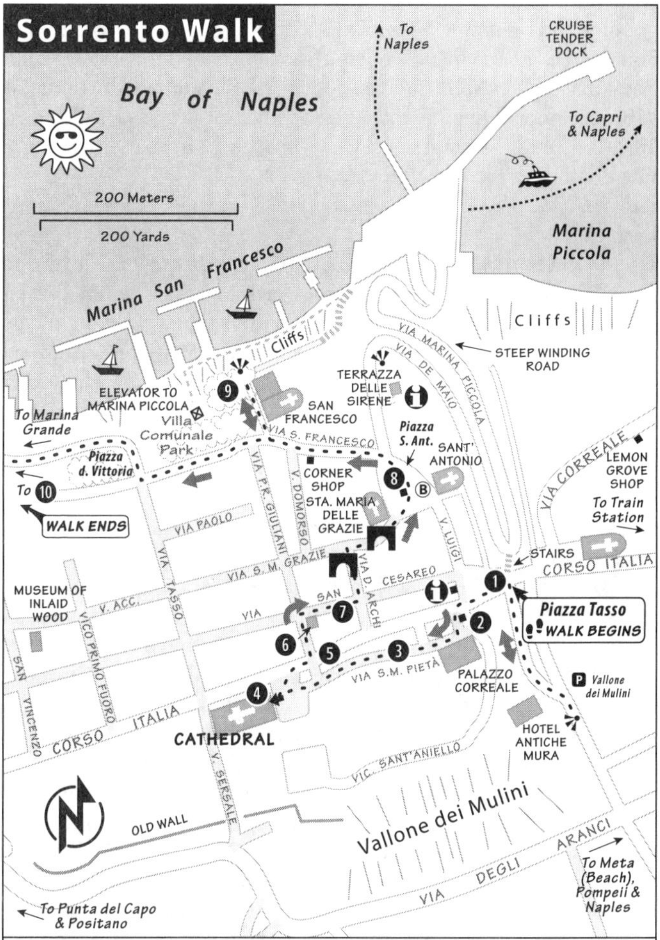

1. Piazza Tasso
2. Statue of Torquato Tasso
3. Via Santa Maria della Pietà
4. Cathedral
5. Corso Italia & Old Town
6. Sorrento Men's Club
7. Via San Cesareo
8. Statue & Basilica of St. Anthony the Abbot
9. Villa Comunale
10. To Ancient Greek Gate & Marina Grande

• *Back at Piazza Tasso, head to the far-left inland corner of the square. You'll find a...*

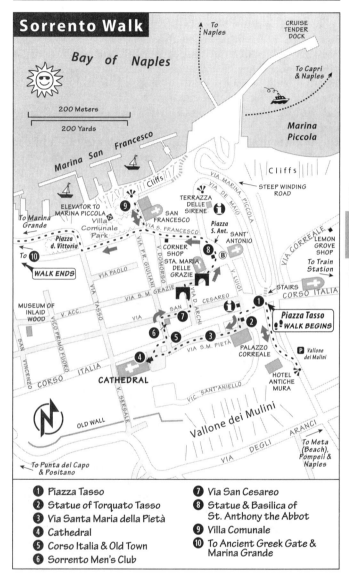

❷ **Statue of Torquato Tasso:** The square's namesake, a Sorrento native, was a lively Renaissance poet—but today he seems only to wonder which restaurant to choose for dinner. Directly behind the statue, pop into the **Fattoria Terranova** shop, one of many fun, family-run, and touristy boutiques. They sell regional goodies and offer free biscuits and tastes of liqueurs, and the shop makes all of its organic products on an *agriturismo* outside the city. The gifty edibles spill into the courtyard of **Palazzo Correale,** at #18 next door. Duck in through the archway to get a feel for an 18th-century aristocratic palace's courtyard. Its patio walls are lined with characteristic tiles from 1772.

• *As you're leaving the courtyard, on your immediate left you'll see the narrow...*

❸ **Via Santa Maria della Pietà:** Here, just a few yards off the noisy main drag, is a street that goes back centuries before Christ. About 100 yards down the lane, at #24 (on the left), find a 13th-century palace (no balconies back then...for security reasons), now an elementary school. A few steps farther on, you'll see a tiny shrine across the street. Typical of southern Italy, it's where the faithful pray to their saint, who contacts Mary, who contacts Jesus, who contacts God. This shrine is a bit more direct—it starts right with Mary.

• *Continue down the lane (passing a recommended kebab shop and trattoria) to reach the delightful...*

❹ **Cathedral:** Walk through the wrought-iron gate, which leads to the church patio. The church is free to enter (daily 8:00-12:30 & 16:30-21:00, except during Masses). Step inside the main door and examine the impressive *intarsio* (inlaid-wood) interior doors. They show religious scenes and depict this very church. Take a cool stroll down the right-hand side of the nave, checking out the intricate inlaid Stations of the Cross. You'll find even more inlaid wood on the side entrance doors. They show scenes of the town and its industry, as well as an old-town map (find Piazza Tasso, trace the fortified walls, and notice the Greek grid street plan). These doors were made to celebrate Pope John Paul II's visit in 1992. Notice the fine inlaid-marble seat of the bishop nearby and how the church's elegance matches that of the town. Before exiting, on the right find the *presepe* (manger scene) with its lovingly painted terracotta figures, each with an expressive face. This takes Bethlehem on that first Christmas and sets it in Sorrento—with pasta, mozzarella, salami, local lemons, the gorge with the Valley of the Mills, and even Mount Vesuvius in the background.

• *Cross the open plaza—where the end of the narrow street you just walked down meets the main drag.*

❺ **Corso Italia and the Old Town:** In the evening, this traffic-free road hosts a wonderful *passeggiata.* Look up to find the cathedral bell tower, then down to see the scavenged ancient Roman columns at its base. Now go left down Via P. Reginaldo Giuliani, following the old Greek street plan. Locals claim the ancient Greeks laid out the streets east-west for the most sunlight and north-south for the prevailing and cooling breeze. Pause at the poster board on your right to see who's died lately. Traditionally, Italian women wore black when a relative died (1 year for an uncle, aunt, or sibling; 2-3 years for a husband or parent). Men got off easy, just wearing a black memorial button.

• *One block ahead, on your right, the 14th-century loggia (called Sedil Dominova) is home to the...*

❻ **Sorrento Men's Club:** Once the meeting place of the town's nobles, for generations now the Sedil Dominova has been a retreat for retired working-class men. Strictly no women—and no phones.

Italian men venerate their mothers. (Italians joke that Jesus must have been a southern Italian because his mother believed her son was God, he believed his mom was a virgin, and he lived at home with her until he was 30.) But Italian men have also built into their culture ways to be on their own. Here, men play cards and gossip under a finely frescoed, 16th-century domed ceiling, with marvelous 3-D scenes.

• *Turn right for a better view of the Men's Club and a historical marker describing the building. Then continue along...*

❼ **Via San Cesareo:** This touristy pedestrian-only shopping street eventually leads back to Piazza Tasso. It's lined with competitive little shops where you can peruse (and sample) lemon products. Notice the huge ancient doorways with their tiny doors—to let the right people in, carefully, during a more dangerous age.

• *After a block, take a left onto Via degli Archi, go under the arch, and then hang a right (under another arch) to the square with the...*

❽ **Statue and Basilica of St. Anthony** (Sant'Antonino): Sorrento's town saint humbly looms among the palms, facing the basilica dedicated to him (free to enter). Step inside the basilica and descend into the crypt (stairs beside main altar), where you'll find a chapel and reliquary containing a few of Anthony's bones surrounded by lots of votives.

In English he is known as St. Anthony the Abbot or St. Anthony the Great (not to be confused with the later St. Anthony of Padua). Locals have long turned to St. Anthony when faced with challenges and hard times. Exploring the room, you'll find countless tokens of appreciation to the saint for his help. Before tourism, fishing was the big employer. The back walls feature paintings of storms with Anthony coming to the rescue. Circle behind the altar with Anthony's relics and study the shiny ex-votos (religious offerings) thanking the saint for healthy babies, good employment, surviving heart attacks and lung problems, and lots of strong legs.

• *Back outside, follow the road that skirts the piazza with St. Anthony's statue (don't go down the street with the line of trees and* Porto *signs). Watch on the left for The Corner Shop, where Giovanni sells a wide variety of wines,* limoncello, *pastas, and other regional products. Soon after, on the right you'll see the trees in front of the Imperial Hotel Tramontano, and to their right a path leading to the...*

❾ **Villa Comunale:** This fine public park overlooks the harbor. Belly up to the banister to enjoy the view of Marina Piccola and the Bay of Naples. Notice Naples' skyline and the boats that commute from here to there in 35 minutes. Imagine the view in AD 79 when Vesuvius blew its top and molten mud flowed down the mountain, burying Pompeii. From here, steps zigzag down to the harbor, where lounge chairs, filled by vacationers working on tans, line the sundecks (there's also the elevator to the harbor). The Franciscan church fronting this square faces a fine modern statue of Francis across the street.

Pop through the archway next to the church to see a dreamy little **cloister.** It's local Gothic—a 13th-century mix of Norman, Gothic, and Arabic styles, all around an old pepper tree. This is an understandably popular spot for weddings and concerts.

At the left side of the cloister, stairs lead to a **photo exhibit:** *The Italians* shows off the work of local photographer Raffaele Celentano, who artfully captures classic Italian scenes from 1990 to 2016 in black and white (€5, daily 10:00 until sunset, closed Jan-Feb, great prints for sale, fun photo-op through the grand tree on their deck, www.gallery-raffaele-celentano.com).

• *From here, you can quit the walk and stay in the town center, or continue another few minutes downhill to the waterfront at Marina Grande. If you take the elevator down, the road to the right leads to Marina Piccola, where boats depart to Capri and other nearby towns. Piers and beaches to the left do not connect to the next stop on this walk.*

❿ To continue to **Marina Grande,** return to the road and keep going downhill. At the next square (Piazza della Vittoria, with a dramatic WWI memorial and another grand view), cut over to the road closest to the water. After winding steeply down for a few minutes, it turns into a wide stairway, then makes a sharp and steep switchback (take the right fork to continue downhill). Farther down, just before reaching the waterfront, you pass under an...

Ancient Greek Gate: This gate fortified the city of Sorrento. Beyond it was Marina Grande, technically a separate town with its own proud residents—it's said that even their cats look different. Because Marina Grande dwellers lived outside the wall and were more susceptible to rape, pillage, and plunder, Sorrentines believe that they come from Saracen (pirate) stock. Sorrentines still scare their children by saying, "Behave—or the pirates will take you away."

• *Now go all the way down the steps into Marina Grande, Sorrento's "big" small-boat harbor.*

Marina Grande: Until recently, this little community was famously traditional, with its economy based on its fishing fleet. To this day, fathers pass their houses and fishing-boat stalls down to their sons.

Two recommended restaurants are on the harbor. **Trattoria da Emilia** has an old newspaper clipping, tacked near the door, about Sophia Loren filming here. **Porta Marina** is smaller, less fancy, and more local but with food every bit as tasty as that of its competition.

• *From here, where the road hits the beach, a minibus returns to Piazza Tasso and the train station once an hour. Or you can walk back up.*

Sights in Sorrento

▲▲Strolling

On balmy evenings Sorrento offers one of Italy's most enchanting *passeggiata* scenes. The old-town stretch of Corso Italia is always traffic-free. Each night in summer and on weekends off-season, the police also close off the stretch east of Piazza Tasso to traffic, making

Sorrento's whole main drag a thriving people scene. The *passeggiata* peaks at about 22:00 in the warmest months. Take time to enjoy the old-town streets between Corso Italia and the sea. The views from Villa Comunale, the public park next to Imperial Hotel Tramontano, are worth the detour.

Lemon Products Galore

Via San Cesareo is lined with hardworking rival shops selling a mind-boggling array of lemon products and offering samples of lots of sour goodies. You'll find *limoncello,* lemon biscuits, lemon pasta, lemon drops, lemon chocolate, lemon perfume, lemon soap, and on and on. Poke around for a pungent experience (and read the "Lemons" sidebar, later). A few produce stands are also mixed in.

▲Lemon Grove Garden (Agruminato)

This lemon and orange grove, lined with shady, welcoming paths, was rescued from development by the city of Sorrento and turned into a park. The family that manages it has seasoned green thumbs and descends from the family that started working here decades ago, when the grove was still in private hands. The garden is dotted with benches, tables, and an inviting little tasting (and buying) stand. You'll get a chance to sniff and taste the varieties of lemons and enjoy free samples of *limoncello,* along with other homemade liqueurs made from mandarins, licorice, or fennel. Check out how they've grafted orange-tree branches onto a lemon tree so that both fruits grow on the same tree.

Cost and Hours: Free, daily 10:00 until sunset, closed in rainy weather, +39 081 878 1888, www.igiardinidicataldo.it. Enter the garden on Corso Italia (where painted tiles show lemon fantasies, across from the recommended Pizzeria da Franco at #265) or at the intersection of Via Capasso and Via Rota (next to Hotel la Meridiana).

Eating: For a cheap and relaxing meal, get a big-enough-to-split *saltimbocca* sandwich to go from the recommended **Pizzeria da Franco** (across the street on Corso Italia) and enjoy it in the lemon grove.

Nearby: The entrepreneurial family's small "factory"—where you can see how they use the lemons, and buy a tasty gelato, *granita,* or lemonade—is just west of the Achille Lauro parking garage entrance at Via Correale 27, next to a smaller lemon grove that's not open to the public.

Museum of Inlaid Wood (Museobottega della Tarsialignea)

Sorrento doesn't have much in the way of museums, but if you want to get out of the heat and crowds, this is a good place to do it. The life's work of an older couple, the museum is not only a collection

Lemons

Around here, *limoni* are ubiquitous: screaming yellow painted on ceramics, dainty bottles of *limoncello,* and lemons the size of softballs at the fruit stand.

The Amalfi Coast and Sorrento area produce several different kinds of lemons. The gigantic, bumpy "lemons" are actually citrons, called *cedri,* and are more for show—they're pulpier than they are juicy, and make a good marmalade. The juicy *sfusato sorrentino,* grown only in Sorrento, is shaped like an American football, while the *sfusato amalfitano,* with knobby points on both ends, is less juicy but equally aromatic. These two kinds of luscious lemons are used in sweets such as *granita* (shaved ice doused in lemonade), *limoncello* (a candy-like liqueur with a big kick, called *limoncino* in the Cinque Terre), *delizia al limone* (a dome of fluffy cake filled and slathered with a thick whipped lemon cream), *spremuta di limone* (fresh-squeezed lemon juice), and, of course, gelato or *sorbetto al limone.*

of inlaid wood but also a painting gallery featuring scenes of 19th-century Sorrento, antique maps, and portraits, and a fine decorative arts collection. The basement displays modern examples of inlaid wood. While pricey, it's serious, thoughtfully presented, and bursting with local pride.

Cost and Hours: €8, daily 10:00-18:30, Nov-March until 17:00, Via San Nicola 28, +39 081 877 1942, www.museomuta.it.

▲Swimming and Sunbathing

If you require immediate tanning, you can rent a chair on a pier by the port. There are no great beaches in Sorrento—the gravelly, jam-packed private beaches of **Marina Piccola** are more for partying than pampering, and there's just a tiny spot for public use. The elevator in Villa Comunale city park (next to the Church of San Francesco) gets you down for €1. There's another humble beach at **Marina Grande.**

The classic, sandy Italian beach two miles away at **Meta** is generally overrun with teenagers from Naples. The local bus goes from the station to Meta beach (last stop, schedule posted for hourly returns; you can also get there on the Circumvesuviana but the Meta stop is a very long walk from the beach). At Meta, you'll find pizzerias, snack bars, and a little free section of beach, but the place is mostly dominated by several sprawling private-beach complexes—if you go, pay for a spot in one of these, such as Lido

Metamare (lockable changing cabins, lounge chairs, +39 081 532 2505). It's a very Italian scene—locals complain that it's "too local" (that is, inundated with riffraff)—with light lunches, a playground, a manicured beach, loud pop music...and no international tourists.

More relaxing beaches are west of Sorrento. Tarzan might take Jane to the wild and stony beach at **Punta del Capo,** a 15-minute bus ride from Sorrento (on the same bus, but in the opposite direction, toward Massa Lubrense; 2/hour, get off at stop on Via Capo just after the Maxim Gorky house, then walk 10 minutes down Calata Punta del Capo, past ruined Roman Villa di Pollio).

Another good choice is **Marina di Puolo,** a tiny fishing town popular in the summer for its sandy beach, surfside restaurants, and beachfront disco (to get here, stay on the bus a bit farther beyond the Punta del Capo stop above—ask driver to let you off at Marina di Puolo—then follow signs and hike down about 15 minutes).

More Activities

Sorrento Food Tours: Tamara—a US expat with many years of experience in Italian food and wine—and her colleagues dish up a fast-paced parade of local edibles interspersed with lots of food history, stopping at eight places in three hours (€75, 15 percent discount for Rick Steves readers, use code "ricksteves"; departures at 10:30 and 16:00 with demand, maximum 14 people; +39 331 304 5666, www.sorrentofoodtours.com, info@sorrentofoodtours.com).

Motorboat Rental: You can rent motorboats big enough for four people (with your back to the ferry-ticket offices, it's to the left around the corner at Via Marina Piccola 43; +39 081 807 2283, www.nauticasicsic.com).

Nightlife in Sorrento

PUBS AND CLUBS

Sorrento is a fun place to enjoy a drink or some dancing after dinner. The crowd is older, and British vacationers have paved the way for you (many have holidayed here annually for decades). Several Irish-style pubs on Corso Italia have big screens and show European soccer.

The **Fauno Bar,** which dominates Piazza Tasso with tables spilling onto the square, is a fine place to make the scene over a drink any time of day.

Terrazza delle Sirene (also known by its old name of **Foreigners' Club**) offers live Neapolitan songs, Sinatra-style classics, and jazzy elevator music with an ocean view nightly at 20:00 throughout the summer. It's just right for old-timers feeling frisky (Via Luigi de Maio 35, entrance just past the TI, +39 081 877 3263).

Daniele's Club is run by DJ Daniele, who tailors music to the audience (including karaoke, if you ask nicely). The scene, while sloppy, is generally comfortable for the 30-to-60-year-old crowd. If you're alone, there's a pole you can dance with (no cover charge, try their signature cocktail, "Come Back to Sorrento," a mojito made with *limoncello;* no food, nightly from 21:30, down the steps from the flags at Piazza Tasso 10, +39 081 877 3992).

THEATER SHOW

At **Teatro Armida,** a hardworking troupe puts on *The Sorrento Musical,* a folk-music show that treats visitors to a schmaltzy dose of Neapolitan Tarantella music and dance—complete with "Funiculì Funiculà" and "Santa Loo-chee-yee-yah." The 75-minute Italian-language extravaganza features a cast playing guitar, mandolin, saxophone, and tambourines, and singing operatically from Neapolitan balconies...complete with Vesuvius erupting in the background. Your €30 ticket includes a drink before the show (€60 with 4-course dinner at attached Basilico Italia restaurant; RS%—Maurizio promises my readers a €5 discount if you buy directly at the box office and show this book, 2 tickets/book; shows run 3-5 nights/week May-Oct at 21:00, bar opens 30 minutes before show, dinner starts at 20:00 and must be reserved in advance—in person or by email; box office open long hours daily, theater seats 500, between Piazza Tasso and the train station at Corsa Italia 219, +39 081 877 2048, www.basilicoitalia.it, info@basilicoitalia.it).

Sleeping in Sorrento

Given the location, hotels here often have beautiful views, and many offer balconies. At hotels that offer sea views, ask for a room *"con balcone, con vista sul mare"* (with a balcony, with a sea view). *"Tranquillo"* is taken as a request for a quieter room off the street.

Hotels listed are either near the train station and city center (where balconies overlook city streets) or on cliffside Via Capo (with sea-view balconies). Via Capo is a 20-minute walk—or short bus ride—from the station.

You should have no trouble finding a room anytime except in August, when the town is jammed with Italians and prices often rise above the regular high-season rates.

IN THE TOWN CENTER

$$$$ Hotel Antiche Mura, with 50 rooms and four-star elegance, offers all the amenities, including an impressive breakfast buffet. Just a block off the main square, it's quieter than some central hotels because it's perched on the edge of a dramatic ravine. The pool and sundeck, surrounded by lemon trees, make a peaceful oasis (RS%, some rooms with balconies, family rooms, air-con, elevator, pay parking, closed Jan-mid-March, a block inland from Piazza Tasso at Via Fuorimura 7, +39 081 807 3523, www.hotelantichemura.com, info@hotelantichemura.com, Luigi).

$$$$ Palazzo Tasso, nicely located near the center, has 12 small, sleek, fashionably designed modern rooms; there's no public space and breakfast is at a nearby bar (some rooms with balconies, air-con, elevator, open all year, Via Santa Maria della Pietà 33, +39 081 807 1594, mobile +39 348 592 1019, www.palazzotasso.com, info@palazzotasso.com, Elena).

$$$$ Plaza Sorrento is a contemporary-feeling, upscale refuge in the very center of town (next door to Antiche Mura but with less expansive grounds). Its 65 rooms mix mod decor with wood grain, and the rooftop swimming pool is inviting (RS%, some rooms with balconies, air-con, elevator, closed Jan-mid-March, Via Fuorimura 3, +39 081 878 2831, www.plazasorrento.com, info@plazasorrento.com).

$$$ Il Palazzo Starace B&B, conscientiously run by Massimo, offers seven tidy, modern rooms in a little alley off Corso Italia, one block from Piazza Tasso (RS%—use code "RSWEL," some rooms with balconies, family room, air-con, lots of stairs, luggage dumbwaiter but no elevator, ring bell around corner from Via Santa Maria della Pietà 9, +39 081 807 2633, mobile +39 349 290 7932, www.palazzostarace.com, info@palazzostarace.com).

$$$ Hotel Mignon rents 22 soothing blue rooms with beautiful, tiled public spaces, a rooftop sundeck, and a small garden surrounded by a lemon grove (RS%—use code "2022RSE" on their website, most rooms have balconies but no views, air-con, closed Jan-mid-March; from the cathedral, walk a block farther up Corso Italia and look for the hotel up a small gated lane to your left; Via Sersale 9, +39 081 807 3824, www.sorrentohotelmignon.com, info@sorrentohotelmignon.com, Paolo).

$$$ Casa Astarita B&B, hiding upstairs in a big building facing the main pedestrian street, has a crazy-quilt-tiled entryway and six bright, tranquil, creatively decorated rooms (three with little balconies). Noise from a nearby bar can spill over...bring earplugs (RS%—use code "RICK23," air-con, open year-round, 50 yards past the cathedral at Corso Italia 67, +39 081 877 4906, mobile +39 331 948 9738, www.casastarita.com, info@casastarita.com, Annamaria and Alfonso).

$$$ Ulisse Deluxe Hostel is basically a hotel, with 56 well-equipped, marble-tiled rooms and elegant public areas, but it also has two single-sex dorm rooms with bunks—hence the name (RS%, family rooms, breakfast buffet extra, air-con, elevator, spa and pool use extra, pay parking, closed Jan-mid-Feb, Via del Mare 22, +39 081 877 4753, www.ulissedeluxe.com, info@ulissedeluxe.com, Chiara). It's a five-minute walk from the old-town action:

From Corso Italia, walk down the stairs just beyond the hospital *(ospedale)* to Via del Mare. Go downhill along the right side of the big parking lot to find the entrance.

$$ Hotel Nice rents 24 simple, straightforward rooms 100 yards in front of the train station on the main drag. It's worth considering only for its very handy-to-the-train-station location. Alfonso promises a quiet room—double-paned windows help dim the hum from the busy street—if you request it when you book by email (RS%, air-con, elevator, sundeck terrace, closed Nov-March, Corso Italia 257, +39 081 878 1650, www.hotelnice.it, info@hotelnice.it).

AT THE EAST END OF TOWN

$$$$ Grand Hotel Ambasciatori is a sumptuous five-star hotel with 100 rooms, a cliffside setting, a sprawling garden, and a pool. This is Humphrey Bogart land, with impressive public spaces, a relaxing stay-awhile ambience, and a free elevator to its "private beach"—actually a sundeck built out over the water (RS%, some view rooms, balconies in all rooms, air-con in summer, elevator, pay parking, closed Nov-March, Via Califano 18, +39 081 878 2025, www.ambasciatorisorrento.com, ambasciatori@manniellohotels.com). It's a short walk from the town center (10-15 minutes from the train station or Piazza Tasso).

WITH A VIEW, ON VIA CAPO

These cliffside hotels are outside of town, toward the cape of the peninsula (from the train station, go straight out Corso Italia, which turns into Via Capo). Once you're set up, commuting into town by bus or on foot is easy. Hotel Minerva is my favorite Sorrento splurge, while Hotel Désirée is a super budget bet with comparable views. If you're in Sorrento to stay put and luxuriate, especially with a car, these accommodations are perfect (although I'd rather luxuriate in Positano—see next chapter).

Getting to Via Capo: From the train station, it's a gradually uphill 20-minute walk (last part is a bit steeper), a €25 taxi ride, or a cheap bus ride (direction: Massa Lubrense). Either take the Sorrento city bus (about 2/hour), or look for one of the long-distance SITA buses that stop on Via Capo on their way to Massa Lubrense (about every 40 minutes; some buses heading for Positano/Amalfi also work—check with the driver; SITA day pass valid). Get off at the Hotel Belair stop for the hotels listed here.

Getting from Via Capo into Town: Buses work great once you get the hang of them (and it's particularly gratifying to avoid the taxi racket). To reach downtown Sorrento from Via Capo, catch any bus heading downhill from Hotel Belair (about 2/hour, buses run all day and evening). Or ask your hotel to call a taxi.

$$$$ Hotel Minerva is a sun-worshipper's temple. The road-level entrance (on a busy street) leads to an elevator that takes you to the fifth-floor reception. Getting off, you'll step onto a spectacular terrace with outrageous Mediterranean views. Bright common areas, a small rooftop swimming pool, and a cold-water Jacuzzi complement 63 large, tiled, colorful rooms with views, half with balconies (3-night peak-season minimum, air-con, pay parking, closed Dec-March, Via Capo 30, +39 081 878 1011, www.minervasorrento.com, info@minervasorrento.com).

$$$$ Hotel la Tonnarella is an old-time Sorrentine villa-turned-boutique-hotel, with several terraces, stylish tiles, and warm wood trim. Eighteen of its 24 rooms have views of the sea, and you can pay extra for a terrace (air-con, pay parking, small beach with private elevator access, closed Nov-March, Via Capo 31, +39 081 878 1153, www.latonnarella.it, info@latonnarella.it).

$$$ Albergo Settimo Cielo ("Seventh Heaven") is an old-fashioned, family-run cliffhanger sitting 300 steps above Marina Grande. The reception is just off the waterfront side of the road, and the elevator passes down through four floors with 50 clean but spartan rooms—all with grand views, and many with balconies. The rooms feel dated for the price—you're paying for the views (family rooms, air-con in summer, parking, inviting pool, sun terrace, closed Nov-March, Via Capo 27, +39 081 878 1012, www.hotelsettimocielo.com, info@hotelsettimocielo.com; Giuseppe, sons Stefano and Massimo, and daughter Serena).

$$ Hotel Désirée is more modest, with reasonable rates, humbler vistas, and no traffic noise. The 22 basic rooms have high, ravine-facing or partial-sea views, and half come with balconies (all the same price). There's a fine rooftop sunning terrace. Owner Corinna (a committed environmentalist), daughter Cassandra, and receptionist Antonio serve an organic breakfast and are helpful with tips on exploring the peninsula (family rooms, air-con, lots of stairs and no elevator, laundry services, free parking, shares driveway and beach elevator with La Tonnarella, closed early Nov-Feb except open at Christmas, Via Capo 31, +39 081 878 1563, www.desireehotelsorrento.com, info@desireehotelsorrento.com).

Eating in Sorrento

GOURMET SPLURGES

In a town proud to have no McDonald's, consider eating well for a few extra bucks. Both of these places are worthwhile splurges run by a hands-on boss with a passion for good food and exacting service. The first is gourmet and playful. The second is classic. Both are romantic. Be prepared to relax and stay awhile.

$$$$ Ristorante il Buco, once the cellar of an old monastery, is now a dressy restaurant—with spacious seating—that serves delightfully presented and creative modern Mediterranean dishes. Peppe holds a Michelin star, and he and his staff love to explain their sophisticated dishes (with an emphasis on seafood). They offer lots of fine wines by the glass. Reserve ahead (RS%; extravagant five- and six-course fixed-price meals for €95-150; Thu-Tue 12:30-14:30 & 19:30-22:30, closed Wed and Jan; just off Piazza Sant'Antonino—facing the basilica, go under the grand arch on the left and immediately enter the restaurant at II Rampa Marina Piccola 5; +39 081 878 2354, www.ilbucoristorante.it).

$$$$ L'Antica Trattoria enjoys a sedate, *romantico,* candlelit ambience, tucked away in its own little world. The cuisine is traditional Italian but with modern flair. Run by the same family since 1930, the restaurant has a trellised garden outside and intimate nooks inside. Aldo and sons will take care of you while Vincenzo—the Joe Cocker-esque resident mandolin player—entertains. Reservations are smart (RS%—10 percent discount on a fixed-price meal or a free *limoncello* if ordering à la carte, €50-90 fixed-price meals, good vegetarian and kids' options; daily 12:00-23:30, closed Jan-Feb; air-con, Via Padre R. Giuliani 33, +39 081 807 1082, www.lanticatrattoria.it).

MIDPRICED RESTAURANTS

$$$ Inn Bufalito specializes in all things buffalo: *mozzarella di bufala* (and other buffalo-milk cheeses), steak, sausage, salami, carpaccio, and buffalo-meat pasta sauce on homemade pasta. The smartly designed space has a modern, borderline-trendy, casual atmosphere and a fun indoor-outdoor vibe (don't miss the seasonal specialties on the blackboard, Thu-Tue 12:00-23:00, closed Wed and Jan-March, Vico I Fuoro 21, +39 081 365 6975).

$$$ At **Donna Sofia,** the six-course tasting menu is a meal you won't forget (€80, minimum 2 people, includes water and *limoncello*). The à la carte options are strong on seafood and include affordable gourmet pizzas. Owners Mario (who lived in New York when young) and his wife Lina (who makes the desserts) serve in a comfy modern dining room and on an upstairs patio. Photos of Sophia Loren (the restaurant's namesake) decorate the walls, and diners watch the open kitchen at work. Reservations are smart for dinner (Wed-Mon 12:00-15:00 & 19:00-23:00, closed Tue; Via Tasso 43, +39 081 877 3532, www.ristorantedonnasofia.com).

$$ Ristorante Pizzeria da Gigino, lively and congested with a sprawling interior and tables spilling onto the alley, makes huge, tasty Neapolitan-style pizzas in their wood-burning oven. Their *linguine gigino* and the seafood salad are favorites (daily 12:00-23:00, closed Jan-mid-March, just off Piazza Sant'Antonino at Via degli Archi 15, +39 081 878 1927, Antonino).

$$ La Cantinaccia del Popolo, rustic and informal, draws a spirited crowd anxious to taste Annalisa's cooking. Her husband Peppe seems well fed, so you know the food is good. Peruse the counter of antipasti displayed under hanging prosciutto, but save room for delicious pasta that's stylishly served in large metal skillets (Tue-Sun 12:00-15:30 & 18:00-23:30, closed Mon and mid-Jan-mid-Feb, no reservations but Peppe pours free homemade wine while you wait, a couple of blocks past the train station at Vico Terzo Rota 3, +39 366 101 5497).

With a Sea View: $$$ Terrazza delle Sirene (also known by its old name, the **Foreigners' Club**) has some of the best sea views in town (with a sprawling terrace under breezy palms), live music nightly at 20:00 (May-mid-Oct), and affordable—if uninspired—meals. It's a good spot for dessert or an after-dinner *limoncello.* You might see wedding banquets here ("snack" menu with light meals, daily, bar opens at 9:30, meals served 11:00-23:00, closed off-season, Via Luigi de Maio 35, +39 081 877 3263). If you'd enjoy eating along the water (rather than just with a water view), see "Harborside in Marina Grande," later.

CHEAP EATS

Pizza: There's nothing fancy about **$ Pizzeria da Franco,** Sorrento's favorite place for basic, casual pizza in a fun atmosphere. Join locals and tourists on benches for great pizzas served on waxed paper in square tins. It's packed to the rafters with a youthful crowd that doesn't mind the plastic cups. Consider their *saltimbocca,* a baked sandwich with top-quality prosciutto and mozzarella on pizza bread—splittable and perfect to go (daily 11:00-late, just across from Lemon Grove Garden, Corso Italia 265, +39 081 877 2066).

Kebabs: The little hole-in-the-wall **$ Kebab Ciampa** has a loyal following among eaters who appreciate Andrea's fresh bread and homemade sauces. This is your best cheap, non-Italian meal in town. Choose beef or chicken and garnish with fries and/or salad (Thu-Tue 17:00-late, closed Wed, near the cathedral at Via Santa Maria della Pietà 23, enter around corner on small side street, +39 081 807 4595).

Picnics: Get groceries at the large **Dodeca** supermarket at Corso Italia 223 (Mon-Sat 8:30-20:00, Sun 9:30-13:00) or at **Carrefour** underneath Hotel Mignon (Via Sersale 5, Mon-Sat 8:00-20:30, Sun from 8:30).

Gelato: Near the train station, **Gelateria David** has many repeat customers (so many flavors, so little time; they make 155 different flavors but have about 30 at any one time). Mario makes his gelato on-site, like his grandfather Augusto Davide, who started the store in 1957. Before choosing a flavor, sample *Profumi di Sor-*

rento (an explosive sorbet of mixed fruits), "Sorrento moon" (white almond with lemon zest), or *brontolo*—salty pistachio (daily 8:00-24:00, shorter hours off-season, closed Dec-Feb, almost in view of the train station at Via Marziale 19, +39 081 807 3649). Mario also offers gelato-making classes (€12/person, 5-person minimum, 1 hour, call or email ahead to reserve, www.gelateriadavidsorrento.it, info@gelateriadavidsorrento.itinfo@gelateriadavidsorrento.it).

At **Gelateria Primavera,** Antonio and Alberta whip up 70 exotic flavors...and still have time to make pastries for the pope and other celebrities—check out the nostalgic photos in their inviting back room, proving this is a Sorrento institution (daily 9:00-24:00, just west of Piazza Tasso at Corso Italia 142, +39 081 807 3252).

HARBORSIDE IN MARINA GRANDE

For a decent lunch or dinner *con vista,* head down to either of these restaurants by Sorrento's small-boat harbor, Marina Grande. To get to Marina Grande, follow the directions from Villa Comunale on my self-guided Sorrento Walk, earlier. It's about a 15-minute stroll from downtown. You can also take the hourly minibus from Piazza Tasso or the station. Be prepared to walk back (last bus leaves at 20:00) or spring for a pricey taxi.

$$ Trattoria da Emilia, at the city-side end of the Marina Grande waterfront, is good for straightforward, typical Sorrentine home cooking, including fresh fish, lots of fried seafood, and *gnocchi di mamma*—potato dumplings with meat sauce, basil, and mozzarella (daily 12:00-15:00 & 18:30-22:00, closed Nov-Feb, no reservations taken, indoor and outdoor seating, Via Marina Grande 62, +39 081 807 2720).

$$ Porta Marina serves fresh-as-can-be seafood in a modest location next door to Trattoria da Emilia, with views every bit as good as more expensive places nearby. Servers will tell you the catch of the day—always the best option—but if grilled octopus is on the menu then think no more (daily, 12:00-21:30, Via Marina Grande 64, +39 349 975 4761).

Sorrento Connections

It's impressively fast to zip by boat from Sorrento to many coastal towns and islands during the summer—in fact, it's quicker and easier by fast boat than by car or train (see "By Boat," later, and the map on page 95).

BY TRAIN AND BUS

At the newsstand in the train station, Ilaria and Gianluigi sell all these tickets and can explain your options (daily from 7:00).

From Sorrento to Naples, Pompeii, and Herculaneum by

Train: The run-down **Circumvesuviana commuter train** runs twice hourly between Naples and Sorrento with crowds, pickpockets, and no air-conditioning (schedules posted widely, www.eavsrl.it). Fares are cheap: Pompeii (35 minutes, €2.40); Herculaneum (55 minutes, €2.90); and Naples (75 minutes, €3.90). If there's a line at the official ticket windows, go to the adjacent snack bar or downstairs to the newsstand.

Four **"Campania Express"** trains per day are no faster than the regular Circumvesuviana but have newer cars with air-conditioning, reserved seats, and some luggage space (€15 in high season to Pompeii, Herculaneum, or Naples; online sales at http://ots.eavsrl.it or buy at the station). For more details, see "Getting Around the Region" on page 62 of the Naples chapter.

From Sorrento to Naples Airport: Curreri buses make the trip in 75 minutes (€10, online reservations wise, 8/day from 6:30-16:30, no service Dec 25 and Jan 1, departs from bay 5 in front of train station, +39 081 801 5420, www.curreriviaggi.it). From Naples Airport to Sorrento, eight buses depart between 9:00 and 19:30 (ask the info desk in the arrivals hall to point you toward the bus departure lot).

From Sorrento to the Amalfi Coast: See page 133.

From Sorrento to Rome: Most people ride the train to Naples, then catch the Frecciarossa or Italo express train to Rome. Another option is the Sorrento-Rome bus: It's cheaper although the departure times can be inconvenient—confirm them in advance (daily at 6:00 and 16:00; off-season Mon-Fri at 6:00, Sat-Sun at 16:00; 4 hours; departs Sorrento from Corso Italia 259B, by Bar Kontatto, a block from the train station, and runs to Tiburtina bus station in Rome; buy tickets at train station newsstand, on website in Italian only, or on board for a surcharge; +39 080 579 0111, www.marozzivt.it).

BY BOAT

The number of boats that run per day varies: The frequency indicated here is for roughly mid-May through mid-October, with more boats per day in the peak of summer and fewer off-season. Check all schedules locally with the TI, your hotel, or online (use the individual boat-company websites—see below—or visit www.capritourism.com, select English, and click "Shipping timetable"). Some ferry companies sell tickets online for an extra fee, but buying tickets at the port is easy (and keeps your departure options open, especially valuable if you're watching the weather); next-day tickets typically go on sale starting the evening before. All boats take several hundred people each and (except for the busiest days) rarely fill up.

From Sorrento to Capri: Boats run at least hourly. Your options are a fast **ferry** (*traghetto* or *nave veloce,* takes cars, 4/day, 30 minutes, Caremar, +39 081 1896 6690, www.caremar.it) or a slightly faster and pricier **hydrofoil** (*aliscafo,* over 20/day, 25 minutes, Gescab, +39 081 807 1812, www.gescab.it). To visit Capri when it's least crowded, buy your ticket at 8:00 and take the 8:30 hydrofoil (try to depart by 9:45 at the very latest). If you make a reservation, it's not changeable. These early boats can be jammed, but it's worth it once you reach the island.

From Sorrento to Other Points: Naples (6/day, more in summer, departs roughly every 2 hours starting at 7:20, few or no boats on winter weekends, arrives at Molo Beverello, 40 minutes), **Positano** (mid-April-mid-Oct only, 4-6/day, 35 minutes), **Amalfi** (mid-April-mid-Oct only, 4-6/day, 1 hour).

Getting to Sorrento's Port (Marina Piccola): It's a 5-minute walk from Piazza Tasso. Go down the steep stairs starting under the flags, then down the road. For fewer stairs, head to the Villa Comunale public park (see my self-guided Sorrento Walk, earlier), where you can pay €1.10 to ride the elevator down (from the bottom, it's a 5-minute walk to the port). Otherwise, catch the minibus from the station or Piazza Sant'Antonino (specify that you're going to the *porto;* buses run 3/hour).

Capri

Capri was made famous as the vacation hideaway of Roman emperors Augustus and Tiberius. In the 19th century, it was the haunt of Romantic Age aristocrats on their Grand Tour of Europe. Later it was briefly a refuge for Europe's artsy gay community: Irish playwright Oscar Wilde, English poet D. H. Lawrence, and company hung out here back when being gay could land you in jail... or worse. And these days, the island is a world-class tourist trap, packed with gawky, nametag-wearing visitors searching for the rich and famous—and finding only their prices.

About 12,000 people live on Capri (although many winter in Naples), and during any given day in high season, the island hosts another 20,000 tourists. The "Island of Dreams" is a zoo in July and August—overrun with tacky group tourism at its worst. At other times of year, though still crowded, it can provide a relaxing and scenic break from the cultural gauntlet of Italy. Even with its crowds, commercialism, fame, and glitz, Capri is a flat-out gorgeous place: Chalky white limestone cliffs rocket boldly from the shimmering blue-and-green surf, and the Blue Grotto sea cave glows with reflected sunlight. Strategically positioned gardens, villas, and viewpoints provide stunning vistas of the Sorrento Peninsula, Amalfi Coast, Vesuvius, and Capri itself.

PLANNING YOUR TIME

This is the best see-everything-in-a-day plan from Naples or Sorrento:

- Take an early hydrofoil to Capri (from Sorrento, buy ticket at 8:00, boat leaves around 8:30 and arrives around 8:50—smart). You'll land at Marina Grande; yes, Capri's port has the same name as the small-boat harbor at Sorrento.
- At the port, select from three boating options: Enjoy the scenic circle-the-island tour with a visit to the Blue Grotto (1.5-2 hours); circle the island without Blue Grotto stop (1 hour); or just visit the Blue Grotto. (There are generally spaces available for departures every few minutes.)
- Arriving back at Marina Grande, catch a bus to Anacapri, which has two or three hours' worth of sightseeing.
- In Anacapri, see the town, ride the chairlift to Monte Solaro and back (or hike down), stroll out from the base of the chairlift to Villa San Michele for the view, and eat lunch.
- Afterward, catch a bus to Capri town, which is worth an hour of browsing.
- Finally, ride the funicular from Capri town down to the harbor and laze on the free beach or wander the yacht harbor while waiting for your boat back to Sorrento.

If you're heading to Capri specifically to see the Blue Grotto, be sure to check weather and sea conditions for the day of your visit. If the tide is too high or the water too rough, the grotto can be closed. Ask the TI or your hotelier. Note that the grotto is also closed in winter. If the Blue Grotto is closed or you're not keen on seeing it, you can still enjoy a leisurely day on the island seeing the sights in Anacapri and Capri town. Or, for the same amount of time and less money, you can skip the Blue Grotto and enjoy circling the entire island by boat (an experience I find even more fun than the famed grotto).

Stormy weather can keep vessels in port. Take care not to get stranded on the island. The website for the sturdy Caremar car ferries, which are the last to be cancelled, shows whether boats are sailing (www.caremar.it).

Efficient travelers can see Capri on the way between destina-

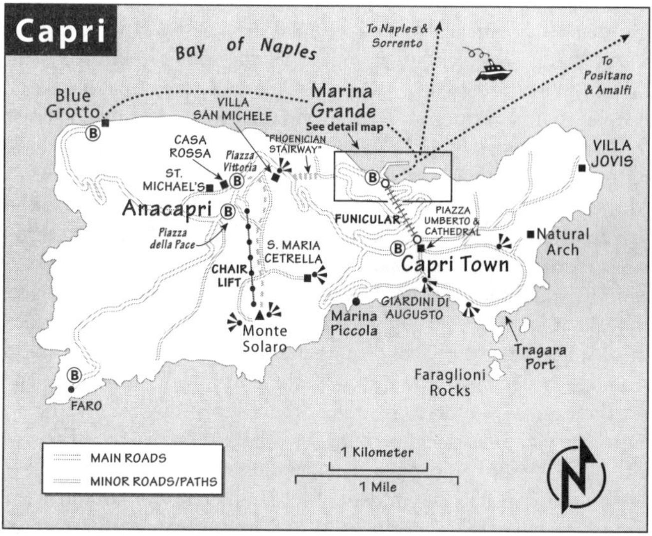

tions: Sail from Sorrento, check your bag at the harbor, see Capri, and take a boat directly from there to Naples or to the Amalfi Coast (or vice versa).

If you buy a one-way boat ticket to Capri (there's no round-trip discount), you'll have maximum schedule flexibility and can take any convenient hydrofoil or ferry back. When you arrive on Capri, double-check the last return trip time at the port ticket office or at www.capritourism.com (it's usually between 18:30 and 19:30). During July and August, however, it's wise to get a round-trip ticket (ensuring you a spot). On busy days, be 20 minutes early for the boat, or you can be bumped.

Starting your day as early as is reasonably possible is key to an enjoyable trip to Capri. Legions of day-trippers on big bus tours come from as far as Rome, combining with cruise-ship excursion groups to create a daily rush hour in each direction (arriving between 10:00 and 11:00, leaving around 17:00) and packing the island through the early afternoon. If you arrive before them, the entire trip to and into the Blue Grotto might take just a half-hour (10 minutes there, 10 minutes in the dinghy going inside, and 10 minutes back); arrive later and you might face a two-hour delay.

GETTING TO CAPRI

For instructions on getting to Capri by **scheduled ferry,** see the "Connections" sections of the Sorrento and Naples chapters, and the "Getting Around the Amalfi Coast" section of the Amalfi Coast chapter.

Another option is to visit Capri by **tour boat.** Consider **Mondo**

Guide, which offers my readers a no-stress, all-day itinerary for €120: You'll be picked up at your Sorrento hotel around 8:00 and driven to the port, where you'll board a small boat (maximum 12 people, shared with other Rick Steves readers) and be taken across to Capri, anchoring by the Blue Grotto (optional entry fee to hop in one of the little rowboats to go inside). Then you'll continue to Marina Grande for about four hours of free time on the island—just enough to head to Anacapri for sightseeing and the Monte Solaro chairlift (island transportation and admissions on your own). Finally, you'll reboard the boat for a lightly narrated circle around the island and pass through the iconic Faraglioni Rocks (includes drinks, a snack, and—conditions permitting—a chance to swim from the boat). For some travelers, the tour may be worth the approximately €45 extra (compared to the cost of doing everything on your own) for a hassle-free, more personalized experience. The trip only goes if enough people sign up, and reservations are required—book online at MondoGuide.it. For details on Mondo and their tours, see page 16. **Tempio Travel**—based at the Sorrento train station—offers a similar trip at a similar price (+39 081 878 2103, www.tempiotravel.com, or drop by their office).

Orientation to Capri

First thing—pronounce it right: Italians say KAH-pree, not kah-PREE like the song (or the pants). The island is small—just four miles by two miles—and is separated from the Sorrentine Peninsula by a five-mile-wide strait. Capri has only two towns to speak of: Capri and Anacapri. The island also has some scant Roman ruins and a few interesting churches and villas. But its chief attraction is its famous Blue Grotto, and its best activity beyond the boat rides is the chairlift from Anacapri up the island's Monte Solaro ("the sunny mount").

TOURIST INFORMATION

Capri's English-speaking TI has three tiny offices in Marina Grande, Capri town, and Anacapri. Their well-organized website has schedules and practical information in English (www.capritourism.com). All have free maps and are open daily in summer (shorter hours on Sun; Mon-Fri only in winter).

The **Marina Grande TI** is in the port office building at the base of the breakwater (+39 081 837 0634).

The **Capri town TI** works out of a closet-like space under the bell tower on Piazza Umberto I and is less crowded than its sister at the port (+39 081 837 0686).

The **Anacapri TI** is at Piazza Vittoria 5, next to the WC near the chairlift entrance (+39 081 837 1524).

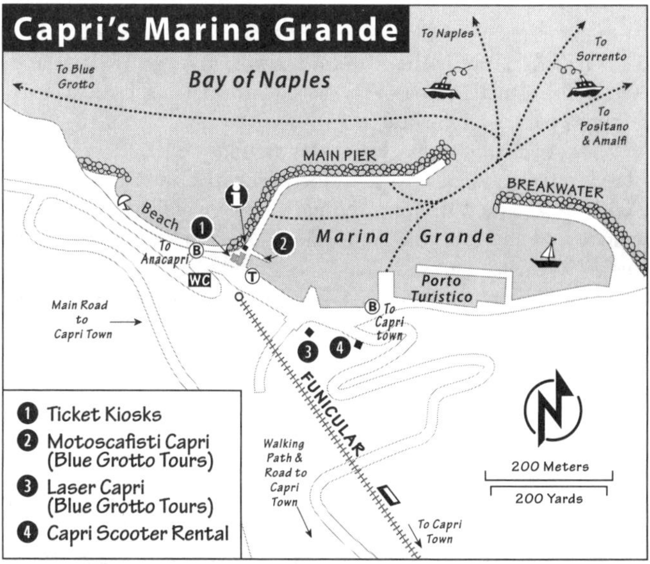

ARRIVAL IN CAPRI

Get oriented on the boat before you dock, as you near the harbor with the island spread out before you. The port is a small community of its own, called **Marina Grande,** connected by a funicular and buses to the rest of the island. **Capri town** fills the ridge high above the harbor. The ruins of Emperor Tiberius' palace, **Villa Jovis,** cap the peak on the left. To the right, the dramatic *"Mamma mia!"* road arcs around the highest mountain on the island **(Monte Solaro),** leading up to **Anacapri** (the island's second town, just out of sight). Notice the old zigzag steps below that road. Until 1874, this was the only connection between Capri and Anacapri. (Though it's quite old, it's nowhere near as old as implied by its nickname, "The Phoenician Stairway.") The white house on the ridge above the zigzags is **Villa San Michele** (where you can go later for a grand view).

Arrival at Marina Grande: Remember that you're arriving with a boatload of other tourists with similar plans. You'll need some patience as you get your bearings. Find the base of the **funicular railway** (signed *funicolare*) that runs up to Capri town, and stand facing it, with your back to the water.

The fourth little clothing-and-souvenir shop to the right of the funicular provides **baggage storage** (€3/bag, look for the awning sign, daily 9:00-18:00, +39 081 837 4575, shorter hours or closed in winter).

Across from the Bar Grotta Azzura are ticket windows for **funicular and bus tickets** (not sold by drivers) and for **boat tickets** to Naples and Sorrento. (Notice the grand electronic departure board on the terminal building listing all boats leaving in the next couple of hours.) Adjacent is the **stop for buses** to the rest of the island. Across the street is a pay **WC,** and a little farther on is Marina Grande's pebbly public beach.

Two companies offer **boat trips** around the island and to the Blue Grotto: **Laser Capri** and **Motoscafisti Capri.** Motoscafisti Capri's ticket shed is along the pier; Laser Capri has two ticket windows along the waterfront. Both offer similar services (see "Sights in Capri," later).

From the port, you can take a boat to the Blue Grotto or around the island, the funicular to Capri town, or a bus to Anacapri or other destinations. The steep paved footpath that connects the port area with Capri town starts a block inland from the ferry dock (follow the signs to *Capri centro;* allow 30 minutes to walk up).

HELPFUL HINTS

Cheap Tricks: A cheap day trip to Capri is tough, as you'll pay about €20 each way just to get there and about €35 to see the Blue Grotto. That's €75 already. But if you picnic and ride buses rather than enjoying restaurants and taxis, you'll find your time on the island itself to be relatively inexpensive. Many of Capri's greatest pleasures are free.

Tread Lightly: Be conscious of your personal impact on this island. More than 2.3 million annual visitors put a strain on local resources. Consider taking any trash out with you and carrying a metal water bottle.

Best Real Hike: Serious hikers love the peaceful and scenic three-hour Fortress Hike, which takes you entirely away from the tourists. You'll walk under ruined forts along the rugged coast, from the Blue Grotto to the *faro* (lighthouse). From there, you can take a bus back to Anacapri (3/hour). The TI has a fine map/brochure. Hiking guru Giovanni Visetti has a great free map of the whole island on his website (www.giovis.com).

Free Beach: Marina Grande has a free pebbly beach (pay at the bar for a shower).

Local Guides: Sorrento-based **Giovanna Donadio** leads good Capri tours (see page 97). Capri resident **Anna Leva** seems to know everybody and every trick (groups of 2-15 people: €160/half-day, €240/day, +39 339 712 7416, www.capritourinformation.com, annaleva@hotmail.it).

GETTING AROUND CAPRI

By Bus and Funicular: Tickets for the island's buses and funicular cost €2 per ride (no transfers allowed). Think about how many tickets you'll need and save time by buying them all at once at the port kiosk. (Tickets are also available throughout the island at newsstands, tobacco shops, and main bus stops.) The €7 all-day bus pass is available only at the terminals. Validate your ticket when you board.

Schedules are clearly posted at all bus stations. Public buses are orange, while gray and blue buses are for private tour groups. Public buses from the port to Capri town, and from Capri town to Anacapri, are frequent (4/hour, 10 minutes). The direct bus between the port and Anacapri runs less often (2/hour, 25 minutes) but is worth the wait if you're following my suggested visit as outlined in "Planning Your Time" at the start of this section. From Anacapri, branch bus lines run to the parking lot above the Blue Grotto and to the lighthouse (*faro;* 3/hour). Buses are teeny (because of the island's narrow roads) and often packed, the aisles filled with people standing. At most stops, you'll see ranks for passengers to line up in. Locals are allowed to cut the line. If the driver changes the bus's display to read *completo* (full), you'll need to wait for the next one.

By Taxi: Taxis have fixed rates, listed at www.capritourism.com (Marina Grande to Capri town-€17; Marina Grande to Anacapri-€23). You can hire a taxi for about €70 per hour—negotiate.

By Scooter: If you're an experienced scooter rider, this is the perfect way to have the run of the island. (For novice riders, Capri's steep and narrow roads aren't a good place to start.) **Capri Scooter** rents bright-yellow scooters with 50cc engines—strong enough to haul couples. Rentals come with a map and instructions with parking tips and other helpful information (€15/hour, €55/day, RS%—10 percent discount on rentals of 2 hours or more with this book; includes helmet, gas, and insurance; daily April-Oct 9:30-18:00, may open in good weather off-season, at Via Don Giobbe Ruocco 55, Marina Grande, +39 338 360 6918).

Sights in Capri

ON THE WATER

You have three boat-tour options: circle the island with a stop at the Blue Grotto, circle only, or Blue Grotto only.

▲▲▲Capri Boat Circle (Giro dell'Isola)

For me, the best experience on Capri is to take the scenic boat trip around the island. It's cheap, comes with good narration and lots of curiosities, and there are plenty of departures from Marina Grande.

Both **Laser Capri** and **Motoscafisti Capri** run trips that circle the island and pass stunning cliffs, caves, and views that most miss when they go only to the Blue Grotto (€20; Motoscafisti Capri—+39 081 837 7714, www.motoscafisticapri.com; Laser Capri—+39 081 837 5208, www.lasercapri.com). The circular tour comes with a live guide and takes about an hour. You'll see quirky sights (a solar-powered lighthouse, tiny statues atop desolate rocks, holes in the cliffs with legends going back to Emperor Tiberius' times), pop into various caves and inlets, power through a tiny hole in the famed Faraglioni Rocks, hear stories of celebrity-owned villas, and marvel at a nonstop parade of staggering cliffs.

With both companies, you can stop at the Blue Grotto at no extra charge (this adds about an hour; check schedules to find out which departures allow a Blue Grotto stop). You can also sail just to the grotto and back (10 minutes each way), but this costs the same as circling the island.

All boats leave daily from 9:00 until at least 13:00 (or later, depending on when the Blue Grotto rowboats stop running—likely 16:00 in summer).

▲▲Blue Grotto (Grotta Azzurra)

Thousands of tourists a day visit Capri's Blue Grotto. I did—early (when the light is best), without the frustration of crowds, and with choppy waves nearly making entrance impossible...and it was great.

The actual cave experience isn't much: a short dinghy ride through a three-foot-high entry hole to reach a 60-yard-long cave, where the sun reflects brilliantly blue on its limestone bottom. But the experience—getting there, getting in, and getting back—is a scenic hoot. You get a fast ride and scant narration on a 30-foot boat partway around the gorgeous island; along the way, you see bird life and dramatic limestone cliffs. You'll understand why Roman emperors appreciated the invulnerability of the island—it's surrounded by cliffs, with only one good access point, and therefore easy to defend.

Just outside the grotto, your boat idles as you pile into eight-foot dinghies that hold up to four passengers each. Next, you'll be taken to a floating ticket counter to pay the grotto entry fee. From there, your ruffian rower will elbow his way to the tiny hole, then pull fast and hard on the cable at the low point of the swells to squeeze you into the grotto (keep your head down and hands in the boat). Then your man rows you around, spouting off a few descriptive lines and singing "O Sole Mio." Depending on the strength of the sunshine that day, the blue light inside can be brilliant.

The grotto was actually an ancient Roman *nymphaeum*—a retreat for romantic hanky-panky. Many believe that, in its day, a tunnel led here directly from the palace, and that the grotto experience was enlivened by statues of Poseidon and company, placed half-underwater as if emerging from the sea. It was ancient Romans who smoothed out the entry hole that's still used to this day.

When dropping you off, your boatman will fish for a tip—it's optional, and €1 is enough (you've already paid plenty). If you don't want to return by boat, ask to be let off at the little dock, where stairs lead up to a café and the Blue Grotto bus stop.

Cost: The €15 entry fee (separate from the €20 ride from Marina Grande and back) includes €10 for the rowboat service plus €5 for admission to the grotto itself. Though some people swim in for free from the little dock after the boats stop running (about 17:00), it's illegal and can be dangerous.

Timing: When waves or high tide make entering dangerous, the boats don't go in—the grotto can close without notice, sending tourists (flush with anticipation) home without a chance to squeeze through the little hole.

If you're coming from Capri's port (Marina Grande), allow 1-2 hours for the entire visit, depending on the chaos at the caves. Going with the first trip (around 9:00) will get you there at the same time as the boatmen in their dinghies—who hitch a ride behind your boat—resulting in less chaos and a shorter wait at the entry point.

If you arrive on the island later in the morning—when the Blue Grotto is already jammed—you could try waiting to visit until about 15:00, when most of the tour groups have vacated. But this may only work by bus (not boat). Confirm that day's closing time with a TI before making the trip.

Going by Bus: To save money, buy the island bus day pass at Marina Grande (€7) and take the **bus** via Anacapri to the small dock next to the grotto entrance. You'll lose time but see a beautiful, calmer side of the island (roughly 3/hour, 10 minutes; buses depart only from the Anacapri bus station at Piazza della Pace—not from the bus stop at Piazza Vittoria 200 yards away). If you're coming from Marina Grande or Capri town and want to transfer to the Blue Grotto buses, don't get off when the driver announces "Anacapri." Instead, ride one more stop to Piazza della Pace. At the Piazza della Pace bus station, notice the two lines: "Grotta Azzurra" for the Blue Grotto, and "Faro" for the lighthouse.

Getting Back from the Blue Grotto by Bus: Even if you've come to the grotto by sea, you can ask your boatman to row you over to the dock and drop you there (for a small tip). From the dock, climb up the stairs to the stop for the bus to Anacapri (you'll still have to pay the full boat fare).

ANACAPRI TOWN AND NEARBY

More interesting than the island's namesake town, Anacapri has two or three hours' worth of sights. Though Anacapri sits higher up on the island ("ana" means "upper" in Greek) than Capri town, there are no sea views at street level in the town center.

When visiting Anacapri by bus, note that there are two stops: at Piazza Vittoria, in the center of town at the base of the Monte Solaro chairlift; and 200 yards farther along at Piazza della Pace (pronounced "PAH-chay"), a larger bus station near the cemetery. Piazza Vittoria gets you closer to the main sights (chairlift and Villa San Michele), while Piazza della Pace is where you transfer to the Blue Grotto bus. When leaving Anacapri for Marina Grande, buses can be packed. Your best chance of getting on board is to catch the bus from Piazza della Pace (the first stop). Another option is to catch a bus to Capri town, visit sights there, then take the funicular down to Marina Grande. Bus tickets can be purchased at the "Moda Mare" souvenir store directly opposite the bus stop in Piazza Vittoria.

Via Orlandi

Anacapri's pedestrianized main drag takes you through the charming center of town. It's just a block or so from either bus stop. (From Piazza Vittoria, the street is right there—just go down the lane to the right of the Anacapri statue. From Piazza della Pace, cross the street and go down the small pedestrian lane called Via Filietto.) Anacapri's **TI** is at Piazza Vittoria, next to the WC by the chairlift.

To see the town, stroll along Via Orlandi for a few minutes. Signs propose a quick circuit that links the Casa Rossa, St. Michael's Church, and peaceful side streets. You'll also find shops and eateries, including good choices for quick, inexpensive pizza, *saltimbocca* (prosciutto and mozzarella on baked pizza bread—great for a filling picnic), *panini,* and other goodies. These two **$** options are both open daily in peak season: **Sciué Sciué** (same price for informal seating or takeaway, at #73, +39 081 837 2068) and **Pizza e Pasta** (takeaway only, lots of benches nearby, just before the church at #157, +39 328 623 8460).

Of the sights below, the first two are in the heart of town (on or near Via Orlandi), while the next two are a short walk away.

Museo Casa Rossa (Red House Museum)

This "Pompeiian-red," eccentric home, a hodgepodge of architectural styles, is the former residence of John Clay MacKowen, a Louisiana doctor and ex-Confederate officer who moved to Capri in the 1870s and married a local woman. (MacKowen and the Villa San Michele's Axel Munthe—see later—loathed each other, and even tried to challenge each other to a duel.) Its small collection of 19th-century paintings of scenes from around the island recalls a time before mass tourism. Don't miss the second floor, with more paintings and four ancient, sea-worn statues, which were recovered from the depths of the Blue Grotto in the 1960s and 1970s.

Cost and Hours: €3.50; discounted to €1 with ticket stub from Blue Grotto, Villa San Michele, or Monte Solaro chairlift; Tue-Sun 10:00-13:30 & 17:30-20:00; shorter hours April-May and Oct; closed Nov-March and Mon year-round; Via Orlandi 78, +39 081 838 7260, http://www.museocasarossa.it.

▲Church of San Michele

This Baroque church in the village center has a remarkable majolica floor showing paradise on earth in a classic 18th-century Neapolitan style. The entire floor is ornately tiled, featuring an angel (with flaming sword) driving Adam and Eve from paradise. The devil is wrapped around the trunk of a beautiful tree. The animals—happily ignoring this momentous event—all have human expressions. For the best view, climb the spiral stairs from the postcard desk. Services are held only during the first two weeks of Advent, when the church is closed to visitors.

Cost and Hours: €2, daily 9:00-19:00; Oct-Nov and mid-Dec-March usually 10:00-14:00, closed late Nov-mid-Dec; in town center just off Via Orlandi—look for *San Michele* signs, +39 081 837 2396, www.chiesa-san-michele.com.

▲Villa San Michele and Grand Capri View

This is the mansion of Axel Munthe, Capri's grand personality, an idealistic Swedish doctor who bought the property (then rundown) in 1887 and lived here until 1946. Munthe was the personal physician of Sweden's Queen Victoria, who often stayed here with him. Munthe enjoyed the avant-garde and permissive scene at Capri, during an era when Europe's leading artists and creative figures gathered here and the island's many gay visitors could be honest about their sexual orientation.

At the very least, walk the path from Piazza Vittoria past the villa to a superb, free viewpoint over Capri town, Marina Grande, and—in the distance—Mount Vesuvius and Sorrento. Paying to enter the villa lets you see a few rooms with period furnishings (follow the one-way route, good English descriptions); an exhibit on Munthe; and one of this region's most delightful gardens, with a chapel, the Olivetum (a tiny museum of native birds and bugs), and a view that's slightly better than the free one outside. Throughout the gardens and the house, you'll see a smattering of original ancient objects unearthed here—and lots and lots of copies. A café (also with a view) serves affordable sandwiches.

Cost and Hours: €10, daily 9:00-18:00, closes earlier Oct-April, +39 081 837 1401, www.villasanmichele.eu.

Getting There: From Piazza Vittoria, walk up the grand staircase and turn left onto Via Capodimonte. At the start of the shopping street, on your right, pass the deluxe Capri Palace Hotel—venture in if you can get past the treacherously eye-catching swimming pool windows (behind the pillars). After lots of overpriced shops, just before the villa, notice the Swedish consulate. In honor of Munthe, Swedes get into the villa for free.

▲▲Chairlift up to Monte Solaro

From Anacapri, you can ride the chairlift *(seggiovia)* to the 1,900-foot summit of Monte Solaro for a commanding view of the Bay of Naples. Work on your tan as you float over hazelnut, walnut, chestnut, apricot, peach, kiwi, and fig trees, past a montage of tourists (mostly from cruise ships; when the grotto is closed—as it often is—they bring passengers here instead). Prospective smoochers should know that the lift seats are all single. As you ascend, consider how Capri's real estate has been priced out of the locals' reach. The ride takes 13 minutes each way, and you'll want at least 30 minutes on top, where there are picnic benches and a café with WCs.

Cost and Hours: €9 one-way, €12 round-trip, daily 9:30-17:00, last run down at 17:30; March-April until 16:00, Nov-Feb until 15:30, +39 081 837 1438, www.capriseggiovia.it. Note that the lift gets more crowded with tour groups in the afternoon.

Getting There: From the Piazza Vittoria bus stop, just climb the steps and look right.

At the Summit: You'll enjoy the best panorama possible: lush cliffs busy with seagulls enjoying the ideal nesting spot. Even if skies aren't clear, the views are spectacular, with clouds surfing over the cliffs. Find the Faraglioni Rocks—with tour boats squeezing through every few minutes—which are an icon of the island. The pink building nearest the rocks was an American R&R base during World War II. Eisenhower and Churchill met here. On the peak closest to Cape Sorrento, you can see the distant ruins of Emperor Tiberius' palace, Villa Jovis. Pipes from the Sorrento Peninsula bring water to Capri (demand for fresh water here long ago exceeded the supply provided by the island's three natural springs). The Li Galli Islands mark the Amalfi Coast in the distance. Cross the bar terrace for views of Mount Vesuvius and Naples.

Hiking Down: A highlight for hardy walkers (provided you have strong knees and good shoes) is the 40-minute downhill hike from the top of Monte Solaro, through lush vegetation and ever-changing views, past the 14th-century Chapel of Santa Maria Cetrella (at the trail's only intersection, it's a 10-minute detour to the right), and back into Anacapri. The trail starts downstairs, past the WCs (last chance). Down two more flights of stairs, look for the sign to *Anacapri e Cetrella*—you're on your way. While the trail is well established, you'll encounter plenty of uneven steps, loose rocks, and few signs.

Lighthouse near Anacapri

The lighthouse *(faro),* at the rocky, arid, and desolate southwestern corner of the island, is a favorite place to enjoy the sunset. This area has a private beach, pool, small restaurants, and a few fishermen. Reach it by bus from Anacapri (3/hour, departs from Piazza della Pace stop).

CAPRI TOWN AND NEARBY

This cute but extremely clogged and touristy shopping town is worth a brief visit, if only for window shopping.

Piazza Umberto I

If you arrive by the funicular, it drops you just around the corner from Piazza Umberto I, the town's main square (named after the second king of Italy). With your back to the funicular, the bus stop is 50 yards straight ahead down Via Roma. The **TI** is under the bell tower on Piazza Umberto (see "Tourist Information," earlier). The footpath to the port starts just behind the TI (follow signs to *Il Porto,* 15-minute walk). A WC and baggage storage are down the stairs by the TI.

Imagine the days when, rather than fancy cafés, the square was filled with a public market. Today, Capri town is traffic-free with only electric service minitrucks scooting here and there. While a coffee costs €1 at any bar, it's €5 at a table on the square.

To the left of City Hall (Municipio, lowest corner), a narrow, atmospheric lane leads into the medieval part of town, which has plenty of eateries and is the starting point for the 45-minute hike to Villa Jovis.

Cathedral

Capri town's multidomed Baroque cathedral, which faces the square, is worth a quick look. Its multicolored marble floor at the altar dates from the first century AD—it was scavenged from Emperor Tiberius' villa and laid here in the 19th century.

"Rodeo Drive"

The lane to the left of the cathedral (past Bar Tiberio, under the wide arch) is a fashionable shopping strip that's justifiably been dubbed "Rodeo Drive" by residents. Walk a few minutes down the street (past Gelateria Buonocore at #35, with its tempting fresh waffle cones—you'll smell them as you approach) to Quisisana Hotel, the island's top old-time hotel (formerly a 19th-century sanitorium). From there, head left for fancy shops and villas, and right for gardens and views. Between the lane and the sea is a huge monastery (Certosa di San Giacomo, described later; access to the left).

Giardini di Augusto

To the right and downhill, a five-minute walk leads to this lovely public garden (€1.50, use machines, daily 9:00-19:30, Nov-March until 17:30, free to enter off-season, no picnicking). While the garden itself is modest, it boasts great views over the famous Faraglioni Rocks—handy if you don't have the time, money, or interest to access the higher vantage points near Anacapri (Monte Solaro, Villa San Michele).

Monastery of San Giacomo

One of the most historic buildings on the island is the Certosa di San Giacomo (€6, Tue-Sun 10:00-16:00, later in summer, closed Mon, Via Certosa 10, +39 081 837 6218). The stark monastery has an empty church and a sleepy cloister. But the finest piece of art on Capri is over the church's front entrance: an exquisite 14th-century fresco of Mary and the baby Jesus by the Florentine Niccolo di Tommaso. Today, the monastery hosts the **Museo Diefenbach,** a small collection of dark and moody paintings by eccentric German artist Karl Wilhelm Diefenbach, who walked around naked in Capri in the early 1900s, when this was a gay, political, and avant-garde place.

Villa Jovis and the Emperor's Capri

Even before becoming emperor, Augustus loved Capri so much that he traded the family-owned Isle of Ischia to the (then-independent) Neapolitans in exchange for making Capri his personal property. Emperor Tiberius spent a decade here, AD 26-37. (Some figure he did so in order to escape being assassinated in Rome.)

Emperor Tiberius' ruined villa, Villa Jovis, is reachable only by a scenic 45-minute hike from Capri town. You won't find any statues or mosaics here—just an evocative, ruined complex of terraces clinging to a rocky perch over a sheer drop to the sea...and a lovely view. You can make out a large water reservoir for baths, the foundations of servants' quarters, and Tiberius' private apartments (fragments of marble flooring still survive). The ruined lighthouse dates from the Middle Ages.

Cost and Hours: €6, Wed-Mon 10:00-18:00, closed Tue, shorter hours and closed off-season—check at Capri TI.

Capri Connections

From Capri's Marina Grande by Boat to: Sorrento (ferry: 4/day, 30 minutes, www.caremar.it; hydrofoil: up to 20/day, 20 minutes, www.gescab.it), **Naples** (roughly hourly, more in summer, hydrofoil: 50 minutes, arrives at Molo Beverello; ferries: 60-90 minutes, arrive at Calata Porta di Massa), **Positano** (mid-April-mid-Oct, 6/day, 40 minutes). Confirm the schedule carefully at TIs or www.capritourism.com (under "Shipping Timetable")—the last boats back to the mainland usually leave around 18:00-20:00. For a steep price, you can always hire a water taxi (weather permitting).

AMALFI COAST & PAESTUM

Amalfi Coast Tour • Positano • Ravello • Paestum

With its stunning scenery, hill- and harbor-hugging towns, and historic ruins, Amalfi is Italy's coast with the most. The breathtaking trip from Sorrento to Salerno is one of the world's great bus or taxi rides. It will leave your mouth open and your camera's memory card full. You'll gain respect for the 19th-century Italian engineers who built the roads—and even more for the 21st-century drivers who squeeze past each other here daily. Cantilevered garages, hotels, and villas cling to the vertical terrain, and beautiful but out-of-reach coves tease from far below. As you hyperventilate, notice how the Mediterranean, a sheer 500-foot drop below, really twinkles. All this beautiful scenery apparently inspires local Romeos and Juliets, with the latex evidence of late-night romantic encounters littering the roadside turnouts. Over the centuries, the spectacular scenery and climate have been a siren call for the rich and famous, luring Roman emperor Tiberius, Richard Wagner, Sophia Loren, Gore Vidal, and others to the Amalfi Coast's special brand of *la dolce vita.*

The two main Amalfi Coast towns (Positano and Amalfi) are pretty, but they're also touristy, congested, and overpriced. (Many visitors prefer side-tripping in from Sorrento.) Most beaches here are private, pebbly, and expensive. Check and understand your bills in this greedy region.

In Paestum, farther south, you can see one of the world's best collections of 2,500-year-old Greek temples, a worthwhile museum with artifacts from the site, and the remains of a Roman town.

Amalfi Coast

The Amalfi Coast is one of those places with a "must see" reputation. Staggeringly picturesque and maddeningly touristy, it can be both rewarding and frustrating. As an antidote to intense Naples, it's the perfect place for a romantic break—if done right and if you can afford it. These towns are the big three sights of the Amalfi Coast: Positano is like a living Gucci ad and has good overnight options; Amalfi evokes a day when small towns with big fleets were powerhouses on the Mediterranean; and Ravello is fun for that tramp-in-a-palace feeling.

PLANNING YOUR TIME

On a quick visit, use Sorrento (see previous chapter) as your home base and do the Amalfi Coast as a day trip. But for a small-town vacation from your vacation, spend a few more days on the coast, sleeping in Positano.

Trying to decide between staying in Sorrento or Positano? Sorrento is larger, with useful services and the best transportation connections and accommodations. Tiny Positano is more touristy, but also more chic and picturesque, with a decent beach.

Naples or Paestum can also work as a base for an Amalfi Coast day trip, if you get an early start and the timetables align. From Naples, you have two options by public transport: train to Salerno, then bus (or boat) to Amalfi town; or, Circumvesuviana train to Sorrento, then bus to Positano and/or Amalfi. (You can go out one way and return the other.) From Paestum, you can take the train to Salerno, then the bus (or boat) to Amalfi or Positano.

GETTING AROUND THE AMALFI COAST

The real thrill here is the scenic drive between Sorrento and Salerno. The stretch from Positano to Amalfi is the best. This is treacherous stuff—even if you have a car, you may want to take the bus or hire a driver. Brave souls enjoy seeing the coast by scooter or motorbike (rent in Sorrento).

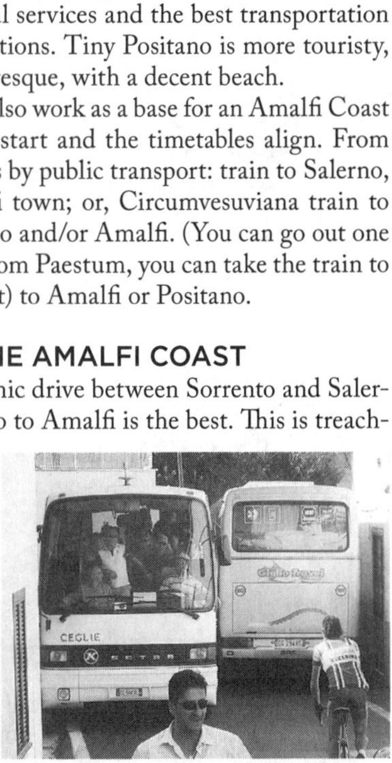

Next, I've outlined your options by bus, boat, and taxi. Many travelers do the Amalfi Coast as a round-trip by bus, but a good strategy is to go one way by land and return by boat. For example, take the bus along the coast to

Getting Around the Amalfi Coast

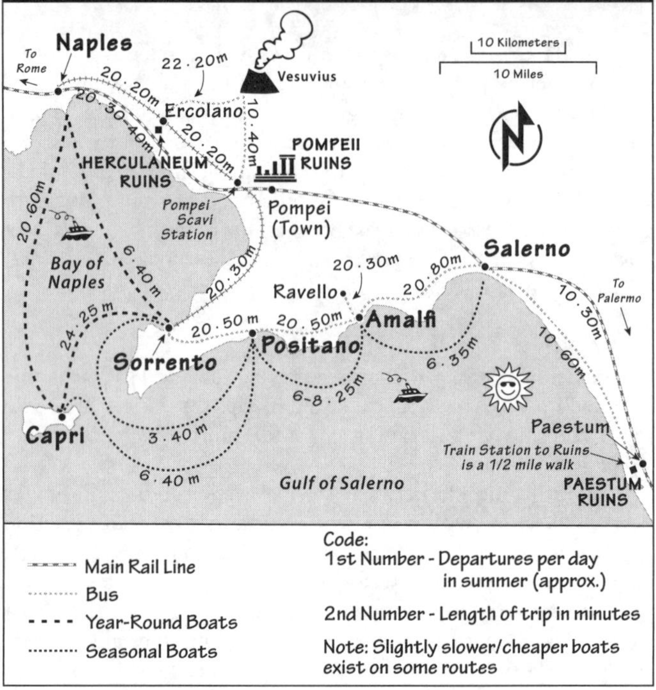

Positano and/or Amalfi, then catch the ferry back. Ferries run less often in spring and fall, and some don't run at all off-season (mid-Oct-mid-April). Boats don't run in stormy weather at any time of year. If boats aren't running directly between Amalfi or Positano and Sorrento, check if you can change boats in Capri.

Looking for exercise? Consider an Amalfi Coast hike (see "Hikes" in the Amalfi Town section, later in this chapter). Numerous trails connect the main coastal towns with villages on the hills. Get a good map before you venture out (local hiker and orienteer Giovanni Visetti has posted free maps and itineraries at www.giovis.com).

By Public Bus

SITA buses from Sorrento to Amalfi, via Positano, are the most common, inexpensive way to see the coast (for schedules, see www.sitasudtrasporti.it or—easier to read—www.positano.com). From Sorrento, the first bus leaves at 6:30; from 8:30 they run roughly every half-hour until 17:00, then hourly until 22:00 in summer or until 20:00 in winter (50 minutes to Positano; another 50 minutes to Amalfi). To reach Ravello (the hill town beyond Amalfi) or Salerno (at the far end of the coast), transfer in Amalfi. When checking the schedule, note that *giornaliero* (G) means daily, *scolastico* (S) means school bus, *feriale* (F) denotes Monday-Saturday, and *festivo* (H) is for Sundays and holidays.

Individual tickets are inexpensive (€2-4). All rides are covered by the 24-hour Costiera SITA Sud pass (€10), which may not save you money but does save time buying tickets. Tickets are sold at tobacco shops and newsstands, not by drivers.

In Sorrento, SITA buses leave from *stalli* (bays) 1-3 at the train station (10 steps down, then join the line). In warm months, look for an extra ticket sales desk under an umbrella.

Leaving Sorrento, grab a seat on the right for the best views. If you return by bus, it's fun to sit directly behind the driver for a box seat with a view over the twisting hairpin action. Sitting toward the front will also help minimize carsickness. If you're unlucky enough to land the occasional bus whose windows are covered by advertising, either sit right up front, or try your luck with the next departure.

Avoiding Crowded Buses: Amalfi Coast public buses are routinely unable to handle demand during summer months and holidays (perhaps because the fares are so cheap). Generally, if you don't get on one bus, you're well positioned to catch the next one. From Sorrento, aim to leave on the 8:30 bus at the latest—earlier if possible. Departures between 9:00 and 11:00 can be frustratingly crowded.

Note that an eight-seater minibus and driver costs about €350 for the day: If you can organize a small group, €50 per person is a very good deal. (For options, see "By Taxi," later.)

When to Stop in Positano: Summer congestion can be so bad—particularly in July and August—that some Amalfi-Sorrento buses don't even stop in Positano (because they fill up in Amalfi). Those trying to get back from Positano to Sorrento are stuck taking an extortionist taxi or hopping a boat...if one's running. When day-tripping from Sorrento to Amalfi, it's safest to make your Positano stop on the outbound leg, then come straight home from Amalfi, where the bus originates. Or consider the hop-on, hop-off bus as an alternative.

By Tour Bus

CitySightseeing's bright red hop-on, hop-off buses travel from Sorrento to Positano to Amalfi and back. While more expensive than public buses, they can be much less crowded and come with a recorded commentary. You'll pay €15 for your outgoing ride (buy tickets onboard) and €6 for the return trip (on the same day). Buses run from the Sorrento train station—confirm times locally (+39 081 1825 7088, www.city-sightseeing.it).

By Boat

A few passenger boats per day link Positano and Amalfi with Sorrento, Capri, and Salerno (generally April-Oct only). The last daily departure can be as early as midafternoon and is never much later than 18:00. Check schedules carefully: Frequency varies from month to month, and boats may be cancelled in bad weather (especially at Positano, where there's no real pier). The companies operating each route change frequently, compete for passengers, and usually claim to know nothing about their rivals' services. The best sources for timetables are www.positano.com (under "Ferry Schedules") and www.capritourism.com (under "Shipping Timetable"). Go to the dock to confirm times and buy tickets. For a summary of sample routes, frequencies, and travel times, see the "Getting Around the Amalfi Coast" map.

If you're going to Capri from Positano, save time and money by finding a boat that goes directly to the Blue Grotto (rather than dropping you at the port in Capri to catch another boat from there). Here's another useful trick: If no boats are going directly between Sorrento and Positano/Amalfi, you can usually still connect the two sides of the peninsula via Capri.

By Taxi

Given the hairy driving, impossible parking, crowded public buses, and potential fun, you might consider splurging to hire your own car and driver for your Amalfi day.

The English-speaking **Monetti family** car-and-driver service—Raffaele, daughter Carolina, and cousin Gianpaolo—have taken excellent care of my readers' transit needs for decades. Sample trips and rates: all-day Amalfi Coast (Positano, Amalfi, Ravello, usually with stops in each town and lunch in Ravello), 8 hours, €350; Pompeii and Paestum, 10 hours, €480; transfer between Naples airport or train station and Sorrento, €160. These prices are for up to three people; you'll pay more for a larger eight-seater van. Though based in Sorrento, they can also pick you up from other places. Payment is cash only (as with most of the car services listed). Reserve directly by email (or by phone on short notice)—don't rely on a web search for the name Monetti, as that might lead you to an impersonator trying to siphon off their business (Raffaele's mobile +39 335 602 9158 or +39 338 946 2860, "office" run by his English-speaking

Finnish wife, Susanna, www.monettitaxi17.com, monettitaxi17@libero.it). If you get into any kind of serious jam in the area, you can call Raffaele for help.

Francesco del Pizzo is another smooth and honest Sorrento-based driver. A classy man who speaks English well, Francesco enjoys explaining things as he drives (9 hours or so in a car with up to 4 passengers, €320; up to 8 passengers in a minibus, €360; +39 333 238 4144, francescodelpizzo@yahoo.it).

Anthony Buonocore, an Amalfi native, specializes in cruise shore excursions, as well as trips anywhere in the region in his eight-person Mercedes van (rates vary, special deals for early booking and in low season, +39 349 441 0336, www.amalfitransfer.com, buonocoreanthony@yahoo.it).

Rides Only: If you're hiring a cabbie off the street for a ride and not a tour, a one-way trip from Sorrento to Positano might cost about €90 (to Amalfi, €150). All Sorrento taxis are white minivans (taking up to eight passengers), sport a taxi sign on top, and use a meter (fares will vary a bit depending on traffic). If there's no meter, it's not an official taxi.

By Shared Minibus

While hiring your own driver is convenient, it's also expensive. To bring the cost down, split the trip—and the bill—with other travelers using this book. Naples-based **Mondo Guide** offers a nine-hour minibus trip that departs from Sorrento and heads down the Amalfi Coast, with brief stops in Positano, Amalfi, and Ravello, before returning to Sorrento (€65/person). They also offer Rick Steves readers shared tours in Pompeii and Naples. For details, see page 16.

Amalfi Coast Tour

The wildly scenic Amalfi Coast drive from Sorrento to Salerno, worth ▲▲▲, is one of the all-time great white-knuckle rides, whether you tackle it by bus, taxi, or shared minibus.

Gasp from the right side of the car or bus as you go out and from the left as you return to Sorrento. (Those on the wrong side really miss out.) Traffic is so heavy that private tour buses are only allowed to go in one direction (southbound from Sorrento). Summer traffic is infuriating. Fluorescent-vested police are

posted at tough bends during peak hours to help fold in side-view mirrors and keep things moving. Here's a loose, self-guided tour of what you're seeing as you travel from west to east.

➲ **Self-Guided Tour:** Leaving **Sorrento,** the road winds up into the hills past lemon groves and hidden houses. The gray-green trees are olives. (Notice the green nets slung around the trunks; these are unfurled in October and November, when the ripe olives drop naturally, for an easy self-harvest.) Dark, green-leafed trees planted in dense groves are the source of the region's lemons (many destined to become *limoncello* liqueur) and big, fat citrons (*cedri,* mostly used for marmalade). The black nets over the orange and lemon groves create a greenhouse effect, trapping warmth and humidity for maximum tastiness, while offering protection from extreme weather (preserving the peels used for *limoncello*).

Atop the ridge outside Sorrento, look to your right: The two small islands are the **Li Galli Islands,** where some say the sirens in Homer's *Odyssey* lived. The largest of these islands was once owned by the famed ballet dancer Rudolf Nureyev; it's now a luxury residence, rented to wealthy visitors for upward of $100,000 per week (bring your own yacht or arrive by helicopter).

When Nureyev bought the island, the only building standing was the stony watchtower—the first of many you'll see all along the coast. These were strategically placed within sight of one another so that a relay of rooftop bonfires could quickly spread word of a pirate attack.

The limestone cliffs that plunge into the sea were traversed by a hand-carved trail that became a modern road in the mid-19th century. Fruit stands sell produce from farms and orchards just over the hill. Limestone absorbs heat and rainwater, making this south-facing coastline a fertile suntrap, with temperatures as much as 10 degrees higher than in nearby Sorrento. The chalky, reflective limestone, which extends below the surface, accounts for the uniquely colorful blues and greens of the water. With the favorable climate, bougainvillea, geraniums, oleander, and wisteria grow like weeds here in the summer. Notice the nets pulled tight against the cliffs—they're designed to catch rocks that often tumble loose after heavy rains.

The dramatic, exotic-looking town of **Positano** is the main stop along the coast. The town is built on a series of man-made terraces, which were carefully carved out of the steep rock, then filled with fertile soil carried here from Sorrento on the backs of donkeys. You can read the history of the region in Positano's rooftops—a mix of Roman-style red terra-cotta tiles and white domes inspired by the Saracens (see sidebar).

If you're getting off here, stay on through the first main stop by the round-domed yellow church (Chiesa Nuova), which is a very long walk above town. Instead, get off at the second main stop,

The Saracens

Along Italy's coast, you'll hear about the Saracens. To understand who they were, go back in time and across the sea to Spain in 1492. That's when Ferdinand and Isabel—Spain's foremost Catholic monarchs—defeated the last Moorish stronghold of Granada. The conquered Muslims were allowed to settle in the mountains to the south. But over time, Catholic intolerance forced most Muslims across the Mediterranean to North Africa.

In the 16th century, the North African coast from Tunisia to Morocco was somewhat united and known as the Barbary States. The displaced Moors (chased from Spain), along with indigenous Berber tribes, were often referred to as Saracens, a term perhaps derived from Arabic, meaning "marauder." Saracens raided Christian ships, capturing and reselling cargo and holding crews for ransom. Christian kingdoms paid bribes to keep shipping lanes open. The Barbary Coast Saracens were loosely aligned with the Ottoman Empire, but that wasn't much help when European powers (plus the United States in its first overseas show of strength) had enough of the raids and declared war. Saracen influence came to an end after their defeat in the Barbary War of 1815, but the Saracen legacy lives on along the Italian coast, with everything from watchtowers to restaurants named after them.

Sponda, then head downhill toward the start of my self-guided Positano Walk (later in this chapter). Sponda is also the best place to catch the onward bus to Amalfi. If you're coming on a smaller minibus, you'll twist all the way down—seemingly going in circles—to Piazza dei Mulini and the start of the walk.

Just south of Positano, **St. Peter's Hotel** (Il San Pietro di Positano, camouflaged below the tiny St. Peter's Church) is just about the poshest stop on the coast. In the adjacent gorge, notice the hotel's terraced gardens (where produce is grown for their restaurant) above an elevator-accessible beach and dock.

Just around the bend, **Praiano** comes into view. Less ritzy or charming than Positano or Amalfi, it's notable for its huge Cathedral of San Gennaro, with a characteristic majolica-tiled roof and dome—a reminder of this region's respected ceramics industry. In spindly Praiano, most of the homes are accessible only by tiny footpaths and staircases. Near the end of town, just before the big tunnel, watch on the left for the big *presepe* (manger scene) embedded into the cliff face. This Praiano-in-miniature was carved by one local man over several decades. At Christmastime, each house is filled with little figures and twinkle lights.

Just past the tunnel, look below and on the right to see another

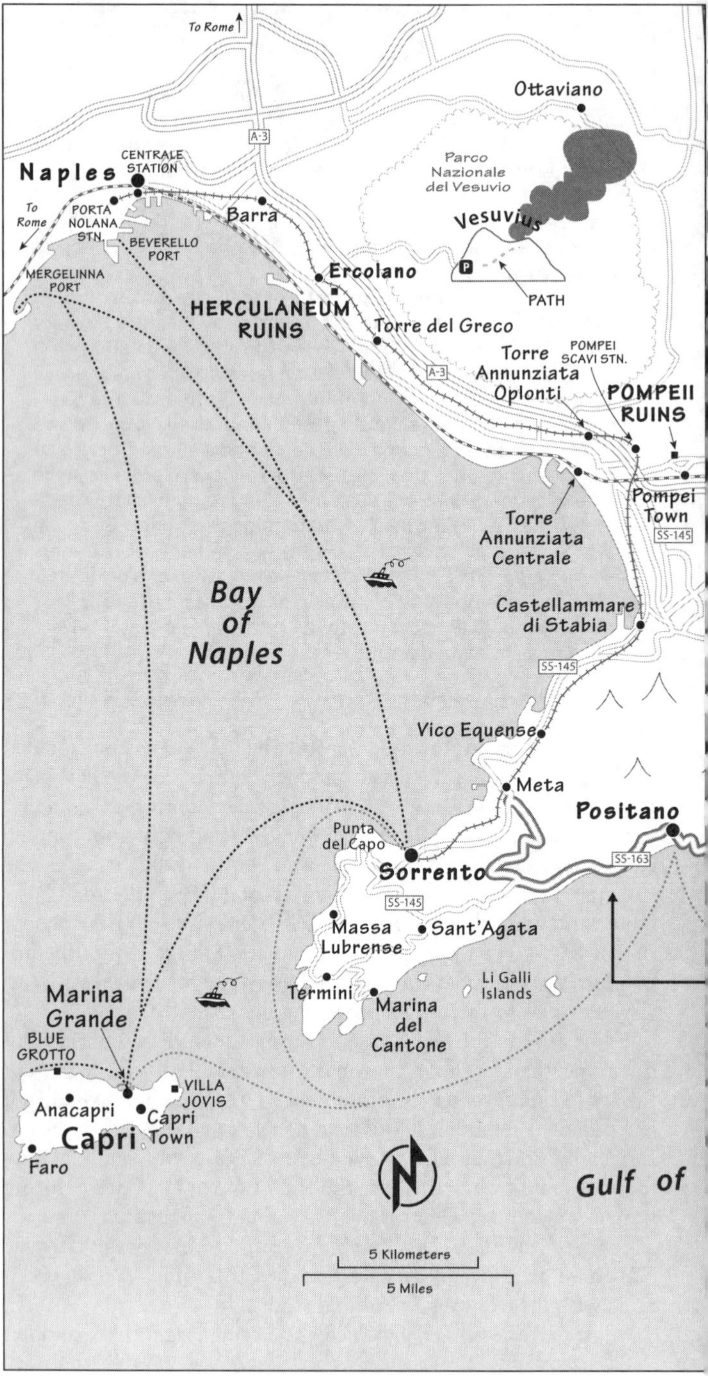
To Rome
Ottaviano
A-3
CENTRALE STATION
Naples
Parco Nazionale del Vesuvio
To Rome
PORTA NOLANA STN.
Barra
Vesuvius
BEVERELLO PORT
P
PATH
Ercolano
MERGELINNA PORT
HERCULANEUM RUINS
Torre del Greco
POMPEI SCAVI STN.
Torre Annunziata Oplonti
A-3
POMPEII RUINS
Pompei Town
Torre Annunziata Centrale
SS-145
Bay of Naples
Castellammare di Stabia
SS-145
Vico Equense
Meta
Positano
Punta del Capo
Sorrento
SS-163
SS-145
Massa Lubrense
Sant'Agata
Li Galli Islands
Termini
Marina del Cantone
Marina Grande
BLUE GROTTO
VILLA JOVIS
Anacapri
Capri Town
Capri
Faro
Gulf of
5 Kilometers
5 Miles

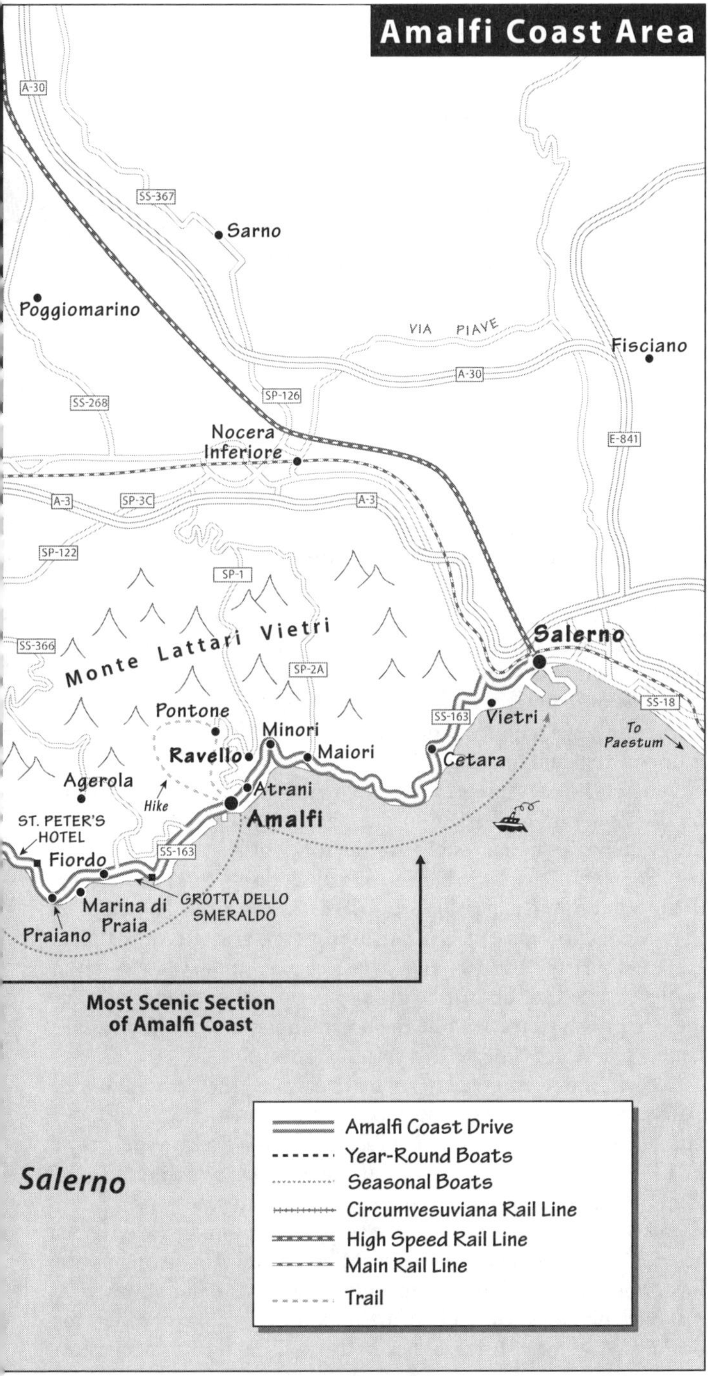
Amalfi Coast Area
A-30
SS-367
Sarno
Poggiomarino
VIA PIAVE
Fisciano
A-30
SS-268
SP-126
E-841
Nocera Inferiore
A-3
SP-3C
A-3
SP-122
SP-1
SS-366
Monte Lattari Vietri
Salerno
SP-2A
Pontone
Minori
SS-163
Vietri
SS-18
To Paestum
Ravello
Maiori
Cetara
Agerola
Atrani
Hike
Amalfi
ST. PETER'S HOTEL
Fiordo
SS-163
Marina di Praia
GROTTA DELLO SMERALDO
Praiano
Most Scenic Section of Amalfi Coast
Salerno
Amalfi Coast Drive
Year-Round Boats
Seasonal Boats
Circumvesuviana Rail Line
High Speed Rail Line
Main Rail Line
Trail

Saracen watchtower. (Yet another caps the little point on the horizon.)

A bit farther along, look down to see the fishing hamlet of **Marina di Praia** tucked into the gorge *(furore)* between two tunnels. If you're driving—or being driven—consider a detour down here for a coffee break or meal. This serene, tidy nook has its own little pebbly beach with great views of the stout bluffs and watchtower that hem it in. A seafront walkway curls around the bluff all the way to the tower.

Just after going through the next tunnel, watch for a jagged rock formation on its own little pedestal. Locals see the face of the Virgin Mary in this natural feature and say that she's holding a flower (the tree growing out to the right). Also notice several caged, cantilevered parking pads sticking out from the road. This stretch of coastline is popular for long-term villa rentals—Italians who want to really settle into Amalfi life.

Look down and left for the blink-or-you'll-miss-it fishing village that's aptly named **Fiordo** ("fjord"), filling yet another gorge. You'll see humble homes burrowed into the cliff face, tucked so far into the gorge that they're entirely in shadow for much of the year. Today these are rented out to vacationers; the postage-stamp beach is uncrowded and inviting.

After the next tunnel, in the following hamlet, keep an eye out for donkeys with big baskets on their backs—the only way to make heavy deliveries to homes high in the rocky hills.

Soon you'll pass the big-for-Amalfi parking lot of the **Grotta dello Smeraldo** ("Emerald Grotto"), a cheesy roadside attraction that wrings the most it can out of a pretty, seawater-filled cave. Passing tourists park here and pay €5 to take an elevator down to sea level, pile into big rowboats, and get paddled around a genuinely impressive cavern while the boatman imparts sparse factoids. Unless you've got time to kill, skip it.

Now you're approaching what might be the most dramatic watchtower on the coast, perched atop a near-island. This tower guarded the harbor of the Amalfi navy until the fleet was destroyed in 1343 by a tsunami caused by an earthquake, which also led to Amalfi's decline (it was once one of Italy's leading powers).

Around the next bend you're treated to stunning views of the coastline's namesake town—**Amalfi.** The white villa sitting on the low point between here and there (with another watchtower at its tip) once belonged to Sophia Loren. Now look up to the very top of the steep, steep cliffs overhead. The hulking former Monastery of Santa Rosa occupies this prime territory. Locals proudly explain that the *sfogliatella* dessert so beloved throughout the Campania region was first created at this monastery. (Today it's a luxury resort, where you can pay a premium to sleep in a tight little former monk's cell.)

Now the bus pulls to a halt—at the end of the line, the waterfront of Amalfi town. Spend some time enjoying this once-powerful, now-pleasant city, with its fine cathedral, fascinating paper museum, and fun-to-explore tangle of lanes (covered later in this chapter).

From Amalfi, you can transfer to another bus to head up to **Ravello** (described later), capping a cliff just beyond Amalfi, or onward to the big city of **Salerno.** Alternatively, buses and boats take you back to Positano and Sorrento.

If you're continuing the trip southward (on the bus to Salerno or Ravello), look up to the left as you leave Amalfi—the white house that clings to a cliff (Villa Rondinaia) was home for many years to writer Gore Vidal. Soon you'll pass through the low-impact, less touristy town of **Atrani** (described later in this chapter). From here, you'll enjoy fine (though slightly less thrilling) scenery all the way to Salerno.

Positano

Specializing in scenery and sand, the easygoing town of Positano hangs halfway between Sorrento and Amalfi town on the most spectacular stretch of the coast. According to legend, the Greek god Poseidon created Positano for Pasitea, a nymph he lusted after, but some think the town's name comes from Poseidon himself.

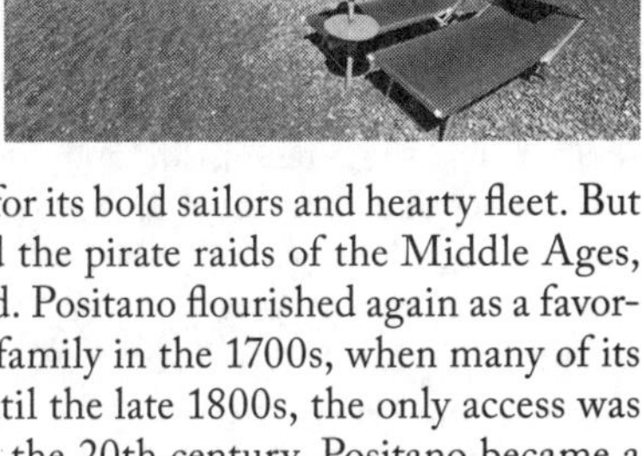

In the early Middle Ages, Positano was part of the Amalfi Republic, famed for its bold sailors and hearty fleet. But after a big 1343 tsunami and the pirate raids of the Middle Ages, its wealth and power declined. Positano flourished again as a favorite under the Bourbon royal family in the 1700s, when many of its fine mansions were built. Until the late 1800s, the only access was by donkey path or by sea. In the 20th century, Positano became a haven for artists and writers escaping Communist Russia and Nazi Germany. In 1953, American writer John Steinbeck's essay on the town popularized Positano among tourists, and soon after it became a trendy stop. That was when the town gave the world "Moda

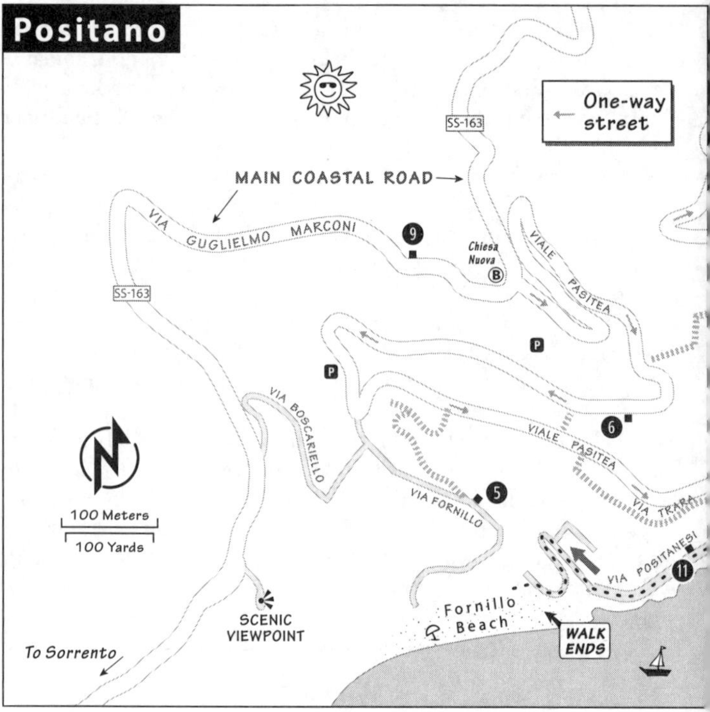

Positano"—a leisurely *dolce vita* lifestyle of walking barefoot; wearing bright, happy, colorful clothes; and sporting skimpy bikinis.

Today, the village, a breathtaking ▲▲▲ sight from a distance, is a pleasant gathering of cafés and expensive stores draped over an almost comically steep hillside. Terraced gardens and historic houses cascade downhill to the stately Church of Santa Maria Assunta and a broad, pebbly beach. Positano is famous for its fashions—and many of its shops are women's clothing boutiques (linen is a particularly popular item).

The "skyline" looks like it did a century ago. Notice the town's characteristic Saracen-inspired rooftop domes. Filled with sand, these provide low-tech insulation—to help buildings, in the days before central air, stay cool in summer and warm in winter. Traditionally, they were painted white in summer and black in winter.

For decades, it's been practically impossible to get a building permit in Positano. Landowners who want to renovate can't make external changes. Endless staircases are a way of life for the hardy locals. Only one street in Positano allows motorized traffic; the rest are narrow pedestrian lanes. While Positano has 4,000 residents, an average of 12,000 tourists visit daily from Easter through October. But because hotels don't take large groups (bus access is too difficult), this town—unlike Sorrento—has been spared the worst

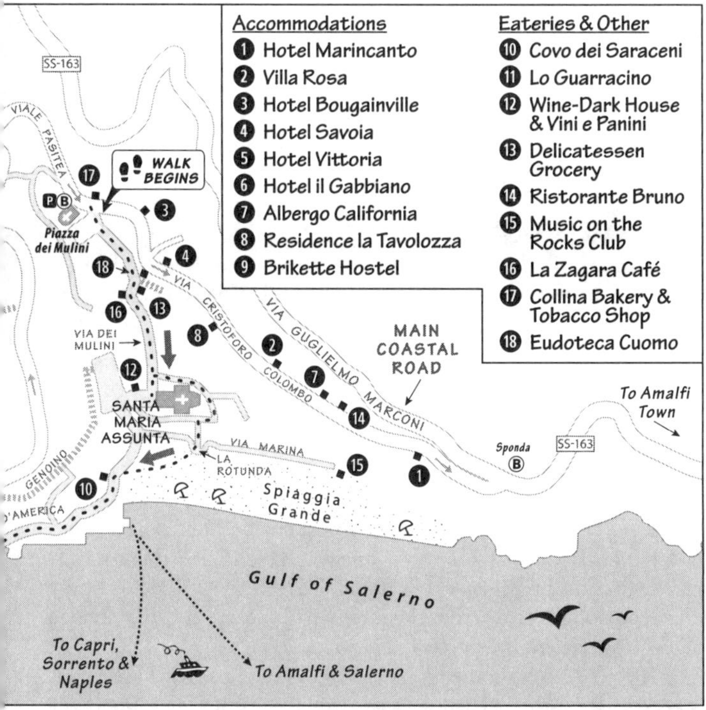

ravages of big-bus tourism. In winter, hotels shut down and the town once again belongs to the locals.

Consider seeing Positano as a day trip from Sorrento: Take the bus out and the afternoon ferry home, but be sure to check boat schedules when you arrive—the last ferry often leaves before 18:00 and doesn't always run in spring and fall. Or spend the night to enjoy the magic of Positano after dark. The town has a local flavor at night, when the grown-ups stroll and the kids play soccer on the church porch.

Orientation to Positano

Squished into a ravine, with narrow alleys that cascade down to the harbor, Positano requires you to stroll, whether you're going up or heading down. The center of town has no main square (unless you count the beach). There's little to do here but eat, window shop, and enjoy the beach and views...hence the town's popularity.

Tourist Information: There's no full-time TI. In summer, the town sets up information stands at the Sponda bus stop, Piazza dei Mulini, and the beach.

Local Guide: Positano native **Lucia Ferrara** (a.k.a. "Zia Lucy") brings substance to this glitzy town. During the day, she leads guided hiking tours, including the "Path of the Gods" high above town (up to 10 people, about 4 miles, 5 hours, €55/person, includes picnic). In the evening, if there's enough demand, she leads a Positano town walking tour (3 hours, departs at 17:00, €30/person). She also offers food tours, and can guide in Amalfi town (+39 339 272 0971, www.zialucy.com).

ARRIVAL IN POSITANO

The main coastal highway winds above the town. Regional SITA buses stop at two scheduled bus stops located at either end of town: **Chiesa Nuova** (at Bar Internazionale, near the Sorrento end of town; use this one only if you're staying at Brikette Hostel) and **Sponda** (nearer Amalfi town). Although both stops are near roads leading downhill through the town to the beach, Sponda is closer and less steep; from this stop, it's a scenic 20-minute downhill stroll/shop/munch to the beach.

Neither bus stop has easy **baggage storage.** Positano does have porter services: A porter can meet you at the Sponda bus stop and watch your bags for €5 apiece—but you have to call them in advance (try Positano Porter, +39 089 875 310). A last resort is to get off at the Sponda stop and roll your bags all the way down to Piazza dei Mulini, where the porters tend to hang out.

If you're catching the SITA bus from Positano, be aware that it may leave from the Sponda stop five minutes before the printed departure time. There's simply no room for the bus to wait, so in case the driver is early, you should be, too. Buy tickets at the tobacco shop in the town center (on Piazza dei Mulini).

To skip the walk up to the stop, take one of the dizzy little **shuttle buses** (marked *Interno Positano*) that constantly loop through Positano, connecting the lower town with the two bus stops up on the highway (2/hour, €1.30 at tobacco shop on Piazza dei Mulini, €1.80 on board, catch it at Piazza dei Mulini). The Collina bakery is just across from the shuttle bus stop, with a fine, breezy terrace to enjoy while you wait.

Coming from the **ferry,** you can give luggage to one of the porter services or lug everything uphill yourself. Follow crowds up wide stairs to the large church, then follow the trellis to Piazza dei Mulini. You'll be doing the reverse of my Positano Walk (described next).

Drivers must go with the one-way flow, entering the town only at the Chiesa Nuova bus stop (closest to Sorrento) and exiting at Sponda (a 20-minute one-way loop). Driving is a headache here. Parking is even worse.

Positano Walk

This short, self-guided stroll downhill will help you get your bearings from top to bottom.

• *Start at...*

Piazza dei Mulini: This "square" is the town center's main junction—as close to the beach as vehicles can get—and the lower stop for the little shuttle bus. The **Collina bakery** is a nice place for gelato or pastries.

Dip into the little yellow **Church of the Holy Rosary** (by the bus stop), with a serene 12th-century interior. Up front, to the right of the main altar, find the delicately carved fragment of a Roman sarcophagus (first century BC). Positano sits upon the site of a sprawling Roman villa, and we'll see a few reminders of that age as we walk.

In summer, look for a popular ***granita* stand** at the top of the lane (across from the church), where the family has been following the same secret lemon slush recipe for generations.

Now continue downhill into town, passing a variety of **shops**—many selling linen and ceramics. These industries boomed when tourists discovered Positano. The beach-inspired Moda Positano fashion label was born as a break from the rigid dress code of the 1950s. (For tips on shopping for linen, see "Shopping," under "Sights in Positano," later). Positano also considers itself an artists' colony, and you'll see many **galleries** featuring the work of area artists.

• *Wander downhill to the "fork" in the road (stairs to the left, road to the right). You've reached...*

Midtown: At **Eudoteca Cuomo** (#3), butchers Pasquale and Rosario stock fine local red wines and are happy to explain their virtues. They also make homemade sausages, *salumi,* and *panini*—good for a quick lunch. The smaller set of stairs leads to the recommended **Delicatessen grocery,** where Emilia can fix you a good picnic.

La Zagara (across the lane from the steps, at #10, with a leafy terrace) is a pricey pastry shop by day and a restaurant by night. Tempting pastries such as the rum-drenched *babà* (a southern Italian favorite) fill the window display. A bit farther downhill, **Brunella** (on the right, at #24) is respected for traditional quality, and Positano-made linens.

Across the street, the ritzy **Hotel Palazzo Murat** fills what was once a grand Benedictine monastery. Napoleon, fearing the power of the Church, had many such monasteries closed during his rule here. This one became a private palace, named for his brother-in-law, who was briefly the King of Naples. Glance into the plush courtyard to appreciate the scene. Continuing on, under a fragrant wisteria trellis, you'll pass "street merchants' gulch," where artisans display their goodies.

• *Continue straight down. You'll run into a fork at the big church. For now, turn right and go downstairs to Piazza Flavio Gioia, facing the big...*

Church of Santa Maria Assunta: This church, which sits upon Roman ruins, was once the abbey of Positano's 12th-century Benedictine monastery. Originally Romanesque, it got an extreme Baroque makeover in the 18th century, when the town was booming and the coast was clear of pirate attacks.

Step **inside** and find these items: In the first chapel on the left is a fine manger scene *(presepe)*. Its original 18th-century figurines give you an idea of the folk costumes of the age. Above the main altar is the Black Madonna, an icon-like Byzantine painting likely brought here from Constantinople by monks in the 12th century. But locals prefer a more romantic origin story for the gilded painting: Saracen pirates had it on their ship as plunder. A violent storm hit—sure to sink the evil ship. The painting of Mary spoke, saying, *"Posa, posa"* (lay me down), and the ship glided safely to this harbor. The pirates were so stricken they became Christians. Locals kept the painting, and the town became known as *Posa-tano* (recalling Mary's command).

To the right of the altar, a small freestanding display case holds a silver-and-copper bust of St. Vitus (along with his bones, now holy relics). He's the town patron, who brought Christianity here in about AD 300. In the adjacent niche (on the right) is a rare 1599 painting by Fabrizio Santafede of Baby Jesus being circumcised, considered the finest historic painting in town.

Back outside, you'll see the **bell tower,** dating from 1707. Above the door, it sports a Romanesque relief scavenged from the original church. The scene—a wolf mermaid with seven little fish—was a reminder to worshippers of how integral the sea was to their livelihood. Nicknamed "our pagan protector," it's a good example of how early Christians incorporated pagan elements into their worship. Notice the characteristic shallow, white "insulation domes" on rooftops in front of the church.

• *Backtrack up the steps, where you'll see a phone-booth-like, glass-walled ticket office for the...*

Roman Villa Complex: The entire town center of today's Positano—from this church all the way up to Piazza dei Mulini, where we started this walk—sits upon the site of a huge Roman villa complex, buried when Mount Vesuvius erupted in AD 79. In 2004, archaeologists made an exciting find under the church crypt: a surviving room from the villa. Now a 30-minute guided tour of the excavated remains (limited to 10 people at a time) will take you down a safe, well-lit stairway to see the walls and floor of what might have been a dining room. The walls are frescoed with decorations not unlike those at Pompeii. Artifacts from the excavation are nicely displayed, and the guide explains the history of the church directly above you, as well as its crypt (pricey at €15, tours daily April-Oct 9:00-21:00, Nov-March until 14:00, Piazza Flavio Gioia 7, +39 331 208 5821, https://marpositano.it).

• *Now circle around the church, and continue descending the steps to the right (following* beach/spiaggia *signs). You'll eventually come to the little square with concrete benches facing the beach, called...*

La Rotonda: This is the town gathering point in the evening, as local boys hustle tourist girls into the nearby nightclub. Step down to beach level. Residents traded their historic baptistery font with Amalfi town for the two iron lions you see facing the beach. Around the staircase, you'll also see some original Roman columns, scavenged from the buried villa. Look up and admire the colorful majolica tiles so typical of church domes in this region.

Positano's **beach,** called Spiaggia Grande, is almost completely private now. It's atmospherically littered with a commotion of fishing boats and recreational craft. The big kiosk on the beach sells excursions to Capri and elsewhere.

Looking out over the beach from this point, you can see three of the **watchtowers** built centuries ago to protect the Amalfi Coast from Saracen pirates: one on the far-left horizon, just below Praiano; a small one on the Li Galli Islands, ahead and right; and the rectangular one far to the right, marking the far end of Fornillo Beach. Defenders used these towers—strategically situated within sight of each other—to relay smoke signals. In more recent times, the tower on the right (near Fornillo Beach) was a hangout for artists, who holed up inside for inspiration. (The people of Positano pride themselves on being artists rather than snazzy jet-setters like those in Capri.)

As you face out to sea, on the far-left side of the beach (below Rada Restaurant) is **Music on the Rocks,** a chic club that's the only remaining piece of the 1970s scene, when Positano really rocked. While it's dead until very late, you're welcome to peek in at the cool troglo-disco interior, or go upstairs to the Fly Bar for the priciest cocktails in town.

• *Now turn right and wander across the beach. Behind the kiosks that sell boat tickets, find the steps to the* ***path*** *that climbs up and over, past a 13th-century lookout fort from Saracen pirate days, to the next beach. It's a worthwhile little five-minute walk through a shady ravine to...*

Fornillo Beach: This is where locals go for better swimming and to escape some of the tourist crowds. Via Positanesi d'America is the lane (lit at night) leading to the beach. It's named for the people who emigrated to America between the 1860s and the 1940s (more than 50 percent of Positano's population) and sent money back to build this path. (Some locals remember when priests used to say at Mass, "And now, let's pray for Positanesi d'America.")

• *Our walk is over. Time to relax. When you're ready to return, go back the way you came to the main beach. Although tempting, Via Fornillo continues straight up the cliffside with a whopping 200-plus stairs...not for the faint of heart.*

Sights in Positano

Beaches

Positano's pebbly and sandy primary beach, **Spiaggia Grande,** is colorful with umbrellas as it stretches wide around the cove. It's mostly private (pay €20-100 to enter, includes lounge chair and umbrella, most expensive near Music on the Rocks). There's a tiny free section near the middle, close to where the boats take off. Look for the pay showers. The nearest WC is beneath the steps to the right (as you face the water).

Fornillo Beach, a less-crowded option just around the bend (to the west) of Spiaggia Grande, is favored by residents, with more affordable chair/umbrella rentals (€15-20) and a wider free area. It has a mellow Robinson Crusoe vibe, with a sturdy Saracen tower keeping watch overhead. This beach has a few humble snack bars and lunch eateries. Note that its position, tucked back in the rocks, means it gets shade earlier in the day than the main beach.

Boat Trips

Boats serving Positano pull up to the dock at the west end of Spiaggia Grande (to the right as you face the sea; booths sell tickets). Also consider renting a rowboat, or see whether they can talk you into taking a boat tour. Passenger boats run to Amalfi, Capri, Salerno, and Sorrento; see "Getting Around the Amalfi Coast" on page 133.

Shopping

Linen: Garments made of **linen** (especially women's dresses) are popular items in Positano. To find a good-quality piece that will last, look for "Made in Positano" (or at least "Made in Italy") on the label, and check the percentage of linen; 60 percent or more is good quality and 100 percent is best. Two companies with top reputations and multiple outlets are **Brunella** and **Pepito's** (each has shops on Via Colombo, near the top of town; along Viale Pasitea, a main drag; and along claustrophobic Via del Saracino, near the bottom of town, parallel to the beach).

Ceramics: One of the oldest ceramics stores in Positano, **Ceramica Assunta** carries colorful Solimene dinnerware and more at two locations (Via Cristoforo Colombo 97 and 137).

Custom Sandals: Positano has a tradition of handmade sandals, crafted to your specifications while you wait (prices start at about €70). One good shop, La Botteguccia, faces a tranquil little square (Piazzetta del Saracino); around the corner, in front of the Capricci restaurant, you'll see Carmine Todisco, who loves to explain how his grandfather shod Jackie O.

Nightlife

The big-time action in the old town center is the impressive club **Music on the Rocks,** literally carved into the rocks on the beach (opens at 23:00 mid-April-Oct, but the party starts even later; there's often a €15-30 cover charge on weekends and in summer, which includes a drink; closed off-season; Via Grotte Dell'Incanto 51, +39 089 875 874, www.musicontherocks.it).

Sleeping in Positano

Most of these hotels are on Via Cristoforo Colombo, which leads from the Sponda bus stop down into the village (ideal for arrival by bus). Most places close in the winter (Dec-Feb or longer). Expect to pay at least €30 per day to park.

$$$$ Hotel Marincanto is a somewhat impersonal four-star hotel with 32 beautiful rooms and a bright breakfast terrace practically teetering on a cliff. Suites seem to be designed for a *luna di miele*—honeymoon (air-con, elevator, pool, stairs down to a private beach, pay parking, closed Nov-March, Via Cristoforo Colombo 50, reception on bottom floor, +39 089 875 130, www.marincanto.it, info@marincanto.it). This is the closest hotel to the Sponda bus stop, 50 yards away.

$$$$ Villa Rosa decorates its 12 spacious rooms plus one apartment with—you guessed it—roses. Most rooms have views plus a terrace, which is the perfect place to have your breakfast served (air-con, no elevator, closed Nov-March, Via Cristoforo Colombo 127, +39 089 811 955, www.villarosapositano.it, info@villarosapositano.it).

$$$$ Hotel Bougainville rents 16 comfortable rooms, half with balconies. Everything's bright, modern, and tasteful (rooms without views are cheaper, air-con, small elevator, closed Nov-March, Via Cristoforo Colombo 25, +39 089 875 047, www.bougainville.it, info@bougainville.it).

$$$$ Hotel Savoia, run by the friendly D'Aiello family, has 39 sizeable, breezy, bright, simple, tiled rooms (RS%, most rooms with balcony or terrace, some cheaper nonview rooms, air-con, elevator, closed Nov-March, Via Cristoforo Colombo 73, +39 089 875 003, www.savoiapositano.it, info@savoiapositano.it).

$$$$ Hotel Vittoria sits just west of the town center with 20 open, spacious rooms and arched ceilings that feel right out of Positano's 1950s boom era. Sprawling up a cliffside, they offer their own free porter service (tips appreciated). All rooms have balconies, most with views overlooking the town (buffet breakfast, uphill from Fornillo Beach on Via Fornillo 19, +39 089 875 049, www.hotelvittoriapositano.it, info@hotelvittoriapostiano.it).

$$$$ Hotel il Gabbiano lies west of the busy town center and has 19 simple but tasteful rooms plus one apartment. All have a view terrace. From here you can explore the many eateries downhill (past the curve) along Viale Pasitea without having to trek into the main part of town (air-con, elevator, closed Nov-March, Viale Pasitea 310, +39 089 875 306, www.ilgabbianopositano.com, info@ilgabbianopositano.com).

$$$$ Albergo California has 15 spacious rooms (all with lofty views), a grand terrace draped with vines, and full breakfasts. The Cinque family—including Maria, Bronx-born son John, and grandchildren Giuseppe and Maria—will welcome you (air-con, pay parking, closed Nov-Feb, Via Cristoforo Colombo 141, +39 089 875 382, www.hotelcaliforniapositano.it, info@hotelcaliforniapositano.it).

$$$ Residence la Tavolozza is an attractive six-room hotel (doubles only), warmly run by Celeste (cheh-LEHS-tay) and English-speaking daughters Francesca and Paola. Each cheerily tiled room comes with a view, a terrace, and silence (lavish à la carte breakfast extra, air-con, confirm by phone if arriving late, closed Dec-Feb, Via Cristoforo Colombo 10, +39 089 875 040, www.latavolozzapositano.it, info@latavolozzapositano.it).

$ Brikette Hostel is your best budget option in this ritzy town. Its 35 dorm beds are pricey by hostel standards, but you're in Positano. It has a great sun and breakfast terrace and a youthful ambience (private and family rooms available, breakfast extra, cheap dinners, air-con, usually open all year, leave bus at Chiesa Nuova stop and backtrack uphill 500 feet to Via G. Marconi 358, www.hostel-positano.com, hostelpositano@gmail.com, Cristiana). The hostel isn't reachable by phone; email instead.

Eating in Positano

Down at the beach, several interchangeable restaurants with view terraces leave people fat and happy, albeit with skinnier wallets (figure €15-20 pastas and *secondi,* plus pricey drinks and sides, and a cover charge). Little distinguishes one place from the next; all are scenic, convenient, and overpriced. **$$$ Covo dei Saraceni** offers the best value on the beach, with good pizza and tables overlooking the action (daily, on the far right as you face the sea, where Via Positanesi d'America starts).

A local favorite for its great views, **$$$ Lo Guarracino** is on

the path to Fornillo Beach, with good food at prices similar to the beachfront places (daily 12:00-15:30 & 18:30-22:30, closed Nov-March, follow path behind the boat-ticket kiosks 5 minutes to Via Positanesi d'America 12, +39 089 875 794). **$$ Wine-Dark House,** tucked around the base of the stairs below the church, fills a cute little piazzetta at the start of Via del Saracino. They serve good pastas and *secondi* and excellent local wines, and are popular with Positano's youngsters for their long list of sandwiches (Wed-Mon 10:00-15:30 & 18:30-22:30, closed Tue, Via del Saracino 6, +39 089 811 925).

Picnics: If a picnic dinner on your balcony or the beach sounds good, sunny Emilia at the **Delicatessen** grocery store can supply the ingredients: *antipasto misto,* pastas, home-cooked dishes, and sandwiches made to order. She'll heat it up for you and throw in the picnic ware. Come early for the best selection (all sold by weight, daily 7:00-22:00, shorter hours off-season, Via dei Mulini 5, +39 089 875 489). **Vini e Panini** (a.k.a. "The Wine Shop"), another small grocery, is a block from the beach just behind the church steps. Daniela, the fifth-generation owner, speaks English and happily makes sandwiches to order. Choose between the "Caprese" (mozzarella and tomato) and the "Positano" (mozzarella, tomato, and prosciutto), or create your own. They also have a nice selection of well-priced regional wines (daily 8:00-20:00, until 22:00 in summer, closed mid-Nov-mid-March, +39 089 875 175).

"Uptown": The unassuming, family-run **$$$ Ristorante Bruno** is handy to my listed hotels on Via Cristoforo Colombo. While expensive, it has nice views and is worth considering if you want a meal without hiking down into the town center (daily 12:00-23:00, closed Nov-Feb, near the top of Via Cristoforo Colombo at #157, +39 089 875 179).

Amalfi Town

After Rome fell, the town of Amalfi was one of the first to trade goods—coffee, carpets, and paper—between Europe and points east. Its heyday was the 10th and 11th centuries, when it was a powerful maritime republic—a trading power with a fleet that controlled this region and rivaled Pisa, Genoa, and Venice. The Republic of Amalfi founded a hospital in Jerusalem and claims to have founded the Knights of Malta order—even giving them the Amalfi cross, which became the famous Maltese cross. Amalfi minted its own coins and established "rules of the sea"—the basics of which survive today.

In 1343, this little powerhouse was suddenly destroyed by a tsunami caused by an undersea earthquake. That disaster, compounded by devastating plagues, left Amalfi a humble backwater. Much of the culture of this entire region was driven by this town—but because it fell from power, Amalfi doesn't always get the credit it deserves. Today its 5,000 residents live off tourism. The coast's namesake is not as picturesque as Positano or as well connected as Sorrento, but it has a real-life feel and a vivacious bustle.

Though generally less touristy than Positano, Amalfi is still packed during the day with big-bus tours (whose drivers pay €80 an hour to park while their groups shop for *limoncello* and ceramics). Amalfi's charms reveal themselves early and late in the day, when the crowds dissipate.

Orientation to Amalfi Town

Amalfi's waterfront is the coast's biggest transport hub. Right next to each other at Piazza Flavio Gioia are the bus station, ferry docks, and a parking lot (€5/hour; if the lot is full, park in the huge Lunarossa garage, burrowed into the hillside just past town and just before the tunnel leading into Atrani). The waterfront hub is overlooked by a statue of local boy Flavio Gioia, the purported inventor of the magnetic compass.

Amalfi's **TI** is just 100 yards up the main road heading east, right before the post office and overlooking the beach (daily 9:00-17:00; Nov-March Mon-Sat until 14:00, closed Sun; pay WC in same courtyard, Corso della Repubbliche Marinare 27; facing the sea, it's to the left; +39 089 871 107, http://incampania.com).

HELPFUL HINTS

Don't Get Stranded: If you're day-tripping to Amalfi from elsewhere in the region, check locally to confirm when the last return bus or boat to Sorrento or Salerno leaves in the evening (in winter this can be as early as 19:00). Don't plan to leave on the last bus or boat of the day in peak season: If that bus or boat is full, your only way home might be a €100 taxi ride.

Baggage Storage and Bus Tickets: You can store your bag safely

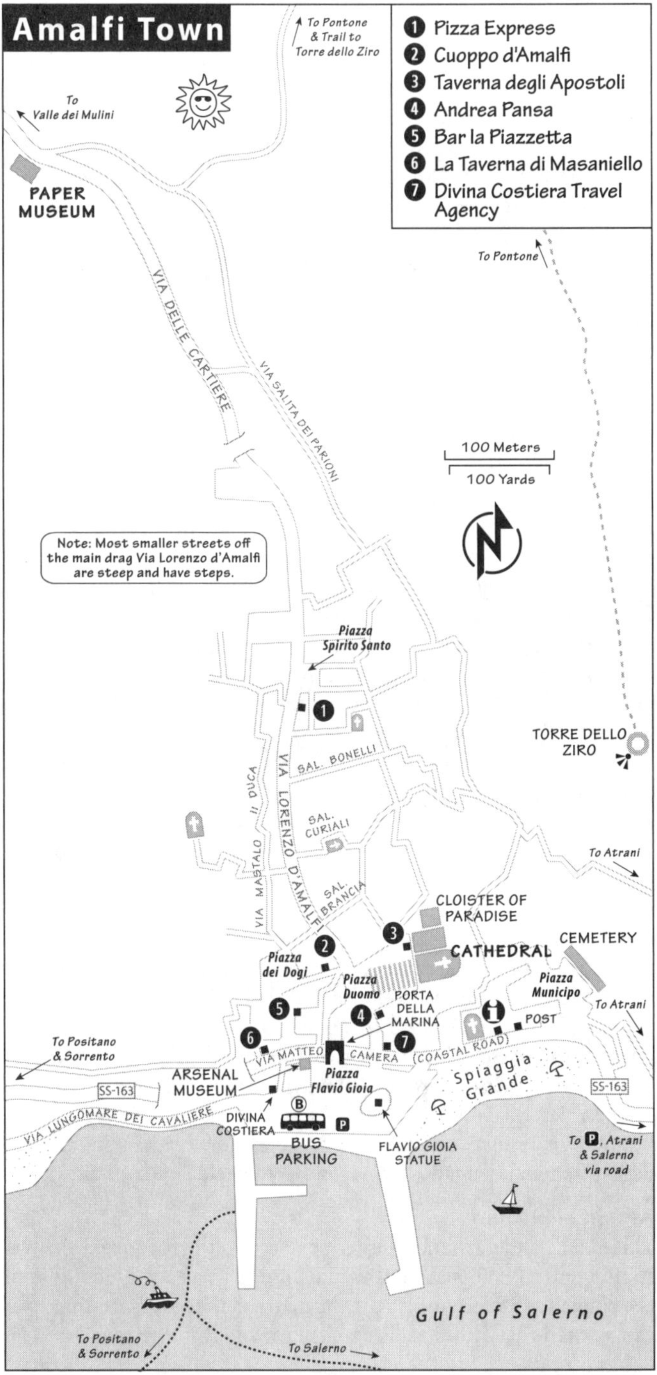
Amalfi Town
1 Pizza Express
2 Cuoppo d'Amalfi
3 Taverna degli Apostoli
4 Andrea Pansa
5 Bar la Piazzetta
6 La Taverna di Masaniello
7 Divina Costiera Travel Agency
To Pontone & Trail to Torre dello Ziro
To Valle dei Mulini
PAPER MUSEUM
To Pontone
VIA DELLE CARTIERE
VIA SALITA DEI PARIONI
100 Meters
100 Yards
Note: Most smaller streets off the main drag Via Lorenzo d'Amalfi are steep and have steps.
Piazza Spirito Santo
TORRE DELLO ZIRO
SAL. BONELLI
VIA LORENZO D'AMALFI
VIA MASTALO II DUCA
SAL. CURIALI
SAL. BRANCIA
To Atrani
CLOISTER OF PARADISE
CATHEDRAL
CEMETERY
Piazza dei Dogi
Piazza Duomo
PORTA DELLA MARINA
Piazza Municipo
To Atrani
POST
To Positano & Sorrento
VIA MATTEO CAMERA (COASTAL ROAD)
ARSENAL MUSEUM
Piazza Flavio Gioia
Spiaggia Grande
SS-163
SS-163
VIA LUNGOMARE DEI CAVALIERE
DIVINA COSTIERA
BUS PARKING
FLAVIO GIOIA STATUE
To P, Atrani & Salerno via road
Gulf of Salerno
To Positano & Sorrento
To Salerno

at the **Divina Costiera Travel Office** facing the waterfront square, across from the bus parking area (€5/4 hours, daily 8:00-20:00, closed Feb, Piazza Flavio Gioia 3, +39 089 871 181). They also sell tickets for the bus to Ravello.

Speedboat Charters: To hire your own boat for a tour of the coastline from Amalfi (or to Capri), consider **Premium Boat Charter** (+39 329 460 3771, www.premiumboatcharter.com).

Sights in Amalfi Town

AMALFI TOWN

Amalfi's one main street runs up from the waterfront through a deep valley, with stairways to courtyards and houses on either side. It's worth walking uphill to the workaday upper end of town. Super-atmospheric, narrow, stepped side lanes branch off, squeezing between hulking old buildings. If you hear water under a grate in the main street, it's the creek that runs through the ravine—a reminder that the town originally straddled the stream but later paved it over to create a main drag.

Before you enter the town, notice the colorful tile above the Porta della Marina gateway, showing off the trading domain of the maritime Republic of Amalfi. Just to the left, along the busy road, a series of arches marks the long, narrow, vaulted halls of Amalfi's arsenal—where ships were built in the 11th century. One of these is now the little Arsenal Museum.

Venture into town, and you'll quickly come to Piazza Duomo, the main square, with the cathedral—the town's most important sight—and a spring water-spewing statue of St. Andrew.

As you get farther away from the water, Amalfi becomes less glitzy and more traditional. The Paper Museum is a 10-minute walk up Via Lorenzo d'Amalfi, the main drag. On the way up to the museum, don't miss the huge, outdoor *presepi* (Nativity scenes) on your left. From the museum, the road narrows and you can turn off onto a path leading to the shaded Valle dei Mulini; it's full of paper-mill ruins that recall this once proud and prosperous industry. The ruined castle clinging to the rocky ridge above Amalfi is Torre dello Ziro, a good lookout point for intrepid hikers (see "Hikes," later).

As you return downhill, be sure to explore up the winding and narrow lanes and arcaded passages on either side of the main street.

Arsenal Museum

This small, underground museum just across the road from the bus station tells a bit about Amalfi's maritime glory years. Stepping into the single long room under the dramatic vaulted stone ceiling, you can just tell that 1,000 years ago, they made ships here.

Cost and Hours: €4; Wed-Thu 10:00-13:00 & 16:00-18:00, Fri-Sun until 20:00, closed Mon-Tue; Piazza Flavio Gioia, +39 089 873 6204, https://arsenalediamalfi.it.

Cathedral

This church is "Amalfi Romanesque" (a mix of Moorish and Byzantine flavors, built c. 1000-1300), with a fanciful Neo-Byzantine facade from the 19th century. Climb the imposing stairway, which functions as a mini Spanish Steps-style hangout zone and a handy outdoor theater. The 1,000-year-old bronze door at the top was given to Amalfi by a wealthy local merchant who had it made in Constantinople. Visitors are directed on a one-way circuit through the cathedral complex with four stops: the cloister, original basilica, crypt, and cathedral.

Cost and Hours: €3, daily 10:00-17:00, open later in summer, closed Jan-March. The cathedral—but not the rest of the complex—can be entered free for prayer or discreet visits daily 7:30-10:00 & 17:00-19:30; it's closed 10:00-17:00 except as part of the paid visit; +39 089 871 324, www.parrocchiaamalfi.com. There's a fine, free WC at the top of the steps (through unmarked green door, just a few steps before ticket booth, ask for key at desk).

Visiting the Cathedral: You'll follow a self-guided, one-way tour of the complex, beginning in a courtyard of 120 graceful columns—the **"Cloister of Paradise."** This was the cemetery for nobles in the 13th century (note their stone sarcophagi). Don't miss the fine view of the bell tower and its majolica tiles.

The original ninth-century church, known as the **Basilica of the Crucifix,** boasts a fine 13th-century wooden crucifix. Today the basilica is a museum filled with the cathedral's art treasures. The Angevin Mitre (Mitra Angioina), with a "pavement of tiny pearls" setting off its gold and gems, has been worn by bishops since the 14th century. Also on display (waist-high, facing the altar) is a carved wooden decoration from a Saracen pirate ship that wrecked just outside of town in 1544 during a freak storm. The church is dedicated to St. Andrew, whom believers credit with causing the storm and saving the town from certain pillage and plunder.

Down the stairs to the right of the basilica's altar is the **Crypt of St. Andrew.** Just as Venice needed St. Mark to get on the pilgrimage map, Amalfi needed St. Andrew—one of the apostles who, along with his brother Peter, left their fishing nets to become the original "fishers of men." Under the huge bronze statue, you'll see a reliquary holding what are believed to be Andrew's remains (kneel at the back of the crypt for a better view). These were brought here from Constantinople in 1206 during the Crusades—an indication of the wealth and importance of Amalfi back then.

Climb the stairs up into the **cathedral** itself. Behind the main altar is a painting of St. Andrew martyred on an X-shaped cross flanked by two Egyptian granite columns supporting a triumphal arch. Before leaving, check out the delicate mother-of-pearl crucifix (right of door in back).

▲Paper Museum (Museo della Carta)

This excellent little museum—worth ▲▲▲ for paper enthusiasts—makes for a good excuse to break free from the crowds and walk up the main drag to a quieter, more local part of town. Paper has been an important industry here since Amalfi's glory days in the Middle Ages. Millworkers would pound rags into pulp in a big vat, pull it up using a screen, and air-dry each sheet (the same technique used to make artisan paper today—look for it at shops in town). At this cavernous, cool museum (an actual paper mill from the 13th century), a multilingual guide collects groups at the entrance (no particular times) for a 25-minute tour. The guide recounts the history and process of papermaking and turns on the museum's vintage machinery. You'll see how the Amalfi River (which you can still hear rumbling underfoot) powered this important industry, and you'll learn the origins of the term "watermark." Kids can dip a screen into the rag pool and make a sheet of paper. It's amazing to think this factory produced paper through 1969 (when it was replaced by a modern facility up the valley).

Cost and Hours: €4.50; daily 10:00-19:00, shorter hours and closed Mon Nov-Jan, closed Feb, last entry 40 minutes before closing; a 10-minute walk up the main street from the cathedral—follow signs to *Museo della Carta* at Via delle Cartiere 23; +39 089 830 4561, www.museodellacarta.it.

HIKES

Amalfi is the starting point for several fine hikes, two of which I've described here. The TI hands out photocopies of Giovanni Visetti's trail maps (or download them from his engaging website, www.giovis.com). The best book on local hikes is Julian Tippett's *Sorrento Amalfi Capri Car Tours and Walks* (2015), with useful color-coded maps and info on public transportation to the trailheads. Lucia Ferrara, a great guide based in Positano, leads hikes around Amalfi (see her listing on page 145).

Hike #1: Pontone

This loop trail leads up the valley past paper-mill ruins, ending in the tiny town of Pontone; you can get lunch there, and head back down to the town of Amalfi (allow 3 hours total). Bring a good map, since it's easy to veer off the main route. Start your hike by following the main road (Via Lorenzo d'Amalfi) away from the sea.

After the Paper Museum, jog right, then left to join the trail, which runs through the shaded woods along a babbling stream. Heed the signs that warn people to stay away from the ruins of paper mills (no matter how tempting they look), since many are ready to collapse on unwary hikers. Continue up to Pontone, where **Trattoria l'Antico Borgo** offers wonderful cuisine and a great view (Via Noce 4, +39 334 748 6611). After lunch, return to Amalfi via a steep stairway.

If you're feeling ambitious and have good shoes, before you head back to Amalfi, add a one-hour detour from Pontone (30 minutes each way) to visit the ridge-hugging **Torre dello Ziro** (a map and trail description are at www.giovis.com). You'll be rewarded with a spectacular view from the headland between Amalfi and Atrani.

Hike #2: Atrani

For an easier walk, head to the nearby town of Atrani. This village, just a 15-minute stroll beyond Amalfi town, is a world apart; its 1,500 residents consider themselves definitely *not* from Amalfi. Leave Amalfi via the main road and stay on the water side until the promenade ends. Cross the street, continue a few more yards, then go up the whitewashed staircase just past the pizzeria. From here, twist up through old lanes to a paved route that takes you over the hill and drops you into Atrani in about 15 minutes.

With relatively few tourists, a delightful town square, and a free, sandy beach (if you drive here, pay for parking at harbor), Atrani has none of Amalfi's trendy resort feel. Piazza Umberto I is the core of town, with cafés, restaurants, and little grocery stores that can make sandwiches. A whitewashed staircase leads up to the serene and beautiful town church (under the clock face).

To save time and sweat on the return walk, follow the promenade just above water level toward Amalfi. Then walk up through the restaurant terrace and find the big, long tunnel next to the parking garage—this will deposit you in the middle of Amalfi.

From Atrani, you could theoretically continue up to **Ravello** (described later in this chapter). But unless you're part mountain goat, you'll probably prefer catching the bus to Ravello from Amalfi town instead.

Eating in Amalfi Town

Quick Bites: Walk five minutes up the main drag; on the right, past the first archway, is **$ Pizza Express,** with honest pies, calzones, and heated sandwiches to go (Thu-Tue 11:00-21:00, closed Wed, Via Capuano 48, +39 329 046 9403). The **Cuoppo d'Amalfi** fried-fish stand at Piazza dei Dogi (described below) is another good option.

On the Main Square, Piazza Duomo: Several pricey places face the cathedral steps. The best of the bunch is tucked just around the left side of the grand staircase, up a smaller flight of stairs: **$$$$ Taverna degli Apostoli,** with colorful outdoor tables and cozy upstairs dining room in what was once an art gallery. The menu is brief but thoughtful, going beyond the old standbys, and everything is well executed (Thu-Tue 12:00-16:00 & 19:00-24:00, closed Wed, cash only, Supportico San Andrea 6, +39 089 872 991). For dessert, the **Andrea Pansa** pastry shop and café, to the right as you face the cathedral steps, is the most venerable place in town—a good spot to try *sfogliatella* (the delicate pastry invented at a nearby monastery) and other desserts popular in southern Italy (daily 7:30-24:00).

Near the Main Square, on Piazza dei Dogi: If you walk straight ahead from the cathedral stairs, go up the little covered lane, and hook right at the fork, you'll pop out in atmospheric little Piazza dei Dogi. Slightly less trampled and more neighborhood-feeling than Piazza Duomo, this has several decent (if forgettable) restaurants aimed squarely at pleasing tourists. The **$ Cuoppo d'Amalfi** fried-fish shop, on the right as you enter the square, fills cardboard cones with all manner of deep-fried sea life. **$$$ Bar la Piazzetta** has tables right in the middle of the square, and **$$$ La Taverna di Masaniello,** tucked at the corner of the square leading to the port, also has good food.

Amalfi Town Connections

Amalfi is connected by bus and boat to all other nearby towns. In season, boats run to Sorrento, Capri, Positano, and Salerno. Amalfi is the terminus for SITA buses to Sorrento (via Positano), Ravello, and Salerno. CitySightseeing buses from Sorrento terminate in Amalfi as well. For details see "Getting Around the Amalfi Coast" on page 133.

Ravello

The Amalfi Coast's version of a hill town, Ravello (a 30-minute bus ride from Amalfi town) sits atop a lofty perch 1,000 feet above the sea. It boasts an interesting church, two villas with stunning gardens, and breathtaking views that have attracted celebrities for generations. Gore Vidal, Richard Wagner, D. H. Lawrence, M. C. Escher, Henry Wadsworth Longfellow, Tennessee Williams, and Greta Garbo all succumbed to Ravello's charms and called it home.

The town is like a lush and peaceful garden floating in a world all its own. It seems to be made entirely of cafés, stonework, old villas-turned-luxury hotels, tourists, and grand views. Ravello feels like a place to convalesce.

GETTING TO RAVELLO

Ravello and Amalfi town are connected by bus along a very windy road (hourly, 30-minute trip, €1.30). Coming from Amalfi, buy your bus ticket at the Divina Costiera travel office facing the waterfront square, or at any tobacco shop. Wait for the bus under the big awning by the statue on the waterfront, just to the left of the statue as you face the water. Coming from Positano or Sorrento, you'll change buses in Amalfi. From Naples or Paestum, you'll change twice (in Salerno and Amalfi), making for a long day.

When returning from Ravello to Amalfi, line up early, since the buses are often crowded (buy ticket in tobacco shop; catch bus 100 yards off main square, by the recommended Ristorante da Salvatore).

Orientation to Ravello

To see the sights listed here, start at the bus stop and walk through the tunnel to the main square, where you'll find Villa Rufolo on the left and the church on the right. Villa Cimbrone is a 10-minute walk from the square (follow the signs).

If you have time for only one villa, consider this: Villa Rufolo is easier to reach (facing the main square) and has a stunning terrace garden. Villa Cimbrone is a 10-minute up-and-down hike from the square, but it's bigger and more rugged and offers even grander views in both directions along the coast.

Tourist Information: From the bus stop, to find the TI, face the church, then walk up the stepped lane to the left and into the Giardino del Vescovo (Bishop's Garden) behind the church (TI open daily 10:00-18:00, closes earlier Nov-April, Viale Richard Wagner 4, +39 089 857 096). The independent website www.ravello.com has helpful information.

Sights in Ravello

Piazza Duomo

Though Ravello is perfectly peaceful today, the weathered watchtower of Villa Rufolo—which once kept an eye out for fires and invasions—is a reminder that it wasn't always postcards and *limoncello.*

The fine umbrella pines on the square provide a shady meeting place for strollers ending up here on the piazza. Opposite the church is a fine view of the terraced hillside and the community of Scala (which means "steps"—historically a way of life there). The terraces—supporting grapevines and lemon trees—mostly date from the 16th century. To the left of the church, Viale Richard Wagner climbs past the TI to the top of town for sea views and ruined villas that are now luxury hotels. The town center is essentially traffic-free.

Duomo

Ravello's cathedral, overlooking the main square, feels stripped-down and Romanesque. The facade of the cathedral is plain because the earlier, fancy west portal was destroyed in a 1364 earthquake. Inside, you'll find tastefully restrained decoration and a floor that slopes upward. The key features of this church are its 12th-century bronze doors (from Constantinople), with 54 biblical scenes; the carved marble pulpit supported by six lions; and the chance to get a close-up look at the relic of holy blood (in the chapel left of main altar). The geometric designs show Arabic influence. In the afternoon, the church's front doors are locked; to enter, you'll need to pay to visit the museum on Viale Richard Wagner, around the left side. The humble museum is two rooms of well-described carved marble that evoke the historical importance of the town.

Cost and Hours: €3 for the museum—which also gets you into the church, daily 12:00-17:00; in the morning and early evening, the church is free to enter.

Villa Rufolo

The villa, built in the 13th-century ruins of a noble family's palace, presents wistful gardens among stony walls, with oh-my-God views. The Arabic/Norman gardens seem designed to frame commanding coastline vistas (you can enjoy some of the same view, without the entry fee, from the bus parking lot just below the villa). It's also one of the venues for Ravello's annual arts festival (July-Sept, www.ravellofestival.com) and music society performances (April-June and Sept-Oct, www.ravelloarts.org). Musicians perch on a bandstand on the edge of the cliff for a combination of wonderful music and dizzying views. Wagner visited here and was impressed enough to set the second act of his opera *Parsifal* in the villa's magical gardens. By all accounts, the concert on the cliff is a sublime experience.

Cost and Hours: €7, daily 9:00-20:00, Oct-April until sunset, may close earlier for concerts, +39 089 857 621, www.villarufolo.it.

Visiting the Villa: From Piazza Duomo, enter through the stout watchtower to buy your ticket and pick up the English booklet explaining the sight. Then, walk through part of the sprawling villa ruins. Check out the short video in the tiny theater at the base of the tower and the exhibit upstairs. The palace itself has little to show, but the gardens and views are magnificent and invite exploration.

▲Villa Cimbrone

This villa offers another romantic garden, this one built upon the ruins of an old convent. Located at the seaward end of Ravello, it was created in the 20th century by Englishman William Beckett. His mansion is now a five-star hotel. The longish walk out rewards you with dreamy landscaping around a villa set on a bluff over the ocean. At the far end, above a sublime café on the lawn, "the Terrace of Infinity" dangles high above the sea.

Cost and Hours: €10, daily 9:00-sunset, +39 089 857 459, www.hotelvillacimbrone.com.

Getting There: Facing the cathedral on Piazza Duomo, exit the square to the right and follow signs. You'll climb up and down (and up and down) the stepped lanes, enjoying a quieter side of Ravello, before reaching the villa at the point.

Visiting the Villa: Buy your ticket and pick up the free map/guide of the gardens. Across from the ticket booth, duck into the old monastery. Then pass the rose-garden terrace and head up the "main boulevard," which leads straight to the stunning Terrace of Infinity, with 360-degree views up and down the coast. If you have the interest and energy, loop back along the more rugged downhill slope (facing the adjacent town of Scala). Tiny lizards scurry underfoot, while mythological statues (Mercury's Seat, Temple of Bacchus, Eve's Grotto) strike their poses before a stunning and serene backdrop.

▲Hike Down to Amalfi Town

Enthusiastic walkers, who have good knees and don't mind lots of uneven stairs, enjoy taking the bus up to Ravello and then making the descent back to Amalfi on foot (there are several ways down). If you plan on this, study your route in advance, get a good map (the free, downloadable one at www.giovis.com will do in a pinch), wear good shoes, allow extra time to give your knees a break, and visit the Ravello TI to check that the paths are open.

The steepest, quickest route starts from Ravello's Villa Cimbrone. From the villa, retrace your steps back toward town. Take the first left, just by the arched entrance gate, onto Via Santa Barbara (this "via" is actually a stairway signposted *Amalfi/Minori*). The stepped path winds its way below the cliff. Pause here to look back up at the rock with a big white mansion—Villa La Rondinaia, where American author Gore Vidal lived for many years. Continue downward, mostly on stone stairs, about 40 minutes to the town of Atrani, where several bars on the main square offer well-deserved refreshments. From here, it's about a 15-minute walk back to Amalfi (see "Hike #2" under "Sights in Amalfi," earlier).

Another route down starts below the Church of Santa Maria a Gradillo (a couple hundred yards down Via Roma from Piazza Duomo). Look for a set of steps called Via Sigilgaida, signposted for *Amalfi*. This path, which has some short stretches on the road (take care), leads you down to Pontone (see "Hike #1" under "Sights in Amalfi"). At Pontone, you can continue directly to Amalfi, or take a fairly level detour through the evocative, ruin-filled Valle delle Ferriere.

Eating in Ravello

Several no-brainer, interchangeable restaurants face Piazza Duomo and line the surrounding streets. To enjoy this fine setting, just take your pick. You can also grab a takeaway lunch at one of the little groceries and sandwich shops that line Via Roma (running off Piazza Duomo). Enjoy your meal at the panoramic benches at the far end of Piazza Duomo (facing the cathedral), or facing even better views just outside of town, near the bus stop and Ristorante da Salvatore. (Picnicking isn't allowed inside the two villas.)

$$$$ Ristorante da Salvatore, near the Ravello bus stop (at the other end of the little tunnel from the Duomo), serves a serious sit-down lunch with great views. Pino, the English-speaking owner of this formal restaurant, serves nicely presented, traditional Amalfi cuisine from a fun, if pricey, menu. Their pasta with potatoes and calamari is a favorite. Be adventurous when ordering and share dishes (Tue-Sun 12:30-15:00 & 19:30-22:00, closed Mon, Via della Repubblica 2, smart to call ahead for reservations—+39 089 857 227).

$$ Trattoria Cumpà Cosimo, a classic indoor family-run restaurant, is a good choice for a quicker, less expensive lunch. For a special treat, get their *piatto misto* with five different pastas for €20 (daily 12:00-15:30 & 18:00-24:00, Via Roma 44, +39 089 857 156).

Paestum

The archaeological park at Paestum (PASTE-oom) includes one of the best collections of Greek temples anywhere—and certainly the most accessible to Western Europe. Serenely situated, Paestum is surrounded by fields and wildflowers. Not quite a village, it also has a bus stop, a church, a TI, a straggle of houses, and a handful of eateries.

This city was founded as Poseidonia by Greeks in the sixth century BC and became a key stop on an important trade route. In the fifth century BC, the Lucanians, a barbarous inland tribe, conquered Poseidonia and tried to adopt the cultured ways of the Greeks. By the time of the Romans, who took over in the third century BC and built a fine town on the site, the name Poseidonia had been simplified to Paestum. The final conquerors of Paestum, malaria-carrying mosquitoes, kept the site wonderfully deserted for nearly a thousand years. The temples were never buried—just ignored. Rediscovered in the 18th century, Paestum today offers the only well-preserved Greek ruins north of Sicily.

While most visitors do Paestum as a day trip (it's 1.25 hours from Naples by convenient direct train), it's not a bad place to overnight. Accommodations offer great value, and you could use Paestum as a base for day trips to Naples or the Amalfi Coast. With more time, there's a beach nearby, and local buffalo-milk dairies that you can visit.

Tourist Information: There's a small TI window at the train station (daily 9:00-13:00 & 14:00-18:00) and a bigger one next to the Paestum Archaeological Museum (daily 9:00-13:00 & 14:00-16:00, +39 0828 811 016).

GETTING TO PAESTUM

A dozen slow milk-run trains to Paestum run directly from Naples via Salerno; from elsewhere, you'll need to transfer at one of those two points. For those transferring in Salerno, see the "Salerno Connections" map, which shows train, bus, and boat stops as well as a few handy eateries if you need to grab a bite. Confirm

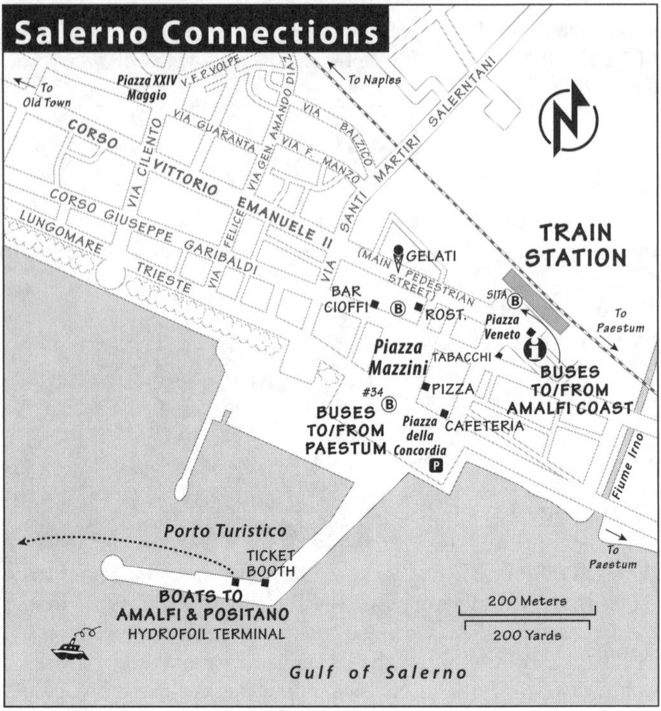

train schedules at www.trenitalia.it and bus schedules at www.sitasudtrasporti.it (or—easier to read—www.positano.com).

From Naples

Direct trains run from Naples' Centrale station to Paestum for €7 (12/day, 1.25 hours, direction: Sapri or Reggio; only the more expensive Intercity trains have a first-class section). Buy tickets online, or from ticket windows or machines at the station. For a day trip from Naples, it's wise to get an early start—especially in warm weather. As of this printing, trains left Naples at 6:50, 7:35, 7:50, and 8:50, then not until 11:45. In the cooler shoulder season, consider arriving for lunch, visiting the museum, then seeing the temples bask in warm afternoon light.

From Sorrento

For a day trip, the smart (if dull) approach is to go bright and early by Circumvesuviana **train** to Naples (70 minutes), catch a direct Naples-Paestum train, and take the same route back (about 3 hours each way). While it's technically possible to do one leg of the trip via an Amalfi Coast SITA **bus,** this makes for a very long day marred by worry about making connections. By **car** from Sorrento, Paestum is 60 miles and at least 3 hours (depending on traffic) via the Amalfi Coast road, but a smooth 2 hours by autostrada. To reach Paestum from Sorrento via the autostrada, drive toward Naples, catch the autostrada (direction: Salerno), skirt Salerno (direction: Reggio), exit at Battipaglia, and drive straight through the roundabout.

From Positano via Salerno

First take a SITA **bus** (2 hours, change in Amalfi) or **boat** (70 minutes) to Salerno, where you can catch the **train** on its way from Naples (30 minutes from Salerno to Paestum). Buses from Amalfi to Salerno terminate at the Salerno train station; boats arrive at a dock a few short blocks from the train station (about a 10-minute, mostly level walk). Once in Salerno, buy your Paestum train ticket at ticket machines or the ticket office in the train station. Note: To start your day trip by bus, you'll need to leave Positano at the crack of dawn—7:00 at the latest—to make the last morning train in Salerno. Check return times from Paestum to Positano carefully in advance; the last possible connection may leave Paestum as early as 16:20.

If you're in a pinch—for example, you've arrived in Salerno during the midday lull in the train schedule—you could take **local CSTP/BusItalia bus #34** from Salerno to Paestum (about hourly, fewer on Sun, 1 hour). It departs from Piazza della Concordia—look for bus shelter between the big parking lot and the main road. This looks convenient to the port, but the closest ticket sales point is the tobacco shop a block in front of the train station. In Paestum, this bus drops you only slightly closer to the ruins than does the train.

To **drive** from Positano to Paestum, you can either follow the Amalfi Coast road to Salerno, or cross back over the peninsula toward Sorrento and then take the expressway. Either way, allow at least 2.5 hours.

Returning from Paestum

Paestum's **train** station is unstaffed but you can buy tickets at machines.

To return to Salerno on local **bus** #34, buy a ticket from one of the bars in Paestum, then go to either of the intersections that flank the ruins (see the "Paestum" map), flag down any northbound bus, and confirm "Salerno?" The last stop is the Salerno waterfront; from here you can catch a boat to Amalfi or Positano, or walk up to the train station to catch an Amalfi-bound SITA bus or a train.

Orientation to Paestum

If you arrive by **train,** cross under the tracks, exit the tiny station, and walk through the ancient city gate; the ruins are a half-mile walk straight ahead, up a dusty road. When you hit the street with hotels and shops, turn right to find the museum and archaeological park entrance. If you'd rather not walk, English-speaking Patrizia Pecora runs a great team of local **taxi** drivers available for transport to hotels or to the ruins (€10-15, +39 392 444 9020). **Buses** from Salerno stop near a corner of the ruins (at a little bar/café). **Drivers** park in the lot by the museum and La Basilica pizzeria (€3). The street between the ruins and museum has been closed off to cars.

Baggage Storage: There's no official baggage storage at the train station or museum. If you're desperate, you can try nicely asking at one of the bars along the main road (they may want a small payment) or at a restaurant you've already patronized.

Local Guide: For an insider's knowledge, Silvia Braggio and her team specialize in Paestum and give a fine two-hour walk of the site and museum (RS%—special €100 rate for my readers, arrange in advance, +39 347 643 2307, www.silviaguide.it, silvia@silviaguide.it). Ask about rounding out the day with a visit to a buffalo farm or another nearby sight. Silvia also offers walking tours of Pompeii and Herculaneum.

Sights in Paestum

PAESTUM ARCHAEOLOGICAL PARK AND MUSEUM

While Paestum is famous for its marvelous Greek temples, most of the structures you see are Roman. Five elements of Greek Paestum survive: three misnamed temples, a memorial tomb, and a circular meeting place (the Ekklesiasterion). The rest, including the wall that defines the site, are the remains of the later Roman town.

Paestum was once a seaport (the ocean is now about a mile away—the wall in the distance, which stretches about three miles, is about halfway to today's coastline). Only about a fifth of the site has been excavated. The original Greek city, which archaeologists figure had a population of about 13,000, was first conquered by Lucanians (distant relatives of the Romans, who spoke a language related to Latin), and then by the Romans (who completely made it over and built the wall you see today).

The remaining Greek structures survive because the Romans were superstitious—they respected sacred areas and didn't mess with temples and tombs. While most old Christian churches are built upon Roman temples (it tends to be what people do when they conquer another culture), no Roman temple is built upon a Greek

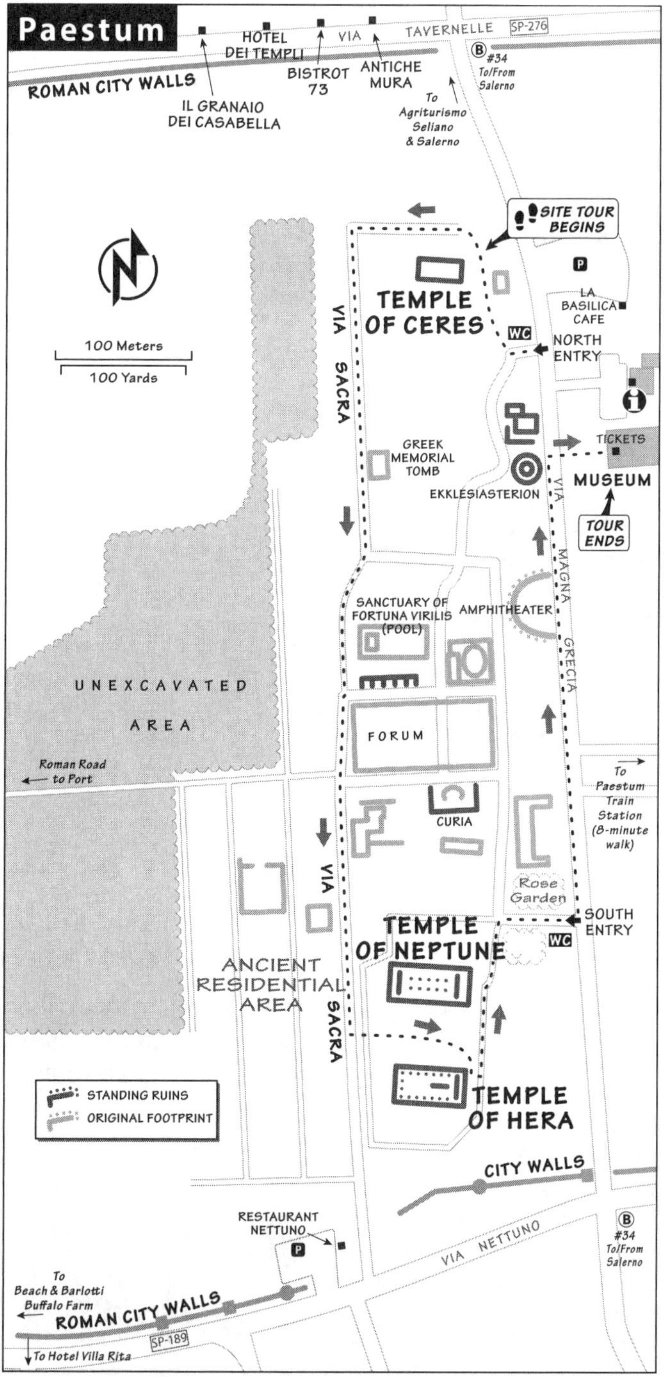
Paestum
HOTEL DEI TEMPLI
VIA TAVERNELLE
SP-276
BISTROT 73
ANTICHE MURA
#34 To/From Salerno
ROMAN CITY WALLS
IL GRANAIO DEI CASABELLA
To Agriturismo Seliano & Salerno
SITE TOUR BEGINS
TEMPLE OF CERES
LA BASILICA CAFE
WC
NORTH ENTRY
100 Meters
100 Yards
VIA SACRA
GREEK MEMORIAL TOMB
TICKETS
MUSEUM
EKKLESIASTERION
VIA MAGNA GRECIA
TOUR ENDS
SANCTUARY OF FORTUNA VIRILIS (POOL)
AMPHITHEATER
UNEXCAVATED AREA
FORUM
Roman Road to Port
To Paestum Train Station (8-minute walk)
CURIA
Rose Garden
SOUTH ENTRY
TEMPLE OF NEPTUNE
ANCIENT RESIDENTIAL AREA
TEMPLE OF HERA
STANDING RUINS
ORIGINAL FOOTPRINT
CITY WALLS
RESTAURANT NETTUNO
VIA NETTUNO
#34 To/From Salerno
To Beach & Barlotti Buffalo Farm
ROMAN CITY WALLS
SP-189
To Hotel Villa Rita

temple. The three Greek temples that you'll see here today have stood for about 2,500 years.

Cost: €12, Dec-Feb-€6, free (and packed) first Sun of each month. Tickets are valid for three days and also cover a nearby archaeological site at Velia.

Hours: Daily 9:00-19:30, last entry one hour before closing.

Information: +39 0828 811 023, www.museopaestum.beniculturali.it.

Getting In: The site and museum have separate entrances. The museum, across the street from the ruins, is in a cluster with the TI and a small early-Christian basilica.

Visitor Information: The following self-guided tours provide all the information you need for both the site and the museum. Skip the museum bookshop's dull audioguide. Renovations are in progress at the museum and ruins; expect changes. You'll enjoy the coolest temperatures in the morning, but the best light and smallest crowds late in the day.

Length of This Tour: Allow two hours to see the ruins and the museum (about an hour for each).

▲▲Paestum Archaeological Site

This tour starts at the site's northern gate (by the museum), visits the Temple of Ceres, goes through the center of the Roman town past the Greek Memorial Tomb, circles around the other two Greek temples, and then leaves the site through the southern gate to walk down the modern road to the Ekklesiasterion (which faces the museum).

➲ Self-Guided Tour

• *Buy your ticket at the museum, then head to the right to find the site's northern gate. (Note that entry is sometimes permitted only through the southern gate: If that's the case, enter the ruins and stroll less than five minutes up to the northern gate and Temple of Ceres to begin this tour.)*

Stand in front of the...

Temple of Ceres: All three Paestum temples have inaccurate names, coined by 19th-century archaeologists who based their "discoveries" on wishful thinking. (While the Romans made things easy by leaving lots of inscriptions, the Greeks did not.) Those 1800s archaeologists wanted this temple to be devoted to Ceres, the goddess of agriculture. However, all the little votive statues found later, when modern archaeologists dug here, instead depicted a woman with

a big helmet: Athena, goddess of wisdom and war. (The Greeks' female war goddess was also the goddess of wisdom—thinking... strategy...female. The Romans' masculine war god was Mars—just fighting.) Each temple is part of a sanctuary—an open, sacred space around the temple. Because regular people couldn't go into the temple, the altar logically stood outside.

The Temple of Ceres dates from 500 BC. It's made of locally quarried limestone blocks. Good roads and shipping didn't come along until the Romans, so the Greeks' buildings were limited to local materials. The wooden roof is long gone. Like the other two temples, this one was once painted white, black, and red, and has an east-west orientation—facing the rising sun. This temple's *cella* (interior room) is gone, cleared out when it was used as a Christian church in the sixth century. In medieval times, Normans scavenged stones from here; chunks of these temples can be found in Amalfi's cathedral.

Walk around to the back side of the Temple of Ceres. The capitals broke in a modern earthquake, so a steel bar provides necessary support. Each of the Paestum temples is Doric style—with three stairs, columns without a base, and shafts that narrow at the top to a simple capital of a round, then a square, block. While there were no carved reliefs, colorful frescoes once decorated the pediments.

As you walk away, look back at the temple. Traditionally, Greeks would build a sanctuary of Athena on a city's highest spot (like the Parthenon in Athens, on the Acropolis). Paestum had no hill, so the Greeks created a mound. The hill was more impressive in its time because the level of the Greek city was substantially lower than the Roman pavement stones you'll walk on today.

• *Follow the path down from behind the temple, and turn left to walk on the paving stones of Via Sacra toward the other Greek temples. After about 100 yards, to the left of the road, you'll see a little half-buried house with a tiled roof.*

Greek Memorial Tomb (Heroon): This tomb (from 500 BC) also survived because the Romans respected religious buildings. But the tomb was most inconveniently located, right in the middle of their growing city. So the practical Romans built a perimeter wall around it (visible today), added a fine tiled roof, and then buried the tomb.

There's a mystery here. Greeks generally buried their dead outside the city (as did Romans)—there are over a thousand ancient tombs outside Paestum's walls—yet this tomb was parked smack-dab in the center of town. When it was uncovered in 1952, no bodies were found inside. The tomb instead held nine perfectly preserved vases (now in the museum). Archaeologists aren't sure what the tomb's purpose was. Perhaps it was a memorial dedicated to some great hero (like a city founder). Or perhaps it was a memorial to those lost when a neighboring community had to evacuate and settle as refugees here.

• *Continue walking down Via Sacra, the main drag of...*

Roman Paestum: Roman towns were garrison towns: rectangular with a grid street plan and two main streets cutting north-south and east-west, dividing the town into four equal sections. They were built by military engineers with a no-nonsense standard design. New excavations (on the left) have uncovered Roman-era lead piping. City administration buildings were on the left, and residential buildings were on the right.

Shortly after the road turns into a dirt path, you'll come to a big **Roman pool** (on the left) that archaeologists believe was a sanctuary dedicated to Fortuna Virilis, goddess of luck and fertility. The strange stones likely supported a wooden platform for priests and statues of gods. Imagine young women walking down the ramp at the far end and through the pool, hoping to conceive a child.

The next big square on the left was the **Roman forum** and ancient Paestum's main intersection. The road on the right led directly (and very practically) to the port. It made sense to have a direct connection to move freight between the sea and the center of town.

Until 2007, the vast field of ruins on the right (between the forum and the next temple) was covered in vegetation. It's since been cleared and cleaned of harmful lichen, which produce acids that dissolve limestone. Study the rocks: Yellow lichen is alive, black is dead. Even the great temples of Paestum were covered in this destructive lichen until 2000, when a two-year-long project cleaned them for the first time.

• *Ahead on the left are the so-called...*

Temples of Neptune and Hera: The **Temple of Neptune** dates from 450 BC and employs the Greek architectural trick where the base line is curved up just a tad to overcome the illusion of sagging caused by a straight base. The Athenians built their Parthenon (with a similar bowed-up base line) just 30 years after this. Many think this temple could have been their inspiration.

The adjacent **Temple of Hera,** dating from 550 BC, is the oldest of Paestum's three temples and one of the oldest Greek temples still standing anywhere. Notice the change 100 years makes in the architectural styles: Archaic Doric in 550 BC versus Classic Doric in 450 BC.

Archaeologists now believe the "Temple of Neptune" was actually devoted to a different god. Votive statues uncovered here suggest that Hera was the focus (perhaps this was a new-and-improved version of the adjacent, simpler, and older Temple of Hera). Or perhaps it was a temple to Zeus, Hera's husband, to honor the couple together.

Together, the two temples formed a single huge sanctuary, with altars outside the temples on the far (east) side. Walk between the temples, then hook right to get a good look at the front of the Temple of Hera. Notice how overbuilt this temple appears. Its columns and capitals are closer together than necessary, as if the builders lacked confidence in their ability to span the distance between supports. Square pillars mark the corners of the *cella* inside. Temples with an odd number of columns (here, nine) had a single colonnade crossing in the center inside to support the wooden roof. More modern temples (such as the Temple of Neptune) had six columns, with two colonnades passing through the *cella*. This left a line of vision open through the middle so that worshippers could see the big statue of the god.

By the way, in 1943, Allied paratroopers dropped in near here during the famous "Landing of Salerno," when the Allies (who had already taken Sicily) invaded mainland Italy. Paestum was part of their first beachhead. The Temple of Hera served as an Allied military tent hospital. From here, the Allies pushed back the Nazis, marching to Naples, Cassino, and finally to Rome.

• *With the Temple of Hera at your back, turn left then right to leave the site (using the exit straight across from the Temple of Neptune). Now turn left onto the modern road...*

Via Magna Grecia: The king of Naples had this Naples-to-Paestum road built in 1829 to inspire his people with ancient temples. While he was modern in his appreciation of antiquity, his road project destroyed a swath of the ancient city, as you'll see as you pass by half of a small **amphitheater.**

• *Just past the amphitheater, you'll find the...*

Ekklesiasterion: Immediately across the street from the museum is what looks like a sunken circular theater. This rare bit of ancient Greek ruins was the Ekklesiasterion, a meeting place where the Greeks would get together to discuss things and vote. Archaeologists believe that the Greek agora (market) was next to here, where the museum stands today.

• *Across the street is the...*

▲▲Paestum Archaeological Museum

Paestum's museum offers the rare opportunity to see artifacts—dating from prehistoric to Greek to Roman times—at the site where they were discovered. These beautifully crafted works (with good English descriptions throughout) help bring Paestum to life. Not everything you see here is from Paestum, though, as the museum also collects artifacts from other nearby sites.

➲ Self-Guided Tour

Before stepping into the museum, notice the proud fascist architecture meant to imitate the structure of the temples you've just seen. Though the building dates from 1954, it was designed in 1938. It seems to command that you *will* enjoy this history lesson.

The exhibit is on several levels. As you follow this tour, expect some location changes due to a recent renovation. You'll likely find mostly Greek pieces on the ground floor (artifacts from the Temple of Hera in front, frescoes from tombs in the back), Paleolithic to Iron Age artifacts on the mezzanine level, and Roman art on the top floor (statues, busts, and inscriptions dating from the time of the Roman occupation). While Roman art is not unique to Paestum, the Greek collection is—so that's what you should focus on.

• *Before exploring the collection, notice the display case (tucked into the far-right corner near the entrance) with the* ***huge book*** *turned to a page with a fine drawing by the Italian artist Giovanni Piranesi, showing his visit to Paestum in 1777. Then look for these museum highlights.*

Temple Reliefs: The museum's center room is designed like a Greek temple inner *cella* and only opened for temporary exhibitions. If it's open, look at the large carvings overhead (known as metopes) that wrap around this inner sanctum. They once adorned a sanctuary of the goddess Hera five miles away. This sanctuary, called Heraion del Sele, was discovered and excavated in 1934. Some of the carvings show scenes from the life of Hercules. You'll get a chance to see the details later in this visit.

• *Along the back wall of this room, find the glass case holding nine perfectly preserved...*

Vases: One ceramic and eight bronze, with artistic handles, these vases were found in Paestum's Greek Memorial Tomb. Greek bronzes are rare because Romans often melted them down to make armor. These were discovered in 1952, filled with still-liquid honey and sealed with beeswax. The honey (as you can see in the display cases below) has since crystallized. Honey was a standard part of a funeral because, to ancient Greeks, honey symbolized immortality...it lasts forever.

• *Enter the room at the far end of the main hall, filled with ancient Greek...*

Votive Offerings: These were dug up at Heraion del Sele (not at Paestum) like the temple reliefs seen earlier. Such offerings are a huge help to modern archaeologists, since the figures that worshippers brought to a temple are clues as to which god the temple honored. These votives depict a woman with a crown on a throne—clearly Hera. The clay votives were simple, affordable, and accessible to regular people.

• *Now continue ahead into the large room (broken up by pillars and interior walls) that holds...*

Relics from the Temples at Paestum: This room displays smaller pieces. Displays tell in which temple each relic was found (videos unfortunately are only in Italian). The Temple of Ceres is often referred to as the Temple of Athena or as the northern *(settentrionale)* sanctuary. The Temples of Neptune and Hera are spoken of as the southern *(meridionale)* sanctuaries.

In a glass case nearby, find the seated statue of **Zeus.** This painted clay Zeus dates from 520 BC. The king of the gods was so lusty with his antics, he's still smirking.

Farther into the room, you can't miss the display case of a statue's **torso** emblazoned with swastikas—a reminder that this symbol (carrying completely different meanings) predated Hitler by millennia.

Across the room, look for the short fragment of a **frieze** with lion heads. Paestum's three temples were once adorned with decorations, such as these ornamental spouts that spurted rainwater out of lions' mouths. Notice the bits of the surviving black, red, and white paint. Reconstructions on the adjacent wall show archaeologists' best guesses as to how the original decorations might have looked.

• *Look out the museum's back window for a good, if distant...*

View of Paestum's Walls: The walls of ancient Paestum reach halfway to the mountain—a reminder that most of the site is still private property and yet to be excavated. The town up on the mountainside is Capaccio, established in the eighth century when inhabitants of the original city of Paestum were driven out by malaria and the city was abandoned.

• *Walk along the corridor at the back of the museum, which shows...*

Objects from Tombs: More than 1,000 tombs have been identified outside the ancient city's wall. About 100 were found decorated with frescoes or containing objects such as these.

• *At the far end of the corridor, turn left to see...*

The Tomb of the Diver: This is the museum's treasure and the most precious Paestum find. Dating from 480 BC, it's not only the sole ancient Greek tomb fresco in the museum—it's the only one ever found in southern Italy. Discovered in 1968, it has five frescoed slabs (four sides and a lid; the bottom wasn't decorated). The Greeks saw death as a passage: diving from mortality into immortality...into an unknown world. Archaeologists believe that the pillars shown on the fresco represent the Pillars of Hercules at Gibraltar, which in ancient times defined the known world. The ocean beyond the Mediterranean was the great unknown...like the afterlife. The Greek banquet makes it clear that this was an aristocratic man.

• *After the Tomb of the Diver, the next room displays...*

Lucanian Tomb Frescoes: The many other painted slabs in the museum date from a later time, around 350 BC, when Paestum fell under Lucanian rule. These frescoes are cruder than their earlier Greek counterpart. The people who conquered the Greeks tried to appropriate their art and style, but they lacked the Greeks' distinctive light touch. Still, these offer fascinating glimpses into ancient life here at Paestum. At the entrance to this room, study the tomb and skeleton of an ancient warrior, who was buried with his armor.

• *Beyond this room, you'll find yourself back at the entrance. Before you leave, go up the stairs by the bookshop for a glimpse at the mezzanine level, which focuses on prehistoric archaeology. Also see the temple friezes at eye level now, with explications of what's happening in almost every scene. The back wall of the mezzanine displays* ***bronze vases,*** *mostly from Gaudo, a half-mile from Paestum.*

MORE SIGHTS IN PAESTUM

Barlotti Caseificio Buffalo Farm

This part of Italy is known for its mozzarella cheese made from buffalo milk. A convenient place to appreciate buffalo mozzarella and other buffalo products is at Barlotti Caseificio, a working buffalo farm about a mile from the Paestum ruins (a 25-minute walk from the museum). Visitors can look around for free, lunch on a buffalo burger or buffalo-cheese ravioli in the café, or buy buffalo gelato and buffalo-based cosmetics in the shop (open daily year-round, shop and gelato counter 8:00-20:00, lunch 12:00-15:00, guided tours available, Via Torre di Paestum 1, +39 0828 811 146, www.barlotti.it).

Sleeping in Paestum

Paestum at night, with views of the floodlit ruins, is magic. Accommodations here offer great value. You can sleep in a mansion for the same price you'd pay for a closet in Positano. For locations see the "Paestum" map earlier in this section.

$$ Hotel Villa Rita is a tidy, quiet country hotel set on two acres of attractive grounds with grassy lawns. A 15-minute walk from the museum and a 20-minute walk from the beach, it has 22 rooms, a kid-friendly swimming pool, and rental bikes (RS%, air-con, lunch or dinner available, free parking, closed Nov-March, Via Nettuno 9, +39 0828 811 081, www.hotelvillarita.it, info@hotelvillarita.it, Luigi and his children Rita and Arnaldo).

$$ Il Granaio dei Casabella, a converted old granary with 14 attractive, reasonably priced rooms, is a 10-minute walk from the museum at the end of the little restaurant strip. It has a beautiful garden and pretty common areas, and four rooms have temple views (RS%, family rooms, air-con, free parking, closed Dec-Feb, 300 yards west of the #34 bus stop closest to Salerno, Via Tavernelle 84, +39 0828 721 014, www.ilgranaiodeicasabella.com, info@ilgranaiodeicasabella.com, hospitable Celardo family).

$$ Hotel dei Templi, with 11 good rooms, is a few doors from Il Granaio dei Casabella (air-con, lots of stairs, pay parking, Via Tavernelle 64, +39 0828 811 747, www.hoteldeitempli.it, info@hoteldeitempli.it).

Outside Town: An offbeat option for drivers, **$$ Agriturismo Seliano** has a huge dining room and lounge with a fireplace, a pool, and 14 spacious rooms on a peaceful, once-elegant farm estate that's been in the same family for 300 years (air-con, closed Nov-March; two miles north of ruins—*Azienda Agrituristica Seliano* sign directs you off the main road down a long, potholed dirt driveway; Via Seliano, +39 0828 723 634, www.agriturismoseliano.it, seliano@agriturismoseliano.it). If you stay here, reserve dinner too—it's served at one long table and made with produce fresh from the garden. They can also organize cooking classes. The place is run by Cecilia, an English-speaking baroness, and her family, including a half-dozen nice and friendly dogs.

Eating in Paestum

Picnics in the ruins aren't allowed. Several eateries cluster around the museum. **$ La Basilica,** facing a pretty little garden between the parking lot and TI, is the most straightforward and reasonable option, with good pizzas and other lunch fare (open daily 12:00-15:00 & 19:00-22:00, Via Magna Grecia 881, +39 0828 811 301).

At the south end of the ruins, **$$$ Ristorante Nettuno** is more elegant, with white tablecloths, a grand piano, and views of the temples; it's built into a surviving tower from the Roman city walls. It has limited hours, though, serving only dinners in summer (mid-June-mid-Sept from 19:30) and lunches in spring and fall (March-mid-June and mid-Sept-Oct 12:00-15:30; closed Tue and Nov-Feb; Via Nettuno 2, +39 0828 811 028).

Just north of the ruins, outside the Roman city wall, Via Tavernelle has been partly blocked off to traffic, creating a fun little restaurant row with casual indoor and outdoor tables. Consider **$$$ Bistrot 73,** with wonderful pasta dishes (at #48, +39 342 526 1393), or **$$$ Antiche Mura,** which accompanies fine grilled meats with an impressive wine list (at #20, +39 0828 199 8535).

PRACTICALITIES

This section covers just the basics on traveling in Italy (for much more information, see *Rick Steves Italy*). You'll find free advice on specific topics at www.ricksteves.com/tips.

MONEY

Italy uses the euro currency: 1 euro (€) = about $1.10. To convert prices in euros to dollars, add about 10 percent: €20 = about $22, €50 = about $55. (Check www.oanda.com for the latest exchange rates.)

You'll use your **credit card** for purchases both big (hotels, advance tickets) and small (little shops, food stands). Visa and Mastercard are universal while American Express and Discover are less common. Some European businesses have gone cashless, making a card your only payment option.

A **"tap-to-pay"** or "contactless" card is the most widely accepted and simplest to use: Before departing, check if you have—or can get—a tap-to-pay credit card (look on the card for the symbol—four curvy lines) and consider setting up your smartphone for contactless payment. Let your bank know that you'll be traveling in Europe, adjust your ATM withdrawal limit if needed, and make sure you know the four-digit PIN for each of your cards, both debit and credit (as you may need to use **chip-and-PIN** for certain purchases). Allow time to receive your PIN by mail.

While most transactions are by card these days, **cash** can help you out of a jam if your card randomly doesn't work, and can be useful to pay for tips and local guides. Wait until you arrive to get euros using your **debit card** (airports have plenty of cash machines). European ATMs accept US debit cards with a Visa or Mastercard logo and work just like they do at home—except they spit out local currency instead of dollars. When possible, withdraw cash from a bank-run ATM located just outside that bank (they usually charge lower fees and are more secure).

Whether withdrawing cash at an ATM or paying with a credit card, you'll often be asked whether you want the transaction processed in dollars or in the local currency. To avoid a poor exchange rate, always refuse the conversion and ***choose the local currency***.

Although rare, some US cards may not work at self-service payment machines (such as transit-ticket kiosks, tollbooths, or fuel pumps). Usually a tap-to-pay card does the trick in these situations. Carry cash as a backup and look for a cashier who can process your payment if your card is rejected.

Before you leave home, let your bank know when and where you'll be using your credit and debit cards. To keep your cash, cards, and valuables safe when traveling, wear a **money belt**.

STAYING CONNECTED

The simplest solution is to bring your own device—mobile phone, tablet, or laptop—and use it just as you would at home (following the money-saving tips below). For more on phoning, see RickSteves.com/phoning. For a one-hour talk covering tech issues for travelers, see RickSteves.com/mobile-travel-skills.

To Call from a US Phone: Phone numbers in this book are presented exactly as you would dial them from a US mobile phone. For international access, press and hold the 0 key until you get a + sign, then dial the country code (39 for Italy) and phone number (including the initial zero when calling Italy). To dial from a US landline, replace + with 011 (US/Canada international access code).

From a European Landline: Replace + with 00 (Europe international access code), then dial the country code (39 for Italy) and phone number (including the initial zero when calling Italy).

Within Italy: To place a domestic call (from an Italian landline or mobile), drop the +39 and dial the phone number (including the initial zero).

Tips: If you bring your mobile phone, consider signing up for an international plan; most providers offer a simple bundle that includes calling, messaging, and data.

Use Wi-Fi whenever possible. Most hotels and many cafés offer free Wi-Fi, and you may also find it at tourist information offices (TIs), major museums, public-transit hubs, and aboard trains and buses. With Wi-Fi you can use your device to make free or low-cost calls via a calling app such as Skype, WhatsApp, FaceTime, and Google Meet. When you need to get online but can't find Wi-Fi, turn on your cellular network (or turn off airplane mode) just long enough for the task at hand.

Most hotels charge a fee for placing calls—ask for rates before

Sleep Code

Hotels in this book are categorized according to the average price of a standard double room with breakfast in high season.

$$$$	**Splurge:** Most rooms over €170
$$$	**Pricier:** €130-170
$$	**Moderate:** €90-130
$	**Budget:** €50-90
¢	**Backpacker:** Under €50
RS%	**Rick Steves discount**

Unless otherwise noted, credit cards are accepted, hotel staff speak basic English, and free Wi-Fi is available. Comparison-shop by checking prices at several hotels (on each hotel's own website, on a booking site, or by email). For the best deal, *book directly with the hotel.* Ask for a discount if paying in cash; if the listing includes **RS%,** request a Rick Steves discount.

you dial. You can use a prepaid international phone card (*carta telefonica prepagata internazionale*—usually available at newsstands, tobacco shops, and train stations) to call out from your hotel.

SLEEPING

I've categorized my recommended accommodations based on price, indicated with a dollar-sign rating (see sidebar). Book your accommodations as soon as your itinerary is set, especially if you want to stay at one of my top listings or if you'll be traveling during busy times. You can do this by checking hotel websites and booking sites such as Hotels.com or Booking.com.

Once your dates are set, compare prices at several hotels. You can do this by checking hotel websites and booking sites such as Hotels.com or Booking.com. After you've zeroed in on your choice, **book directly with the hotel itself.** This increases the chances that the hotelier will be able to accommodate special needs or requests (such as shifting your reservation). And when you book on the hotel's website, by email, or by phone, the owner avoids the commission paid to booking sites, giving them wiggle room to offer you a discount, a nicer room, or a free breakfast.

For family-run hotels, it's generally best to book your room directly via email or phone. Here's what they'll want to know: number and type of rooms; number of nights; arrival date; departure date; any special requests; and applicable discounts (such as a Rick Steves discount, cash discount, or promotional rate). Use the European style for writing dates: day/month/year.

Room prices can fluctuate significantly with demand and amenities (size, views, room class, and so on), but relative price

Restaurant Code

Eateries in this book are categorized according to the average cost of a higher-end pasta or typical main course. Drinks, desserts, and splurge items can raise the price considerably.

$$$$	**Splurge:** Most main courses over €25
$$$	**Pricier:** €20-25
$$	**Moderate:** €15-20
$	**Budget:** Under €15

Pizza by the slice and other takeaway food is **$;** a basic trattoria or sit-down pizzeria is **$$;** a casual but more upscale restaurant is **$$$;** and a swanky splurge is **$$$$.**

categories remain constant. City taxes vary from place to place (figure €2-5 per person, per night). Some hoteliers will ask to collect the tax in cash to make their bookkeeping and accounting simpler.

Some hotels extend a discount to those who pay cash or stay longer than three nights. And some accommodations offer a special discount for Rick Steves readers, indicated in this guidebook by the abbreviation "**RS%.**"

EATING

I've categorized my recommended eateries based on the average price of a typical main course, indicated with a dollar-sign rating (see sidebar). Italy offers a wide array of eateries. A ***ristorante*** is a high-end, sit-down restaurant, while a ***trattoria*** or ***osteria*** is a notch below a *ristorante* in price, but the food is often just as good, if not better. *Trattorie* and *osterie* are generally family-owned and serve home-cooked meals at moderate prices. Italian **bars** are not so much taverns as small, inexpensive cafés selling sandwiches, coffee, and other drinks. An ***enoteca*** is a wine bar with snacks and light meals that's generally an inexpensive option for lunch. Takeaway food from a pizza shop or a deli *(rosticceria)* are great for assembling a picnic.

Italians eat dinner a bit later than we do; better restaurants start serving around 19:00. A full meal consists of an appetizer *(antipasto)*, a first course (*primo piatto,* generally pasta, soup, rice—usually risotto, or polenta), and a second course (*secondo piatto,* expensive meat and fish/seafood dishes). Vegetables *(verdure)* may come with the *secondo*, but more often must be ordered separately as a side dish *(contorno)*. Desserts *(dolci)* are typically tiramisu and *panna cotta,* or other local favorites. For most travelers this is too much food, and the euros can add up in a hurry. My approach is to share dishes family-style with my dinner partners, mixing *antipasti* and *primi* courses while skipping *secondi.*

Or, for a basic value, look for a *menù del giorno* (menu of the day), a three- or four-course, fixed-price meal deal (avoid the cheapest ones, often called a *menù turistico*).

At bars and cafés, getting a drink while standing at the bar *(al banco)* is cheaper than drinking it at a table *(al tavolo)*. This tiered pricing system is often posted near the cashier. You'll usually pay at a cash register, then take the receipt to another counter to claim your drink.

Good service is relaxed (slow to an American). You won't get the bill until you ask for it: *"Il conto?"* Many (but not all) restaurants in Italy add a cover charge *(coperto)* of €1.50-3 per person to your bill.

Tipping: A 10- to 15-percent service charge *(servizio)* that goes to the server is most likely included in a restaurant's prices—you'll see *servizio compreso* or *servizio incluso* on the menu. (At places that do levy a separate *servizio* charge, you don't need to leave an additional tip.) However, if you're pleased with the service, it's polite to add a small tip *(una mancia)*, usually by rounding up the bill. A common tip at a simple restaurant or pizzeria is €1 per person. At a finer restaurant, leave a few euros per person. If paying with a credit card, you'll need to tip with cash or coins; credit card receipts don't have a tip line.

TRANSPORTATION

By Train: To see if a rail pass could save you money, check RickSteves.com/rail. To research train schedules, visit Italy's state-run rail company Trenitalia's website (www.trenitalia.com) or private train company Italo's site (www.italotreno.it; domestic journeys only), or use their apps. For international trips, use Bahn.com (Germany's all-Europe schedule website, which reflects national railways but not private companies like Italo).

It's easy to buy tickets online or download the Trenitalia or Italo app to your smartphone—both have English versions. It's also easy to buy tickets at train stations (at the ticket window, though beware of lines, or at machines with English instructions) or from travel agencies. If your ticket includes a seat reservation on a specific train *(biglietto con prenotazione)*, you're all set and can just get on board. The same is true for any ticket bought online or with the Trenitalia or Italo apps; these tickets are considered already validated.

An open ticket (generally for a slower, regional train) bought from a ticket desk or machine must be validated (date-stamped) before you board (the ticket may say *da convalidare* or *convalida*). To validate it, before getting on the train, stamp your ticket in the small machine near the platform.

Strikes, which are common, generally last a day (often a Friday). Train employees will simply explain, *"Sciopero,"* strike. However, a few sporadic trains still run—ask around.

By Bus: Long-distance buses are catching on in Italy as an alternative to the train. They are usually cheaper, modern, and often have free Wi-Fi. Some of the operators you'll see are Flixbus (http://global.flixbus.com) and Marozzi (www.marozzivt.it).

By Plane: Covering long distances on a budget flight can be cheaper than a train or bus ride (though it leaves a larger carbon footprint). Check the cost of a flight on one of Europe's airlines, whether a major carrier or a no-frills outfit like EasyJet or Ryanair. Kayak is the top site for flights to and within Europe, easy-to-use Google Flights has price alerts, and Skyscanner includes many inexpensive flights within Europe.

By Car: It's cheaper to arrange most car rentals from the US. For tips on your insurance options, see RickSteves.com/cdw. Theft insurance is mandatory in Italy ($15-20/day). In Italy, most car-rental companies' rates automatically include Collision Damage Waiver (CDW) coverage. Even if you try to decline CDW when you reserve your Italian car, you may find when you show up at the counter that you must buy it after all.

You're also technically required to have an International Driving Permit—an official translation of your license (sold at AAA offices for about $20 plus the cost of two passport-type photos; see AAA.com).

You'll pay tolls for some stretches of freeway (autostrada; for costs, use the trip-planning tool at www.autostrade.it). Be warned that car traffic is restricted in many city centers—don't drive or park in any area that has a sign reading *Zona Traffico Limitato* (*ZTL*, often shown above a red circle). If you do, your license plate will be photographed and a hefty (€80-plus) ticket mailed to your home.

Italians are aggressive drivers. Turn signals are optional. If a driver is tailgating you on the highway, pull to the side to let them pass, even if that means driving on the shoulder. Otherwise, local road etiquette is similar to that in the US. Ask your car-rental company for details, or check the US State Department website (www.travel.state.gov, search for your country in the "Learn About Your Destination" box, then click "Travel and Transportation").

A car is an expensive headache in major cities—park it safely (get tips from your hotelier). As break-ins are common, be sure your valuables are out of sight and locked in the trunk, or even better, with you or in your hotel room.

HELPFUL HINTS

Travel Advisories: Before traveling, check updated health and safety conditions, including restrictions for your destination, on the travel pages of the US State Department (www.travel.state.gov) and Centers for Disease Control and Prevention (www.cdc.gov/travel). The US embassy website for Italy is also a good source of information (see below).

Covid Vaccine/Test Requirements: It's possible you'll need to present proof of vaccination against the coronavirus and/or a negative Covid-19 test result to board a plane to Europe or back to the US. Carefully check requirements for each country you'll visit well before you depart, and again a few days before your trip. See the websites listed above for current requirements.

Emergency and Medical Help: For any emergency service—ambulance, police, or fire—call **112** from a mobile phone or landline. If you get sick, do as the Italians do and go to a pharmacist for advice. Or ask at your hotel for help—they'll know the nearest medical and emergency services.

For **passport problems,** call the **US Embassy** (Rome—appointment required, dial +39 06 46741, http://it.usembassy.gov) or **Consulate** (Milan—dial +39 02 290 351; Florence—dial +39 055 266 951; or Naples—dial +39 081 583 8111), or the **Canadian Embassy** (Rome—dial +39 06 854 442 911, www.italy.gc.ca) or **Consulate** (Milan—dial +39 02 626 94238).

ETIAS Registration: The European Union may soon require US and Canadian citizens to register online with the European Travel Information and Authorization System (ETIAS) before entering Italy and other Schengen Zone countries (quick and easy process). For the latest, check www.etiasvisa.com.

Theft or Loss: Italy has particularly hardworking pickpockets—wear a money belt. Assume beggars are pickpockets and any scuffle is simply a distraction by a team of thieves. If you stop for any commotion or show, put your hands in your pockets before someone else does.

To replace a passport, you'll need to go in person to an embassy or consulate (see above). Cancel and replace your credit and debit cards by calling these 24-hour US numbers with a mobile phone: Visa (dial +1 303 967 1096), Mastercard (dial +1 636 722 7111), and American Express (dial +1 336 393 1111). From a landline, you can call these US numbers collect by going through a local operator.

File a police report either on the spot or within a day or two; you'll need it to submit an insurance claim for lost or stolen items, and it can help with replacing your passport or credit and debit cards. For more information, see RickSteves.com/help.

Time: Italy uses the 24-hour clock. It's the same through 12:00 noon, then keep going: 13:00, 14:00, and so on. France, like most of continental Europe, is six/nine hours ahead of the East/West Coasts of the US.

Business Hours: Traditionally, Italy used the siesta plan, with people working from about 9:00 to 13:00 and from 15:30-16:00 to 19:00-19:30, Monday through Saturday. Siesta hours are no longer required by law, so offices and many shops stay open through lunch or later into the evening, especially larger stores in tourist areas. Still, expect small towns and villages to be more or less shut tight during lunch. Stores are also usually closed on Sunday, and often on Monday.

Sightseeing: Many popular sights come with long lines—not to get in, but to buy a ticket. Visitors who buy tickets online in advance (or who have a museum pass covering these key sights) can skip the line and waltz right in. Advance tickets are generally timed-entry, meaning you're guaranteed admission on a certain date and time.

For some sights, buying ahead is required (tickets aren't sold at the sight and it's the only way to get in). At other sights, buying ahead is recommended to skip the line and save time. And for many sights, advance tickets are available but unnecessary: At these uncrowded sights you can simply arrive, buy a ticket, and go in.

Use my advice in this book as a guide. Note any must-see sights that sell out long in advance and be prepared to buy tickets early. If you do your research, you'll know the smart strategy.

Given how precious your vacation time is, I'd book in advance both where it's required (as soon as your dates are firm) and where it will save time in a long line (in some cases, you can do this even on the day you plan to visit).

Holidays and Festivals: Italy celebrates many holidays, which can close sights and attract crowds (book hotel rooms ahead). For information on holidays and festivals, check Italy's website: www.italia.it. For a simple list showing major—though not all—events, see RickSteves.com/festivals.

Numbers and Stumblers: What Americans call the second floor of a building is the first floor in Europe. Europeans write dates as day/month/year, so Christmas 2024 is 25/12/24. Commas are decimal points and vice versa—a dollar and a half is 1,50, and there are 5.280 feet in a mile. Italy uses the metric system: A kilogram is 2.2 pounds; a liter is about a quart; and a kilometer is six-tenths of a mile.

RESOURCES FROM RICK STEVES

This Snapshot guide is excerpted from my latest edition of *Rick Steves Italy,* one of many titles in my series of guidebooks on European travel. I also produce a public television series, *Rick Steves' Europe,* and a public radio show, *Travel with Rick Steves.* My free online video library, Rick Steves Classroom Europe, offers a searchable database of short video clips on European history, culture, and geography (Classroom.RickSteves.com). My website, RickSteves.com, offers free travel information, a forum for travelers' comments, guidebook updates, my travel blog, an online travel store, and information on European rail passes and our tours of Europe. If you're bringing a mobile device, you can download my free Rick Steves Audio Europe app that features dozens of self-guided audio tours of the top sights in Europe—including sights in Rome, Florence, Venice, Milan, Naples, Pompeii, Siena, and Assisi—and travel interviews about Italy. For more information, see RickSteves.com/audioeurope. You can also follow me on Facebook, Twitter, and Instagram.

ADDITIONAL RESOURCES

Tourist Information: www.italia.it
Passports and Red Tape: www.travel.state.gov
Packing List: www.ricksteves.com/packing
Travel Insurance: www.ricksteves.com/insurance
Cheap Flights: www.kayak.com or www.google.com/flights
Airplane Carry-on Restrictions: www.tsa.gov
Updates for This Book: www.ricksteves.com/update

HOW WAS YOUR TRIP?

To share your tips, concerns, and discoveries after using this book, please fill out the survey at RickSteves.com/feedback. Thanks in advance—it helps a lot.

Italian Survival Phrases

Hello. (informal)	Ciao. chow
Good day.	Buongiorno. bwohn-**jor**-noh
Do you speak English?	Parla inglese? **par**-lah een-**gleh**-zay
Yes. / No.	Si. / No. see / noh
I (don't) understand.	(Non) capisco. (nohn) kah-**pees**-koh
Please.	Per favore. pehr fah-**voh**-ray
Thank you.	Grazie. **graht**-see-ay
You're welcome.	Prego. **preh**-go
I'm sorry.	Mi dispiace. mee dee-spee-**ah**-chay
Excuse me.	Mi scusi. mee **skoo**-zee
No problem.	Non c'è problema. nohn cheh proh-**bleh**-mah
Goodbye.	Arrivederci. ah-ree-veh-**dehr**-chee
one / two / three	uno / due / tre **oo**-noh / **doo**-ay / tray
four / five / six	quattro / cinque / sei **kwah**-troh / **cheeng**-kway / **seh**-ee
seven / eight	sette / otto **seh**-tay / **oh**-toh
nine / ten	nove / dieci **noh**-vay / dee-**ay**-chee
How much is it?	Quanto costa? **kwahn**-toh **koh**-stah
Write it?	Me lo scrive? may loh **skree**-vay
Is it free?	È gratis? eh **grah**-tees
Is it included?	È incluso? eh een-**kloo**-zoh
Where can I buy / find...?	Dove posso comprare / trovare...? **doh**-vay **poh**-soh kohm-**prah**-ray / troh-**vah**-ray
I'd like / We'd like...	Vorrei / Vorremmo... voh-**reh**-ee / voh-**reh**-moh
...a room.	...una camera. **oo**-nah **kah**-meh-rah
...a ticket to ___.	...un biglietto per ___. oon beel-**yeh**-toh pehr ___
Is it possible?	È possibile? eh poh-**see**-bee-lay
Where is...?	Dov'è...? doh-**veh**
...the train station	...la stazione lah staht-see-**oh**-nay
...tourist information	...informazioni turisti een-for-maht-see-**oh**-nee too-**ree**-stee
...the bathroom	...il bagno eel **bahn**-yoh
men / women	uomini, signori / donne, signore **woh**-mee-nee, seen-**yoh**-ree / **doh**-nay, seen-**yoh**-ray
left / right / straight	sinistra / destra / sempre dritto see-**nee**-strah / **deh**-strah / **sehm**-pray **dree**-toh
What time does this open / close?	A che ora apre / chiude? ah kay **oh**-rah **ah**-pray / kee-**oo**-day
At what time?	A che ora? ah kay **oh**-rah
Just a moment.	Un momento. oon moh-**mehn**-toh
now / soon / later	adesso / presto / tardi ah-**deh**-soh / **preh**-stoh / **tar**-dee
today / tomorrow	oggi / domani **oh**-jee / doh-**mah**-nee

In an Italian Restaurant

I'd like / We'd like...	Vorrei / Vorremmo...	voh-**reh**-ee / voh-**reh**-moh
...to reserve a table for one / two.	...prenotare un tavolo per uno / due.	preh-noh-**tah**-ray oon **tah**-voh-loh pehr **oo**-noh / **doo**-ay
...the menu (in English).	...il menù (in inglese).	eel meh-**noo** (een een-**gleh**-zay)
Is this seat free?	È libero questo posto?	eh **lee**-beh-roh **kweh**-stoh **poh**-stoh
service (not) included	servizio (non) compreso	sehr-**veet**-see-oh (nohn) kohm-**pray**-zoh
cover charge	(pane e) coperto	(**pah**-nay ay) koh-**pehr**-toh
to go	da portar via	dah **por**-tar **vee**-ah
with / without	con / senza	kohn / **sehnt**-sah
and / or	e / o	ay / oh
breakfast / lunch / dinner	(prima) colazione / pranzo / cena	(**pree**-mah) koh-laht-zee-**oh**-nay / **prahn**-zoh / **chay**-nah
fixed-price meal (of the day)	menù (del giorno)	meh-**noo** (dehl **jor**-noh)
specialty of the house	specialità della casa	speh-chah-lee-**tah** **deh**-lah **kah**-zah
appetizer	antipasto	ahn-tee-**pah**-stoh
first course	primo (piatto)	**pree**-moh (pee-**ah**-toh)
main course	secondo (piatto)	seh-**kohn**-doh (pee-**ah**-toh)
side dishes	contorni	kohn-**tor**-nee
cold cuts / bread / cheese	salumi / pane / formaggio	sah-**loo**-mee / **pah**-nay / for-**mah**-joh
sandwich	panino	pah-**nee**-noh
soup / salad	zuppa / insalata	**tsoo**-pah / een-sah-**lah**-tah
meat / chicken	carne / pollo	**kar**-nay / **poh**-loh
fish / seafood	pesce / frutti di mare	**peh**-shay / **froo**-tee dee **mah**-ray
fruit / vegetables	frutta / verdure	**froo**-tah / vehr-**doo**-ray
dessert	dolce	**dohl**-chay
tap water	acqua del rubinetto	**ah**-kwah dehl roo-bee-**neh**-toh
mineral water	acqua minerale	**ah**-kwah mee-neh-**rah**-lay
still / sparkling	naturale / frizzante	nah-too-**rah**-lay / freet-**zahn**-tay
(orange) juice	succo (d'arancia)	**soo**-koh (dah-**rahn**-chah)
coffee / tea / milk	caffè / tè / latte	kah-**feh** / teh / **lah**-tay
wine / beer	vino / birra	**vee**-noh / **bee**-rah
red / white	rosso / bianco	**roh**-soh / bee-**ahn**-koh
glass / bottle	bicchiere / bottiglia	bee-kee-**eh**-ray / boh-**teel**-yah
Cheers!	Salute! / Cin cin!	sah-**loo**-tay / cheen cheen
The bill, please.	Il conto, per favore.	eel **kohn**-toh pehr fah-**voh**-ray
Do you accept credit cards?	Accettate carte di credito?	ah-cheh-**tah**-tay **kar**-tay dee **kreh**-dee-toh
Delicious!	Delizioso!	day-leet-see-**oh**-zoh

For more user-friendly Italian phrases, check out *Rick Steves Italian Phrase Book* or *Rick Steves French, Italian, & German Phrase Book*.

INDEX

A
Accommodations: *See* Sleeping
Agriturismo, near Paestum: 177
Airport, in Naples: 65–66, 116
Air travel: 184, 187
Amalfi Coast: 132–178; maps, 134, 140–141; planning tips, 133; self-guided tour, 137–143; tours, 16–17; transportation, 133–137. *See also* Positano; Sorrento
Amalfi Town: 142–143, 153–160; eating, 160; helpful hints, 154, 156; map, 155; orientation, 154; sights/activities, 156–159; tourist information, 154; transportation, 160
Amalfi Town Cathedral: 157–158
Ambulance: 185
Amphitheater (Paestum): 170
Amphitheater (Pompeii): 85
Anacapri: 117, 120, 126–129; sights/activities, 126–129; tourist information, 120; transportation, 121–123, 131
Anacapri Lighthouse (Faro): 129
Andrew, Saint: 156, 157
Anthony, Saint: 103–104
Antica Pizzeria da Michele (Naples): 36, 58
Apps: messaging, 180; payment, 179; trains, 183
Aqueduct (Pompeii): 81
Archaeological museums: Paestum, 174–176. *See also* Naples Archaeological Museum
Archaeological sites: Capri, 131; Herculaneum, 87–91; Naples, 35, 38–39; Paestum, 168–173; Pompeii, 73–85
Armida Theater Cinema (Sorrento): 109
Arrival: *See* Transportation
Arsenal Museum (Amalfi): 156–157
ATMs: 179–180
Atrani: 143, 159; hiking, 159, 164
Audio Europe, Rick Steves: 187
Augustus: 117, 131

B
Baggage storage: Amalfi Town, 154, 156; Capri, 121; Herculaneum, 86–87; Naples, 7; Paestum, 168; Pompeii, 72; Positano, 146; Sorrento, 97
Bakery and Mill (Pompeii): 83
Banca Intesa Sanpaolo (Naples): 41
Banco di Napoli (Naples): 41
Barbary Coast Saracens, about: 139
Bar Nilo (Naples): 33–34
Basilica (Pompeii): 76–77
Baths of the Forum (Pompeii): 79–80
Beaches: Capri, 122, 129; Marina di Praiano, 142; Marina di Puolo, 108; Positano, 147, 149–150; Punta del Capo, 108; Sorrento, 107–108
Bellini Theater (Naples): 26–27
Blue Grotto (Capri): 124–125
Boating: Amalfi Town, 156; Positano, 150; Sorrento, 108
Boat travel (ferries): 63; Amalfi Coast, 136; Capri, 119, 121–122, 123–124, 131; map, 63; Naples, 15, 65; Positano, 146, 150; Sorrento, 96, 116–117
Bookstores: Naples, 11; Sorrento, 97
Borgo Marinaro (Naples): 42, 50–51
Brothel (Pompeii): 83
Buses (bus tours): 62, 184; Amalfi Coast, 134–135; Amalfi Town, 160; Capri, 122–123; map, 63; Mount Vesuvius, 92–93; Naples, 14; Paestum, 166–167, 168; Pompeii, 68; Positano, 146; Ravello, 161; Sorrento, 96, 97–98, 115–116. *See also* CitySightseeing; Mondo Guide
Business hours: 185–186

C
Cable cars: *See* Funiculars
Cabs: *See* Taxis
Campania ArteCard: 6, 11, 62
Campania Express: 62; map, 63;

Naples, 7, 62; Pompeii, 68; Sorrento, 116
Capodimonte (Naples): 46–50
Capodimonte Museum (Naples): 46–49
Capodimonte Park (Naples): 46
Cappella Sansevero (Naples): 32, 37–38
Capri: 117–131; beaches, 122, 129; helpful hints, 122; maps, 95, 119, 121; orientation, 120; planning tips, 118–119; shopping, 129–130; sights/activities, 123–131; tourist information, 120; tours, 17; transportation, 119–120, 131
Capri Boat Circle: 124–125
Capri Cathedral: 130
Capri City Hall: 130
Capri town: 117, 120–125, 129–131; sights/activities, 129–131; tourist information, 120; transportation, 121–123
Caravaggio: 35, 40, 49
Car insurance: 184
Carracci, Annibale: 48
Car rentals: 184
Carthusian Monastery of San Martino (Naples): 53
Car travel (driving): 184; Mount Vesuvius, 92; Paestum, 166–167, 168; Pompeii, 68; Positano, 146; Sorrento, 96–97
Caruso, Enrico: 94, 100
Casa dei Cervi (Herculaneum): 90
Casa dei Vettii (Pompeii): 82
Casa del Fauno (Pompeii): 81–82
Casa del Poeta Tragico (Pompeii): 80–81
Casa di Menandro (Pompeii): 84
Casa di Nettuno e Anfitrite (Herculaneum): 89–90
Casa Rossa (Capri): 126–127
Castel dell'Ovo (Naples): 42
Castel Nuovo (Naples): 43
Castel Sant'Elmo (Naples): 52–53
Catacombs of San Gaudioso (Naples): 45
Catacombs of San Gennaro (Naples): 49–50
Cemetery of the Fountains (Naples): 45
Centrale funicular (Naples): 13, 41, 52
Centrale Station (Naples): 7, 36; eating near, 58, 61, 64; sleeping near, 55
Ceramics, shopping for, in Positano: 147, 150
Certosa e Museo di San Martino (Naples): 53
"Chapel of Maradona" (Naples): 33–34
Chiesa Nuova: 146
Churches and cathedrals: Amalfi Town Cathedral, 157–158; Cappella Sansevero (Naples), 32, 37–38; Capri Cathedral, 130; Gesù Nuovo (Naples), 31, 36–37; Holy Rosary Church (Positano), 147; Naples Duomo, 39–40; Pio Monte della Misericordia (Naples), 35, 40; Ravello Duomo, 162; San Francesco di Paola (Naples), 41; San Michele Church (Capri), 127; Santa Chiara Church (Naples), 31, 37; Santa Maria Assunta (Positano), 148; Santa Maria delle Grazie (Sorrento), 97; Sant Antonino Basilica (Sorrento), 103–104; Sorrento Cathedral, 97, 102
Cimitero delle Fontanelle (Naples): 45
Circumvesuviana Train: 62; Herculaneum, 86; Naples, 64; Pompeii, 68; Sorrento, 96, 115–116
CitySightseeing: 62; Amalfi Coast, 135, 160; Naples, 14, 62, 69; Pompeii, 62, 69
Civic Museum (Naples): 43
College of the Augustali (Herculaneum): 89
Consulates: 185
Cooking classes: 177
Corno: 34
Corso Italia (Sorrento): 95, 102–103
Covid vaccine/test requirements: 185
Credit cards: 179–180
Crime: *See* Theft alert

INDEX

Cuisine: 55, 58, 182–183. *See also* Gelato; Pizza
Currency and exchange: 179–180

D
Dancing Faun: 21
Debit cards: 179–180
Diefenbach (Wilhelm) Museum (Capri): 130–131
Doriforo: 24
Driving: *See* Car travel

E
Eating: 182–183; Amalfi Town, 160; Italian restaurant phrases, 190; Naples, 55–64; Paestum, 177–178; Pompeii, 72–73; Positano, 152–153; Ravello, 164–165; Sorrento, 112–115. *See also* Gelato; Pizza
Ekklesiasterion (Paestum): 173
Embassies: 185
Emerald Grotto: 142
Emergencies: 185
Ercolano: *See* Herculaneum
Ercolano Scavi: 62, 86, 92
ETIAS (European Travel Information and Authorization System): 185
Euro currency: 179–180

F
Faraglioni Rocks: 120, 128–129
Farnese Collection (Naples): 18, 20–21
Farnese Cup: 21
Farnese Hercules: 20–21
Faro (Capri): 129
Ferries: *See* Boat travel
Festivals: 186
Fiordo: 142
Fish market, in Naples: 50
Flavio Gioia: 154
Food: *See* Cooking classes; Eating; Gelato; Groceries; Markets; Pizza
Food tours: 108, 146
Foreigners' Club (Sorrento): 96, 108, 114
Fornillo Beach (Positano): 149–150
Forum (Pompeii): 74, 76, 78–79
Funiculars (cable cars): Capri, 121–123, 128–129; Naples, 13, 41, 52

G
Galleria Borbonica (Naples): 44
Galleria Principe di Napoli: 25–26
Galleria Umberto I (Naples): 43–44
Galli Islands: 129, 138
Garden of the Fugitives (Pompeii): 85
Garibaldi Station (Naples): 7, 62, 64
Gelato: Naples, 35–36; Paestum, 176; Positano, 147; Sorrento, 114–115
Gesù Nuovo Church (Naples): 31, 36–37
Giardini di Augusto (Capri): 130
Giro dell' Isola (Capri): 124–125
Gold shops, in Naples: 34
Gran Caffè Gambrinus (Naples): 43
Greek Gate (Sorrento): 105
Greek Memorial Tomb (Paestum): 171–172
Groceries: Naples, 64; Positano, 153; Sorrento, 114
Grotta Azzurra (Capri): 124–125
Grotta dello Smeraldo: 142

H
Hanging Gardens (Naples): 42
Helpful hints: 184–186; Amalfi Town, 154, 156; Capri, 122; Naples, 10–11; Paestum, 168; Sorrento, 97
Herculaneum: 86–91; map, 88; orientation, 86–87; self-guided tour, 87–91; transportation, 86
Hiking: Amalfi Town, 158–159; Atrani, 159, 164; Capri, 122, 127–128, 129; Ravello, 163–164
Holidays: 186
Holy Rosary Church (Positano): 147
Hotel Palazzo Murat (Positano): 147–148
Hotels: *See* Sleeping
House of Menander (Pompeii): 84
House of Neptune and Amphitrite (Herculaneum): 89–90
House of Relief of Telephus (Herculaneum): 90

House of the Deer (Herculaneum): 90
House of the Faun (Pompeii): 81–82
House of the Tragic Poet (Pompeii): 80–81
House of the Vettii (Pompeii): 82

I
Information: *See* Tourist information
Italian restaurant phrases: 190
Italian survival phrases: 189

L
La Feltrinelli (Naples): 11
La Rotonda (Positano): 149
Laundry: Naples, 11; Sorrento, 97
Lemon Grove Garden (Sorrento): 106
Lemons: 106, 107
Li Galli Islands: 129, 138
Limoncello: 106, 138
Linen, shopping for, in Positano: 150
Loren, Sophia: 142–143
Luggage storage: *See* Baggage storage
Lungomare (Naples): 50–51
Lupanare (Pompeii): 83

M
MADRE (Naples): 40–41
Madre del Buon Consiglio (Naples): 49–50
Maps: Amalfi Coast, 134, 140–141; Amalfi Town, 155; Capri, 95, 119, 121; Herculaneum, 88; Naples, 8–9, 12–13, 26–27, 56–57; Paestum, 169; Pompeii, 68, 70–71, 75; Positano, 144–145; Salerno, 166; Sorrento, 95, 98–99, 101
Maradona (Diego) Chapel (Naples): 33–34
Marina di Praiano: 142
Marina di Puolo: 108
Marina Grande (Capri): 120; beach, 122; map, 121; tourist information, 120; transportation, 121–123, 131
Marina Grande (Sorrento): 96, 104–105; eating, 115
Marina Piccola (Sorrento): 96, 104, 107, 117
Markets, in Naples: 30, 50
Medical help: 185
Mergellina (Naples): 51
Meta Beach: 107–108
Metric system: 186
Metro, in Naples: 7, 11–13, 65; map, 12–13; tickets, 11
Mobile phones: 180
Monastery of San Giacomo (Capri): 130–131
Mondo Guide: 16–17, 63; Amalfi Coast, 17, 137; Capri, 17, 119–120; Naples, 14, 16–17; Pompeii, 16, 72; Sorrento, 97
Money: 179–180
Money belts: 180, 185
Monte Solaro (Capri): 128–129
Moscati, Giuseppe: 36
Motor scooters: *See* Scooter rentals
Mount Vesuvius: 76, 91–93; eruption of (79 A.D.), 67–68, 76, 77, 78, 87
Munthe, Axel: 127–128
Museo Archeologico (Naples): 15–24, 25; eating near, 59, 61; map, 19; orientation, 15–18; self-guided tour, 18–24
Museobottega della Tarsialignea (Sorrento): 106–107
Museo Casa Rossa (Capri): 126–127
Museo Civico (Naples): 43
Museo della Carta (Amalfi): 158
Museo di Capodimonte (Naples): 46–49
Museo Diefenbach (Capri): 130–131
Museum of Inlaid Wood (Sorrento): 106–107
Music on the Rocks (Positano): 149, 151

N
Naples: 3–66; arrival in, 6–7; helpful hints, 10–11; history of, 32–33; maps, 8–9, 12–13, 26–27, 56–57; Naples, 55–64; orientation, 5; planning tips, 5; shopping, 25–26, 28–29, 34, 43–44; sights/activities,

INDEX

36–53; sleeping, 54–55; tourist information, 6; tours, 14–15, 16–17; transportation, 6–7, 11–14, 64–66; walking tours, 25–36; Lungomare *passeggiata,* 50–51; Museo Archeologico, 15–24
Naples Archaeological Museum: 15–24, 25; eating near, 59, 61; map, 19; orientation, 15–18; self-guided tour, 18–24
Naples Civic Museum: 43
Naples Duomo: 39–40
Naples Hanging Gardens: 42
Naples Harbor: 42–43; eating, 61
Naples International Airport: 65–66, 116
Napoli Sotterranea: 35, 38–39
Naval Museum (Naples): 53

O
Opera, in Naples: 43

P
Packing list: 187
Paestum: 165–178; eating, 177–178; helpful hints, 168; map, 169; maps, 140–141; orientation, 168; sights, 168–176; sleeping, 176–177; tourist information, 165; transportation, 165–167
Paestum Archaeological Museum: 168, 170
Paestum Archaeological Site: 168–173
Palazzo Correale (Sorrento): 102
Palazzo Reale (Naples): 41–42
Palazzo Venezia (Naples): 31
Paper Museum (Amalfi): 158
Passeggiata: 50–51, 105–106
Passports: 185, 187
Phones: 180–181
Piazza Bellini (Naples): 27–28
Piazza Capuana (Naples), market: 50
Piazza Carità (Naples): 30–31
Piazza Dante (Naples): 28
Piazza dei Dogi (Amalfi), eating: 160
Piazza dei Mulini (Positano): 147
Piazza della Pace (Capri): 125, 126
Piazza della Vittoria (Sorrento): 104–105
Piazza del Plebiscito (Naples): 41
Piazza Duomo (Amalfi): 156, 162; eating, 160
Piazza Duomo (Ravello): 162, 164
Piazza Flavio Gioia (Positano): 148
Piazza Gesù Nuovo (Naples): 31
Piazza San Domenico Maggiore (Naples): 31–32
Piazza Sette Settembre (Naples): 29
Piazza Tasso (Sorrento): 95, 99–102, 105–106, 108
Piazza Umberto I (Capri): 129–130
Piazza Vittoria (Capri): 126
Piazza Vittoria (Naples): 51
Picnics: 64, 72–73, 114, 153, 182
Pio Monte della Misericordia Church (Naples): 35, 40
Pizza (pizzerias): 58; Amalfi Town, 160; Capri, 126; Naples, 36, 58–59; Positano, 152; Sorrento, 106, 113, 114
Planning tips: Amalfi Coast, 133; Capri, 118–119; Naples, 5; Sorrento, 95
Police: 185
Polo Nord Gelateria (Naples): 35–36
Pompeii: 67–85; background of, 73, 78; eating, 72–73; maps, 68, 70–71, 75; orientation, 70–73; self-guided tour, 73–85; tourist information, 70; tours, 16, 72; transportation, 68–70
Pompeiian Mosaics (Naples): 21–22
Pontone: 159
Porta della Marina (Amalfi): 156
Porta Marina (Pompeii): 74
Porta Marina (Sorrento): 105, 115
Porta Nolana Open-Air Fish Market (Naples): 50
Posillipo Hill (Naples): 51
Positano: 138–139, 143–153; eating, 152–153; map, 144–145; nightlife, 151; orientation, 145–146; shopping, 147, 150–151; sleeping, 151–152; tourist information, 145; transportation, 134–135, 146; walking tour, 147–150

Praiano: 139
Presepi: 34, 44, 53, 156
Punta del Capo: 108

R
Raimondo de Sangro: 37–38
Ravello: 143, 159, 161–165; eating, 164–165; sights/activities, 162–164; tourist information, 162; transportation, 161
Ravello Duomo: 162
Reader feedback: 187
Red House Museum (Capri): 126–127
Resources from Rick Steves: 186–187
Restaurants: *See* Eating
"Rodeo Drive" (Capri): 130
Roman Villa Complex (Positano): 148–149
Rome: embassies, 185; transportation, 64, 116
Royal Apartments (Naples): 48
Royal Palace (Naples): 41–42

S
Safety: *See* Theft alert
St. Peter's Hotel: 139
Sale Moscati (Naples): 36
Salerno: 17, 143; map, 166; transportation, 64, 133, 165–167
San Carthusian Monastery and Museum (Naples): 53
Sandals, shopping for, in Positano: 150–151
San Domenico Maggiore (Naples): *See* Cappella Sansevero
San Francesco di Paola Church (Naples): 41
San Gaudioso Catacombs (Naples): 45
San Gennaro, Catacombs of (Naples): 49–50
San Giacomo Monastery (Capri): 130–131
Sanità (Naples): 44–45
San Martino (Naples): 51–53
San Martino Carthusian Monastery and Museum (Naples): 53
San Michele Church (Capri): 127
Sansevero Chapel (Naples): 32, 37–38
Santa Chiara Church (Naples): 31, 37
Santa Lucia (Naples): 42, 50–51; eating, 61; sleeping, 61
Santa Maria a Gradillo (Ravello): 164
Santa Maria Assunta Church (Positano): 148
Santa Maria della Sanità (Naples): 45
Santa Maria delle Grazie (Sorrento): 97
Sant Antonino Basilica (Sorrento): 103–104
Santa Restituta Chapel (Naples): 40
Saracens, about: 139
Scooter rentals: Capri, 123; Sorrento, 98
Secret Room (Naples): 22
Sfogliatella: 43, 143, 160
Shopping: Capri, 129–130; hours, 185–186; Naples, 25–26, 28–29, 34; Positano, 147, 150–151; Sorrento, 101–102, 103, 106. *See also* Markets, in Naples
Sightseeing: general tips, 186. *See also specific sights and destinations*
Silver shops, in Naples: 34
Sleep code: 181
Sleeping: 181–182; Naples, 54–55; Paestum, 176–177; Positano, 151–152; Sorrento, 109–112
Smartphones: 180
Soccer: 33–34
Sorrento: 94–117, 138; arrival in, 96–97; eating, 112–115; helpful hints, 97; maps, 95, 98–99, 101; nightlife, 108–109; orientation, 95–96; planning tips, 95; shopping, 101–102, 103, 106; sights/activities, 105–108; sleeping, 109–112; tourist information, 96; tours, 17, 108; transportation, 96–97, 97–100, 115–117; walking tour, 99–105
Sorrento Cathedral: 97, 102
Sorrento Food Tours: 108
Sorrento Men's Club: 103

Sorrento Musical: 109
Spaccanapoli (Naples): 29, 36, 41; eating, 59–61; sleeping, 54–55
Spanish Quarter (Naples): 30
Spiaggia Grande (Positano): 149, 150
Sponda: 138–139, 146
Suburban Baths (Herculaneum): 90
Subway, in Naples: 7, 11–13, 65; map, 12–13; tickets, 11

T
Tasso, Torquato: 101–102
Taxis: 63; Amalfi Coast, 136–137; Capri, 123; Mount Vesuvius, 92; Naples, 7, 14; Sorrento, 98–99
Teatro di San Carlo (Naples): 43
Telephones: 180–181
Temple of Ceres (Paestum): 170–171
Temple of Hera (Paestum): 172–173
Temple of Isis (Pompeii): 84
Temple of Jupiter (Pompeii): 76
Temple of Neptune (Paestum): 172–173
Terme del Foro (Pompeii): 79–80
Theater (Pompeii): 84
Theft alert: 185; Naples, 10
Tiberius: 48, 117, 131
Time zones: 185
Tipping: 183
Titian: 47
Tomb of the Diver (Paestum): 175–176
Toro Farnese: 18, 20
Torre dello Ziro: 159
Tour guides: Amalfi Coast, 136–137; Capri, 122; Naples, 14; Paestum, 168; Pompeii, 72; Positano, 145–146; Sorrento, 97
Tourist information: 187; Amalfi Town, 154; Capri, 120; Herculaneum, 86; Naples, 6; Paestum, 165; Pompeii, 70; Positano, 145; Ravello, 162; Sorrento, 96
Tours: Capri, 119–120; Herculaneum, 86; Naples, 14–15, 16–17; Pompeii, 72; Sorrento, 97, 108. *See also* Mondo Guide; Walking tours, self-guided
Traffic safety, in Naples: 10–11
Train travel: 62–63, 183; Herculaneum, 86; map, 63; Naples, 6–7, 64; Paestum, 168; Pompeii, 68–69; Salerno, 165–167, 167; Sorrento, 96, 115–116. *See also* Campania Express; Circumvesuviana Train
Transportation: 62–63, 183–184; Amalfi Coast, 133–137; Amalfi Town, 160; Capri, 119–120, 131; Herculaneum, 86; map, 63; Mount Vesuvius, 91–92; Naples, 6–7, 11–14, 64–66; Paestum, 165–167; Pompeii, 68–70; Positano, 146; Ravello, 161; Salerno, 165–167; Sorrento, 96–97, 97–100, 115–117
Travel advisories: 184–185
Travel insurance: 187

U
Underground Naples: 35, 38–39

V
Vallone dei Mulini: 100
Vesuvio Express: 92
Vesuvius: 76, 91–93; eruption of (79 A.D.), 67–68, 76, 77, 78, 87
Via Abbondanza (Pompeii): 77
Via Arena della Sanità (Naples): 45
Via Capo (Sorrento): 95, 108, 109, 111; sleeping, 111–112
Via Colombo (Positano): 150
Via Crocelle (Naples): 45
Via degli Archi (Sorrento): 103
Via dei Tribunali (Naples): 35; pizza, 58–59
Via Forcella (Naples): 35
Via Francesco Caracciolo (Naples): 42–43, 51
Viale Richard Wagner (Ravello): 162
Via Maddaloni (Naples): 29
Via Magna Grecia (Paestum): 173
Via Nazario Sauro (Naples): 50–51
Via Orlandi (Capri): 126
Via Pignasecca Market (Naples): 30, 50
Via Posillip (Naples): 51
Via Roma (Capri): 129

Via San Cesareo (Sorrento): 103, 106
Via San Gregorio Armeno (Naples): 34–35
Via Santa Maria della Pietà (Sorrento): 102
Via Sant'Antonio Abate (Naples), market: 50
Via Toledo (Naples): 28–29; eating, 59–61; sleeping, 54–55
Via Vicaria Vecchia (Naples): 35–36
Vidal, Gore: 143, 164
Villa Cimbrone (Ravello): 163
Villa Comunale (Sorrento): 104
Villa Jovis (Capri): 121, 131
Villa La Rondinaia (Ravello): 164
Villa Rufolo (Ravello): 162–163
Villa San Michele (Capri): 127–128
Visitor information: *See* Tourist information
Vitus, Saint: 148

W

Walking tours, self-guided: Herculaneum, 87–91; Naples, 25–36; Lungomare *passeggiata,* 50–51; Museo Archeologico, 15–24; Paestum, 168–176; Pompeii, 73–85; Positano, 147–150; Sorrento, 99–105

Start your trip at

Our website enhances this book and turns

Explore Europe

At ricksteves.com you can browse through thousands of articles, videos, photos and radio interviews, plus find a wealth of money-saving travel tips for planning your dream trip. And with our mobile-friendly website, you can easily access all this great travel information anywhere you go.

TV Shows

Preview the places you'll visit by watching entire half-hour episodes of *Rick Steves' Europe* (choose from all 100 shows) on-demand, for free.

ricksteves.com

your travel dreams into affordable reality

Radio Interviews

Enjoy ready access to Rick's vast library of radio interviews covering travel tips and cultural insights that relate specifically to your Europe travel plans.

Travel Forums

Learn, ask, share! Our online community of savvy travelers is a great resource for first-time travelers to Europe, as well as seasoned pros.

Travel News

Subscribe to our free Travel News e-newsletter, and get monthly updates from Rick on what's happening in Europe.

Classroom Europe®

Check out our free resource for educators with 500 short video clips from the *Rick Steves' Europe* TV show.

Rick Steves has

Experience maximum Europe

Save time and energy

This guidebook is your independent-travel toolkit. But for all it delivers, it's still up to you to devote the time and energy it takes to manage the preparation and logistics that are essential for a happy trip. If that's a hassle, there's a solution.

Rick Steves Tours

A Rick Steves tour takes you to Europe's most interesting places with great

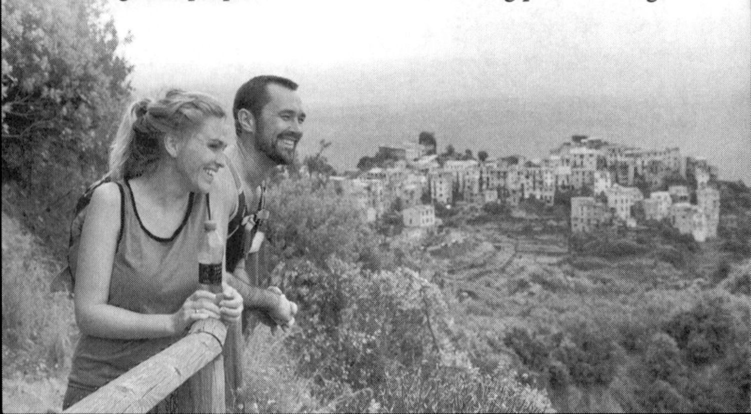

A Guide for Every Trip

Rick Steves
BEST OF ITALY
Rick Steves
BEST OF SPAIN

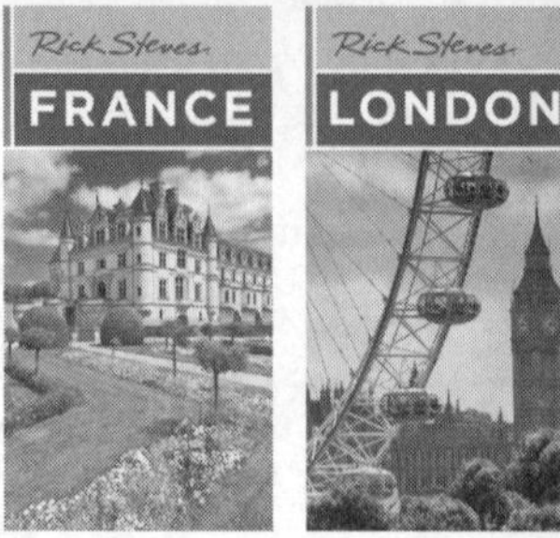

Rick Steves
FRANCE
Rick Steves
LONDON

BEST OF GUIDES

Full-color guides in an easy-to-scan format. Focused on top sights and experiences in the most popular European destinations

Best of England
Best of Europe
Best of France
Best of Germany
Best of Ireland
Best of Italy
Best of Scotland
Best of Spain

E BEST OF ROME
of the Eternal City where Caesars walked can make tourists wilt. Recharge by taking siestas, gelato breaks, and after-dark walks, strolling from one atmospheric square to another in the refreshing evening air.

COMPREHENSIVE GUIDES

City, country, and regional guides printed on Bible-thin paper. Packed with detailed coverage for a multi-week trip exploring iconic sights and venturing off the beaten path

Amsterdam & the Netherlands
Barcelona
Belgium: Bruges, Brussels, Antwerp & Ghent
Berlin
Budapest
Croatia & Slovenia
Central Europe
England
Florence & Tuscany
France
Germany
Great Britain
Greece: Athens & the Peloponnese
Iceland
Ireland
Istanbul
Italy
London
Paris
Portugal
Prague & the Czech Republic
Provence & the French Riviera
Rome
Scandinavia
Scotland
Sicily
Spain
Switzerland
Venice
Vienna, Salzburg & Tirol

Rick Steves books are available from your favorite bookseller. Many guides are available as ebooks.

POCKET GUIDES

Compact color guides for shorter trips

Amsterdam
Athens
Barcelona
Florence
Italy's Cinque Terre
London
Munich & Salzburg
Paris
Prague
Rome
Venice
Vienna

SNAPSHOT GUIDES

Focused single-destination coverage

Basque Country: Spain & France
Copenhagen & the Best of Denmark
Dublin
Dubrovnik
Edinburgh
Hill Towns of Central Italy
Krakow, Warsaw & Gdansk
Lisbon
Loire Valley
Madrid & Toledo
Milan & the Italian Lakes District
Naples & the Amalfi Coast
Nice & the French Riviera
Normandy
Northern Ireland
Norway
Reykjavík
Rothenburg & the Rhine
Sevilla, Granada & Southern Spain
St. Petersburg, Helsinki & Tallinn
Stockholm

CRUISE PORTS GUIDES

Reference for cruise ports of call

Mediterranean Cruise Ports
Scandinavian & Northern European Cruise Ports

Complete your library with...

TRAVEL SKILLS & CULTURE

Study up on travel skills and gain insight on history and culture

Europe 101
Europe Through the Back Door
Europe's Top 100 Masterpieces
European Christmas
European Easter
European Festivals
For the Love of Europe
Italy for Food Lovers
Travel as a Political Act

PHRASE BOOKS & DICTIONARIES

French
French, Italian & German
German
Italian
Portuguese
Spanish

PLANNING MAPS

Britain, Ireland & London
Europe
France & Paris
Germany, Austria & Switzerland
Iceland
Ireland
Italy
Scotland
Spain & Portugal

Photo Credits

Front Cover: Positano © Freeartist, Getty Images/iStockphoto

Title Page: Amalfi Coast © Cameron Hewitt

Dreamstime.com: 2 (top left) © Mondan80; 2 (left vertical) © Jenifoto406; 2 (middle right) © Padebat; 2 (bottom) © Prostogugs

Additional Photography: Dominic Arizona Bonuccelli. Photos are used by permission and are the property of the original copyright owners.

Avalon Travel
Hachette Book Group
1700 Fourth Street
Berkeley, CA 94710

Portions of this book originally appeared in *Rick Steves Italy*, 27th Edition.

Printed in Canada by Friesens
7th Edition. Second printing July 2023.

ISBN 978-1-64171-521-8

For the latest on Rick's talks, guidebooks, tours, public television series, and public radio show, contact Rick Steves' Europe, 130 Fourth Avenue North, Edmonds, WA 98020, +1 425 771 8303, RickSteves.com, rick@ricksteves.com.

Rick Steves' Europe
Managing Editor: Jennifer Madison Davis
Assistant Managing Editor: Cathy Lu
Editors: Glenn Eriksen, Julie Fanselow, Suzanne Kotz, Rosie Leutzinger, Teresa Nemeth, Jessica Shaw, Carrie Shepherd
Editorial & Production Assistant: Megan Simms
Researchers: Cameron Hewitt, Suzanne Kotz, Gretchen Strauch, Cary Walker, Ian Watson
Contributor: Gene Openshaw
Graphic Content Director: Sandra Hundacker
Maps & Graphics: Orin Dubrow, David C. Hoerlein, Lauren Mills, Mary Rostad, Laura Terrenzio

Avalon Travel
Senior Editor and Series Manager: Madhu Prasher
Associate Managing Editor: Jamie Andrade
Editor: Rachael Sablik
Proofreader: Patrick Collins
Indexer: Stephen Callahan
Production and Typesetting: Christine DeLorenzo, Lisi Baldwin, Rue Flaherty, Jane Musser, Ravina Schneider
Cover Design: Kimberly Glyder Design
Maps & Graphics: Kat Bennett